M000221596

This practical guide not only provides a bibl_____
includes helpful strategies for gospel shari_____
will be helpful for all who desire to see th_____
followers of Jesus.

—ED STETZER, Billy Graham Distinguished Chair, Wheaton College

Every Christian has an implicit theology: a set of beliefs about God and about what God was doing in Jesus Christ. To communicate this good news—the gospel—to others is every believer's privilege and responsibility. Sam Chan's book helpfully shows how to do this in a way that fits our twenty-first-century multicultural contexts.

—KEVIN J. VANHOOZER, Research Professor of Systematic
Theology, Trinity Evangelical Divinity School

If you are looking for an evangelism textbook with biblical foundations, strong theology, real-life illustrations, passion for the heart of God, and tools to move people out into a skeptical world with the good news of Jesus, look no further. Sam has done a masterful job of taking evangelism from concept and theory to practice and action.

—REV. DR. KEVIN G. HARNEY, author, Organic Outreach trilogy;
founder and visionary leader, Organic Outreach International

This is an important book. In it, one of Christianity's smartest voices, Sam Chan, shows us how to bring our secular neighbors into a lifegiving encounter with the gospel. Highly recommended for use in universities, seminaries, and churches.

—BRUCE RILEY ASHFORD, provost and professor of theology
and culture, Southeastern Baptist Theological Seminary

Sam Chan has written the evangelism manual we've needed. *Evangelism in a Skeptical World* combines cultural understanding, theological acumen, and practical apologetics to equip the church to bear witness to the gospel in a secular age. It is lucidly written and full of real-world wisdom. I expect it to be a featured text for ministry students for many years to come.

—JOSHUA D. CHATRAW, executive director, Center for Apologetics
and Cultural Engagement, School of Divinity, Liberty University

This book provides readers a comprehensive theological overview of evangelism, challenges outdated high-profile models, and offers new models centered in Scripture and applicable to multiple contexts. A masterful contribution.

—TOM STEFFEN, emeritus professor of intercultural studies,
COOK School of Intercultural Studies, Biola University

How do we express a transcultural gospel to an enculturated audience in postmodernity? Chan provides a biblical foundation with more than forty different means to engage communities, contexts, and common grounds. This is a superb work, undergirded by Scripture, rich in relevant methods, and impressive in contextual scope of audiences. Finally, we have a go-to resource in the twenty-first century.

—REV. SAMUEL E. CHIANG, president and CEO,
The Wycliffe Seed Company

Chan has written a helpful resource for sharing the gospel in our world. He helps students of evangelism think through ways to present the good news, as well as means to handle skeptics' objections. His stories and insights show that his words are more than theory; he has practiced this! I recommend this contribution to the literature on evangelism which every serious student should read.

—DAVID M. GUSTAFSON, chair of mission and evangelism
department, Trinity Evangelical Divinity School

This is one of the most thoughtful books on evangelism I've read. It is both theologically sound and informed by practice. Chan avoids oversimplifying the gospel. At the same time, he never makes evangelism feel complex and cumbersome. His approach is balanced and flexible. If I could recommend just one book on evangelism, this would be it.

—JACKSON WU, seminary professor; author,
*One Gospel for All Nations*

This book is a brilliant and practical explanation of how to show the beauty of Jesus' gospel to a world that thinks it has "moved on." From understanding the many aspects of the gospel's engagement with a dying world to the practicalities of "shaping a gospel talk," this book will help the pastor, the evangelist, and any Christian to speak about Jesus in a way that can be heard by people who have become deaf to a message they consider irrelevant.

—AL STEWART, City Bible Forum, Australia

# EVANGELISM
## in a
# SKEPTICAL WORLD

How to Make the Unbelievable News
About Jesus More Believable

## SAM CHAN

ZONDERVAN

*Evangelism in a Skeptical World*
Copyright © 2018 by Samuel Chan

This title is also available as a Zondervan ebook.

ISBN 978-0-310-53471-6 (International Trade Paper Edition)

Requests for information should be addressed to:
Zondervan, *3900 Sparks Dr. SE, Grand Rapids, Michigan 49546*

---

Library of Congress Cataloging-in-Publication Data

Names: Chan, Sam, 1966— author.
Title: Evangelism in a skeptical world : how to make the unbelievable news about Jesus more
    believable / Sam Chan.
Description: Grand Rapids, MI : Zondervan, [2018]
Identifiers: LCCN 2017050512 | ISBN 9780310534679 (hardcover)
Subjects: LCSH: Evangelistic work--Study and teaching. | Witness bearing (Christianity)
Classification: LCC BV3796 .C43 2018 | DDC 269/.2--dc23 LC record available at https://lccn
    .loc.gov/2017050512

---

*Cover design: Kirk DouPonce, DogEared Design*
*Cover photo: iStockphoto.com*
*Interior design: Kait Lamphere*

---

*Printed in the United States of America*

---

19 20 21 22 23 24 25 26 27 28 /DCI/ 15 14 13 12 11 10 9 8 7

*To my wife, Stephanie, who generously*
*gives me space to explore and create*

*To my sons, Toby, Cooper, and Jonty,*
*who show me fun, beauty, and joy*

*To my parents, Winnie and Joseph, who*
*taught me to know and love Jesus*

# CONTENTS

# FOREWORD

Fifty or sixty years ago, most Christians in the Western world who chose to be involved in evangelism were trying to win people to Christ who already enjoyed some knowledge of the Bible, people who, culturally speaking, were not too dissimilar from us. Whether we were involved in "personal work" (as one-on-one evangelism was then labeled) or speaking more formally to groups, the barriers to communication did not seem insuperable. Of course, we all recognized that what was needed was a work of the Spirit of God: it is impossible simply to talk people into the kingdom. But most of the time it seemed we were, if not on the same page, at least in the same country and talking the same language.

All of this has changed. For a start, owing not least to worldwide immigration patterns, most of our cities are hives of racial and cultural diversity, including many people from places that provided little instruction in the Bible or the Christian faith. Meanwhile, rising biblical illiteracy characterizes the majority of people in the West. The assumptions of the current form of secularism dictate that every individual enjoys not only the right but the obligation to choose their own path and identity: it is ugly and foolish to submit to self-proclaimed authorities, and those authorities that try to tell you who you are and what you must do—religious, traditional, governmental—are narrowminded, corrupt, and intolerant.

This means that most of the themes that tie the Bible together have little resonance in our world. Such themes as covenant, truth, sacrifice, temple, resurrection, priest, sin, atonement, and justification are not common topics of conversation when we gather for some Thai food or munch on a burrito. Worse, in almost every case, the limited religious vocabulary of the contemporary Western world means something a little different from what those words mean in the Bible—faith, spiritual, truth, salvation, conversion. Seventy-five years ago, questions like "Where will you spend eternity?" and "Did you know that Jesus died to save sinners?" might not have been welcomed, but they weren't displaced in the culture with questions like "What gender am I?" and "What is better for me, Netflix or Amazon Prime?"

The result of these changes is that it often feels as if Christians who share their faith, and the people with whom they are sharing, live in different worlds. To change the metaphor, even brief conversations about religion feel a bit like two ships slipping past each other in the night, neither quite comprehending that the other is there.

Enter Sam Chan. Sam has thought deeply about what the gospel is, but also about what makes contemporary culture tick. He has a distinctive take on postmodernism and can talk knowledgeably about skepticism and plausibility structures, but he is driven by the gospel. No less important, he loves people and is himself engaged in both personal evangelism and public evangelism. Here is a helpful guide and stimulus to get on with the evangelism we know we should be doing but have sometimes abandoned because we feel intimidated. No more intimidation: the gospel is still the power of God that brings salvation, and Sam helps us recover that confidence.

—*D. A. Carson*

# ACKNOWLEDGMENTS

No person is an island. We all stand on the shoulders of others. And we are shaped by our friends and family.

My thinking about and practice of evangelism have been profoundly shaped by John Chapman, Sydney's champion evangelist, who taught the subject of evangelism to me at Bible college.

I've also benefitted from the examples and thoughts of creative evangelists such as John G. (can't mention his full name), Aaron Koh, Andrew Wong, Lawrence Tan, Morgan Powell, Jon Dykes, Andrew Bardsley, Ariel Kurilowicz, Christine Dillon, Phil Nicholson, and Tim Chen. They have shared and demonstrated to me their insights on contextualization and evangelism.

Huge thanks to my employer, City Bible Forum, who has a massive heart for evangelism. City Bible Forum has given me a safe haven to explore fresh ideas and methods of evangelism. They understand me. They give me a long leash. And they graciously give me the freedom to fail.

A big shout out to their own gifted team of evangelists, including Tho Luu, Lachlan Orr, Alan Stewart, Russell Matthews, Caroline Spencer, Peter Kaldor, Craig Josling, Lish Lo, Grace Huang, and Mark Leong, to name a handful. Thank you for putting up with me and my eccentricities.

A big nod to my parents, Winnie and Joseph. Their generosity in supporting my PhD studies at Trinity Evangelical Divinity School is what has made all of this possible. In God's providence I was exposed to the thinking (and hospitality) of great professors such as Graham Cole, Don Carson, Kevin Vanhoozer, John Woodbridge, Harold Netland, Paul Feinberg, John Feinberg, Paul Hiebert, Willem VanGemeren, and Peter Cha. More important, these great thinkers modeled humility and how to be gracious to people who have different viewpoints.

But most of all, my evangelism is possible because of my wife, Stephanie. She is one of the world's keenest and most competent evangelists. She shares the gospel to so many friends in so many different ways. She is evidence that hospitality provides the space and foundation for evangelism. She doesn't just *do* evangelism. Her whole life *is* evangelism.

# CHAPTER 1

# A THEOLOGY OF EVANGELISM

## What must I do for my friend to be saved?

Anne is a stay-at-home mom who helps to run the play group at her church. After dropping off her two older sons at school, she brings her youngest son to the play group. Anne enjoys watching her son play with other four-year-olds while she has coffee with other parents.

One of the aims of the play group is to create opportunities for evangelism. Many of the parents and children don't come from churched backgrounds, so the play group offers a unique opportunity to tell them the gospel of Jesus Christ.

Anne does this by mixing stories from the Bible with well-known children's storybooks. For story time, the children might hear about Little Red Riding Hood, the Cat in the Hat, and David and Goliath. Next, Anne incorporates Bible stories into the craft activities. So far, the children have made slingshots to go with the David and Goliath story, long-haired wigs to go with the Samson story, and bandages to go with the story about Jesus raising Lazarus.

Anne is excited by the play group's success. But lately there have been complaints from the Christian parents. They're frustrated that the gospel isn't being communicated. Why isn't Anne using the Four Spiritual Laws, which is how many of the Christian parents first heard the gospel? And why hasn't Anne talked about Jesus' substitutionary death on the cross?

Has Anne been doing evangelism at all? Has she been communicating the gospel of Jesus Christ? In what sense is the play group an evangelistic play group?

What counts as evangelism? What is the gospel? These words carry a lot of baggage, tradition, and emotion. Many well-meaning Christians remember fondly how they were told the gospel at some evangelistic event. For them, that will remain the only recognizable form of evangelism.

You may be coming to this book with a well-developed sense of what you mean by the word evangelism, or you may come with your own questions. To answer some of these questions, we will start by exploring a theology of evangelism. We will do this by surveying how the Bible describes evangelism and then applying this to our contemporary settings. So let's begin with some definitions. What is evangelism according to the Bible?

## WHAT IS EVANGELISM?

I want to be clear that while many people use the word evangelism in different ways, we are looking to understand evangelism as an idea that we get from the Bible. There is just one problem. There is no direct-equivalent word for our English word evangelism in the Bible. There is no noun that matches how we use the term in English.

The Bible uses these Greek words: *euangelion*—"gospel"—to describe what is said (Mark 1:14–15); *euangelistes*—"evangelist"—to describe the person who is telling the gospel (Acts 21:8; Eph. 4:11); and *euangelizo*—"to proclaim the gospel"—to describe the activity of telling the gospel (Rom. 10:15). The best way to understand the term evangelism is that it is our attempt to describe what happens when someone tells the *euangelion* or gospel.

### What Do the Terms *Euangelion* and Gospel Mean?

*Euangelion*, or gospel, usually refers to the "good news" about Jesus Christ. It is the story of God saving his people and judging his enemies by sending Jesus Christ. In this sense, *euangelion* or gospel is more broadly both good news and bad news.[1]

---

1. For more on this double aspect—good news and bad news—of the gospel, see Broughton Knox, "What Is the Gospel?" *The Briefing* 343 (April 2007), 10–13.

## Hebrew

In the Old Testament, the Hebrew terms are *besorah* (noun) and *basar* (verb), which the Septuagint translates into Greek as *euangelion* and *euangelizo* respectively. These terms refer to the activity of bringing significant news in any general sense (1 Sam. 4:17; 1 Kings 1:42; Jer. 20:15). But they also come to mean significant news in a specific sense—God's acts of salvation, especially the promised eschatological salvation of his people (Ps. 40:9; 68:11; 96:2; Isa. 40:9; 41:27; 52:7; 61:1; Joel 2:32; Nah. 1:15).[2]

## Greek

Outside of the Bible, the Greek word *euangelion* (in the neuter singular) hardly occurs. And when we do find it being used, it doesn't mean "good news" until several centuries after the New Testament.

But in the New Testament, *euangelion* recalls what we saw in the Old Testament's use of *basar*—"to bring good news." The word is used seventy-six times in the New Testament—sixty times by Paul alone. It typically refers to the story about Jesus Christ (1 Cor. 15:1; Gal. 1:11; 2:2) or of someone telling this story (1 Cor. 9:14; 2 Cor. 2:12; 8:18).[3]

## English

The English word gospel comes from the Anglo-Saxon word God-spell—literally, "God's story." It is used in our English Bibles to translate the Greek word *euangelion*. When William Tyndale translated the Bible into English, he used gospel to mean "good news."

## What Does the Concept of Evangelism Mean?

Evangelism is a term we use in English for the act of communicating the gospel. This idea is conveyed in the New Testament by the verb *euangelizo* ("to bring good news"). But the concept should be broadly understood to include several different ways of bringing that good news to people. It includes any form of communicating the gospel, and there are several New Testament verbs that convey this idea, such as *martureo* ("to testify" or "bear witness"), *kerusso* ("to herald"), *parakaleo* ("to exhort"), *katangelo* ("to proclaim"), or *propheteuo* ("to prophesy"), and *didasko* ("to teach").[4]

---

2. Douglas Moo, *The Epistle to the Romans*, New International Commentary on the New Testament (Grand Rapids, Mich.: Eerdmans, 1996), 43n16.

3. Moo, *Epistle to the Romans*, 43n16.

4. Klaas Runia, "What Is Preaching according to the New Testament?" *Tyndale Bulletin* 29 (1978): 3–48.

### Evangelism Is Defined by Its Message

While several terms indicate the variety of ways we communicate the gospel, the essence of evangelism is in the message, the gospel of Jesus. Evangelism is the event of communicating this message, or we might say that evangelism is defined by its message. The essence of evangelism is not the method (preaching, singing, acting) nor the medium (a person, a book, a song) nor the occasion (church service, commencement speech, school camp) nor the audience (believers and nonbelievers).

### Evangelism Has Broad and Narrow Senses

In a broad sense, evangelism communicates the gospel to both believers and nonbelievers. We find this sense of evangelism, for example, when Paul says, "[Christ] is the one we proclaim, admonishing and teaching everyone with all wisdom, so that we may present everyone fully mature in Christ" (Col. 1:28). Paul communicates (evangelizes) the gospel to the believers, those who already know and follow Jesus. In this broad sense, evangelism is the basis of preaching, teaching, and ethical exhortations to believers. Without the gospel message, our preaching, teaching, and exhortations to believers would be reduced to legalism and moral aphorisms.

In the midtwentieth century, C. H. Dodd wrongly made it fashionable to distinguish between preaching to believers and evangelizing nonbelievers. But this distinction cannot be supported biblically, because in the New Testament the gospel is the basis of both activities. Both believers and nonbelievers are being preached to and evangelized with the gospel.[5]

However, we can also define evangelism in a narrow sense as communicating the gospel to nonbelievers to urge them to believe in Jesus (Acts 8:35; Rom. 10:14–15). For the rest of this book, we will use the term evangelism in this sense.

### Evangelism Is Not Defined by Its Method

In the Bible, there is no single method of communicating the gospel; instead there is a variety of methods. In the New Testament alone, we find:

- Parables by Jesus
- Songs
- Creeds
- Letters to churches

---

5. For a further critique of Dodd's thesis, see Runia, "What Is Preaching?" 13–16.

- One-on-one conversations
- Sermons in formal worship gatherings
- Discussion meetings
- Public speeches
- Apocalyptic literature
- Miracles

Unfortunately, well-meaning Christians often get stuck on one particular method and end up believing it is the only or best method. Usually this is the method that we have become an expert in. Or it is the method that was effective in our own conversion. Or it is the method that distinguishes our tradition or denomination from others.

For example, my American friends tell me that for a long time, much of North American evangelism utilized tent-style crusades. Or it relied on crisis evangelism, sharing the gospel in a way that emphasized making a decision at that moment.[6] While it's understandable why we might use one method for a long time, it does mean that we miss out on the strengths of other methods. And we risk becoming legalistic and reductionist by insisting on one method, confusing orthodoxy (the message) with orthopraxy (the method).

My hope is that this book will help us to be aware of our prejudices about methods of evangelism and to explore different methods and appreciate their strengths.

## WHAT IS THE GOSPEL?

We have defined evangelism as an event where the gospel is communicated. But what exactly is this gospel? How do we describe it? How do we understand it? To answer these questions, we will look at the gospel from three different but complementary perspectives.

### 1. The Gospel according to the New Testament Writers

Let's say we're trained as New Testament exegetes. We would answer the question "What is the gospel?" by describing what New Testament writers such as Paul say about it. From passages such as Romans 1:1–5 and 1 Corinthians 15:1–4, we can observe four things:

---

6. Wayne Grudem, *Systematic Theology* (Leicester, UK: Inter-Varsity, 1994).

1.  The gospel is the story about Jesus Christ: who he is and what he has done.
2.  Our access to the gospel is through the Scriptures.
3.  The gospel, which demands a response of faith and obedience, brings salvation.
4.  The gospel is communicated to both believers and nonbelievers.

---

## GOD'S GOSPEL OR MY GOSPEL?

In Romans 1:1, the apostle Paul tells us that the gospel is "the gospel of God"; it is God's gospel.* This means the story belongs to God; it is not our story to invent, modify, or embellish. We should also trust in its power. We do not need to add anything to it to make it more powerful.

At the same time, in Romans 16:25 Paul tells us that the gospel is "my gospel, the message I proclaim about Jesus Christ"; it is Paul's gospel as proclaimed by him. So even though the story belongs to God, it is told by a human evangelist. In this sense, it is our story to tell. It has to come through our personality, culture, language, idioms, emotions, limitations, and experiences.

There is always this tension to the act of evangelism. We have a timeless story from God, which is true for all peoples of all cultures and in all places. But at the same time, it has to be told by a person who is in a time, culture, and place. Throughout this book, we will return to this tension again and again, and we'll explore it in greater detail in later chapters.

---

\* This was drummed into my head by one of Sydney's champion evangelists, John Chapman. I can still hear his distinctive voice saying, "It is *God's gospel.*"

---

## 2. The Gospel according to Theologians

Let's say we're trained as systematic theologians. We would answer the question "What is the gospel?" by prescribing systematized biblical ideas for our contemporary setting. Most approaches to evangelism in the West use some type of theological grid to communicate and explain Christian beliefs. For example, we could break down the gospel story into a variation on the following main points:[7]

---

7. I owe this observation to a talk I heard by Timothy Keller called "Dwelling in the Gospel,"

1. God created us.
2. We have sinned against God.
3. Jesus saves us from our punishment.
4. We now have a decision to make.

These main points are fleshed out with our theologies of creation, sin, salvation, and conversion. This has been the predominant approach to evangelism over the last century, commonly found in methods like Evangelism Explosion, the Four Spiritual Laws, Bridge to Life, and Two Ways to Live. Perhaps you can think of others.

## 3. The Gospel according to Storytellers

Let's say we're trained as storytellers, in particular as biblical theologians. We would answer the question "What is the gospel?" by tracing the story of what God has done, and continues to do, to save his people. As an example of this approach, Timothy Keller suggests the following storytelling grid:[8]

1. Manger
2. Cross
3. King

We would begin by telling the story of how Jesus came to us in a manger. God the Son came to us as a human being, a servant. He ate and drank with the poor, the marginalized, and the outcast. Theologians call this act the incarnation. It illustrates the new ethic and reversal of values described by New Testament writers: "The last will be first, and the first will be last" (Matt. 20:16), "Blessed are the meek" (Matt. 5:5), and "He made himself nothing" (Phil. 2:7).

Next, we tell the story of how Jesus died for us on a cross. God the Son saves us from our sins by dying in our place. This is an act of grace. We are saved not by our goodness but by this gift from God. Theologians call this act substitutionary atonement. It is the salvation by grace described by New Testament writers: "All have sinned . . . all are justified freely by his grace through the redemption that came by Christ Jesus" (Rom. 3:23–24).

Finally, we tell the story of how Jesus will come again as king. God

---

presented at the New York City Dwell Conference, April 30, 2008.

8. Timothy Keller borrows this from Simon Gathercole. This is from Keller's talk "Dwelling in the Gospel."

the Son is coming again to renew this world. He will right all wrongs and wipe away every tear. The renewed life that we enjoy now in the gift of God's Spirit will be enjoyed forever, more fully, in a renewed world. This is what theologians call restoration. It is the consummation described by New Testament writers: "The kingdom of the world has become the kingdom of our Lord" (Rev. 11:15).

## WHAT ARE THE ROLES IN EVANGELISM?

In an orchestra, there are different parts to play. Some people play the violin. Some play the trumpet. In my high school orchestra, I played the percussion instruments—the triangle and tambourine. In the same way, there are different roles in evangelism. Let's unpack this idea by looking at a passage from Paul's first letter to the church at Thessalonica.

In 1 Thessalonians 1:4–10, Paul describes when he evangelized the Christians in Thessalonica. We can note that in this passage, six different roles are being played:

1. God's role is to *choose* people for salvation (v. 4). God has a sovereign role in salvation. This is the theological idea of calling, election, and predestination.
2. Jesus' role is to *save* people from wrath (v. 10). He is responsible for dying for people and their sins, rising from the dead, and one day coming back to judge people. Jesus' other role is that the gospel story is about him (v. 8). The gospel is a message about who Jesus is and what he's done to save people from their sins.
3. Paul's role is to *communicate the gospel* (v. 5). He did this both with words and actions, not just what he said but also how he lived. Paul gives more details about his model life in 1 Thessalonians 2:6–12.
4. The Holy Spirit's role is to *empower* the person who is communicating the gospel (v. 5). Perhaps this means that the Spirit gives the person the gift of effective communication or the words to say. And the Spirit also *illuminates* the person hearing the gospel by convicting them (v. 5) and opening their heart to receive the gospel with joy (v. 6).
5. The Thessalonians *hear* the gospel and *welcome* it with joy (v. 6b). They respond with faith (v. 8b) by turning from their idols to God (vv. 8b–9). Now they imitate Paul (v. 6a) and are models for other believers (v. 7) while they wait for Jesus to return (v. 10).

6. The gospel is a *message about Jesus* (v. 8). It is the means by which the Holy Spirit convicts people of their sins (v. 5) and enables them to welcome God's salvation with joy (v. 6).

We can describe these different roles in evangelism using theological categories:

| God | Chooses (v. 5) | Election |
| --- | --- | --- |
| Jesus | Saves (v. 10) | Atonement |
| Paul (the evangelist) | Brings the gospel (v. 5) | External call |
| Holy Spirit | Power, suffering, joy (vv. 5–6) | Internal call |
| Thessalonians (hearers) | Faith and repentance (vv. 8–9) | Conversion |
| Gospel message | Story of Jesus (v. 8) | Instrument |

And when we look elsewhere in the New Testament, we find similar roles—multiple, different, complementary—in Philip's evangelism of the Ethiopian (Acts 8:26–40) and Paul's evangelism of the gentiles (Acts 13:48).

When I work as a medical doctor at the hospital, the doctors and nurses are given multiple, different, and complementary roles in a surgical operation. The surgeon's role is to perform the knee surgery. The anesthesiologist's role is to keep the patient asleep and pain free. The nurse's role is to pass the surgical instruments to the surgeon. My role, as the surgical assistant, is to hold the leg. It's important that I stay focused on my role so that I can do it well. It's also important that I don't try to perform someone else's role, because that will burden me with a responsibility that isn't mine. At the same time, I do everything I can to cooperate with the others on our team, helping them to do their roles, complementing what they do, and trying not to get in their way.

It's the same with evangelism. Our role is to communicate the gospel both in words and actions. But our role is not God's: we are not sovereignly choosing who gets saved. Our role is not Jesus': we are not saving people from their sins. Our role is not the Holy Spirit's: we cannot force people to believe. Instead we must stay focused on our role as the evangelist and do it well. We do everything we can to cooperate with God, complement what he does, and not create obstacles to evangelism.

## God's Sovereignty and Human Responsibility

This brings us to a question about the relationship between God's sovereignty in evangelism and our responsibility as the human evangelist. Many Bible passages emphasize God's sovereignty in the task of evangelism. (See 2 Tim. 2:10 and Matt. 9:37–38 as examples.) But there are also Bible passages that emphasize the human evangelist's responsibility (Rom. 10:14–15; 2 Tim. 4:5).

This is another of those healthy tensions in the Bible. If we emphasize only God's sovereignty and remove our responsibility, we become lazy fatalists: "God will do something if he wants to." But if we emphasize only our responsibility and remove God's sovereignty, we become overburdened with guilt for not evangelizing enough, despairing that not enough are responding to our message, and disappointed with our inadequate gifts. We might even feel the need to coerce or manipulate people into belief. Even worse, we might become proud when our efforts are rewarded by people responding to our message.

But if we get the tension right, we will praise God when people respond to the gospel, because it's God who chooses people for salvation. We will also pray to God to open the hearts of the hearers, because that is something only God can do. We will also be encouraged to do the work of an evangelist no matter how unrewarding it is, because we know that God is in control. At any moment, he might use our gospel message, no matter how poorly gifted we are, as the natural means to bring someone to salvation. For our part, we should do everything within our strength, gifting, and circumstances to communicate the gospel clearly, frequently, and persuasively.

## The External and Internal Call of the Gospel

The Protestant Reformers gave us the useful categories of the external and internal calls of the gospel to help us understand the relationship between God's sovereignty and human responsibility in evangelism.

When an evangelist communicates the gospel, this is the external call of the gospel. It is open, public, and resistible. For example, if I tell my friend Larry about Jesus, this is the external call. It's happening openly: I know I'm doing it; Larry knows I'm doing it. It's publicly verifiable: anyone watching can verify that I'm telling Larry about Jesus. And it's resistible: Larry can choose not to believe my message.

The internal call of the gospel occurs if God effectively uses the gospel to open the heart of the nonbeliever, moving that person from unbelief to belief. For example, when I tell my friend Larry about Jesus, if God sovereignly chooses, the Holy Spirit will apply my words to Larry's heart. Larry is illuminated: he hears and understands; he sees and believes. His heart is regenerated so that he can respond to the gospel call by moving to faith and repentance. This work of the Holy Spirit is hidden: I don't know whether it's happening. It is private: I have no access to what's going on. And it is effectual: God sovereignly cooperates with Larry's free will so that he chooses to believe the gospel.

As with much of theology, the exact terms—external and internal calls of the gospel—are not found in the Bible, but they express biblical ideas and concepts. In some Bible passages, we have evidence of the external call of the gospel, which is resisted (Matt. 22:14; John 5:39–40). In other passages, we see the internal call of the gospel, which is hidden, private, and effectual (John 3:8; 10:3; Acts 16:14).

My friend Andrew once invited his nonbelieving friend to hear Billy Graham preach the gospel. Graham was preaching somewhere in a studio in the USA, and the message was being broadcast to TV sets all over the world.

Andrew and his friend sat in front of a small TV to hear Graham. But Graham was much weakened by the effects of age and disease. He was no longer the powerful and gifted speaker that most of us remember. Even worse, the picture was tiny and the sound quality was poor.

Andrew was embarrassed that he had asked his friend to listen to this gospel presentation. So when Billy Graham invited people to respond to the message by getting up out of their chairs, kneeling, and praying with him, Andrew hardly expected any response from his friend. But to Andrew's surprise, his friend got up out of his chair, knelt, and prayed to become a believer.

The lesson for Andrew and for us is that if God sovereignly chooses, he can use our gospel presentation, the external call—no matter how unimpressive—to internally call someone to faith.

## Is Evangelism Something God Does? Or Something I Do?

If I want my friend Larry to become a Christian, do I pray to God that the Holy Spirit will open Larry's heart so that he believes and follows Jesus? Or do I have to tell Larry the gospel and urge Larry to respond to it with faith and repentance? Or is it both God's work and my efforts that help Larry become a Christian? And how does that happen?

We ask these questions because there is often confusion between the Spirit's supernatural personal agency and our natural means. These are two real phenomena, but they are complementary rather than contradictory.

For example, when we read in Exodus 14:21–22 that God parted the Red Sea, we can ask, "What caused the Red Sea to part?" On the one hand, we have a supernatural explanation: God parted the sea. But on the other, we also have a natural explanation: a wind blew back the sea. And we have an instrumental explanation: Moses stretched out his hand!

What's really going on here? We have God's supernatural personal agency performing a miracle with the natural means of the wind, which is orchestrated by the instrumental means of Moses' stretching out his hand. And it's the same with evangelism. If God saves my friend Larry, it's because of the Spirit's supernatural personal agency opening Larry's heart with the natural and instrumental means of my telling Larry the gospel. So we shouldn't pit our efforts against God's efforts, as if by evangelizing our friends we are not trusting in God's sovereign power. The opposite is true. In his sovereignty, God uses our human efforts as the natural and instrumental means of converting people into followers of Jesus.

## A DEFINITION OF EVANGELISM

After considering all of these factors, we can arrive at this definition of evangelism:

> The essence of evangelism is the message that Jesus Christ is Lord. Evangelism is our human effort of proclaiming this message—which necessarily involves using our human communication, language, idioms, metaphors, stories, experiences, personality, emotions, context, culture, locatedness—and trusting and praying that God, in his sovereign will, will supernaturally use our human and natural means to effect his divine purposes.
>
> In a general sense, evangelism refers to our human efforts of proclaiming this message to any audience of believers and nonbelievers. In a narrower sense, evangelism refers to our human efforts of proclaiming this message to nonbelievers. But in both senses, we proclaim the gospel with the hope that our audience responds by trusting, repenting, and following and obeying Jesus.

An earlier book I wrote on preaching, called *Preaching as the Word of God*, applies something called speech-act theory to the preaching of the gospel.[9] Speech-act theory, as developed by J. L. Austin and John Searle, proposes that meaning is located not in the words we say *per se* but in the speech act that we perform. To speak is to perform an act, and it is a false dichotomy to distinguish between stating facts and performing an action.[10]

According to J. L. Austin, a speech act consists of three actions:

1. *Locution:* the act *of* saying something. It is the *meaning*—sense and reference—of what I say.
2. *Illocution:* the act *in* saying something. It is the *force*—the action performed—of what I say.
3. *Perlocution:* the act *by* saying something. It is the *effect*—the result—of what I say.

For example, if I say, "Close the door!" the locution is my statement, "Close the door." The illocution is a command. And the perlocution is that you close the door. But there is a problem with this formulation. Although, as the speaker, I might have an intended perlocution—that you close the door—I can't guarantee that you will do so. You might ignore me. Or you might close the door.

For this reason, John Searle better formulizes a speech act as *F(p)*. The *p* refers to the locution—the propositional information being communicated. And the *F* refers to the illocutionary force—the action performed. According to Searle, a propositional utterance can never exist alone. For example, even if I merely utter, "The door is closed," I have performed an illocutionary action of uttering. There is no such thing as a free-floating propositional statement. It is always accompanied by an illocutionary force of some sort.

On the flip side, the same *p* (the information communicated) can be accompanied by multiple, different *F*s (the action performed). So, for example, let's say *p* is, "The door is closed." If *F* is a question, we have, "Is the door closed?" If *F* is a command, we have, "Close the door." If *F* is a promise, we have, "I promise I will close the door."

---

9. My work was inspired by Kevin Vanhoozer's *Is There a Meaning in This Text? The Bible, the Reader, and the Morality of Literary Knowledge* (Grand Rapids, Mich.: Zondervan, 1998).

10. Sam Chan, *Preaching as the Word of God: Answering an Old Question with Speech-Act Theory* (Eugene, Ore.: Pickwick, 2016); Vanhoozer, *Is There a Meaning in This Text? The Bible, the Reader, and the Morality of Literary Knowledge* (Grand Rapids, Mich.: Zondervan, 1998); J. L. Austin, *How to Do Things with Words: The William James Lectures Delivered at Harvard University in 1955*, ed. J. O. Urmson and Marina Sbisa (Cambridge, Mass.: Harvard Univ. Press, 1962); John R. Searle, *Speech Acts: An Essay in the Philosophy of Language* (New York: Cambridge Univ. Press, 1969).

What does any of this have to do with evangelism? If we apply this concept to evangelism, then $p$ is the propositional idea that "Jesus is Lord," or what we refer to in shorthand as the gospel. But what is $F$? What is the illocutionary force of evangelism? What action are we performing? Here we find more than one answer. Is the action we perform to communicate the gospel teaching, proclaiming, heralding, witnessing, urging, beseeching, calling, commanding, promising, blessing, warning, prophesying, exhorting, edifying, or encouraging?

And more than this. There is more than one way of performing the same speech act. It can be done through utterances, drama, song, poetry, stained-glass windows, puppet shows, and art. This is because the essence of communication is neither the words themselves nor the methods of communication, but the speech act itself.

I hope the answer is clear. The essence of evangelism is the locution—$p$—the good news of Jesus. It is not defined by its method or audience. And we can even say that evangelism is not entirely defined by its illocutionary force. This implies that we don't have to restrict our understanding of evangelism to only one illocutionary force. Depending on the audience and context, we are free to choose an appropriate illocutionary force. It might be that we communicate the gospel through urging. Or by encouraging. Or it might be by blessing. Or through a warning. And it can be performed through speaking. Or singing. Or drama. Or a puppet show.

## HOW DOES SOMEONE BECOME A CHRISTIAN?

People like to ask how my wife and I met. I usually reply, "Whose story do you want?" Because the reality is that my wife and I have two different perspectives of how we met. Both are true, yet they are different and complementary.

The same principle is at work when we're asked how someone becomes a Christian. We can reply, "Whose story do you want?" Because God and the convert have two different yet complementary stories to tell.

### God's Side of the Story: I *Regenerate* Them

From God's perspective, someone becomes a Christian because God regenerates them. Regeneration literally means "to be born again." God gives an individual a supernatural new birth in which the new believer moves from spiritual death to a new life (John 3:3; Titus 3:5; 2 Cor. 5:17;

1 Peter 1:3). Although regeneration is instantaneous, it is continuous with God's other activities in bringing salvation to a believer:

1. Internal call
2. **Regeneration**
3. Progressive sanctification
4. Preservation
5. Glorification

Although it's useful to distinguish between the different activities, they are all related because they are all supernatural works of God, internal and transformative, and they affect the entire person.

God's supernatural work of regeneration is effected through the natural means of someone hearing the gospel (James 1:18; 1 Peter 1:23). So we can say that the cause of regeneration is the supernatural work of God, but the instrumental means is someone hearing the gospel. Although regeneration happens through the supernatural and miraculous work of God, it happens through the ordinary speaking of the gospel by finite and fallible people like you and me.

## The Power of Words

Philosophers like to talk about the interface between God and his creation. They ask, How does God sustain the universe? How does God do miracles? How does God make it rain? How does God answer prayer? How does God get me to do what he wants?

For a long time, because of the influence of Greek philosopher Aristotle, we talked about the causal link between God and his creation. When God parted the Red Sea, God was the primary cause, but the wind was the secondary cause. But the problem with this model is it treats the entire universe—rocks, plants, animals, angels, humans—as inanimate objects. Human beings are no different from tennis balls bouncing off each other. God is the giant tennis ball, while everything else in the universe, including people, are little tennis balls.

But human beings are more than inanimate objects. We are agents with free will. More than that, we are persons with stories, emotions, and personalities. So how does God interact with persons? How does God get persons to do what he wants?

Well, we might begin to answer this question by asking, "How does anyone get a person to do something?" Let me give you an example. Once a week, it is my turn to take out the trash. How does my wife get me to take out the trash? If I were an object, she could try throwing a tennis ball at my head. Maybe the force of her throw would move me to take out the trash. But I am more than an object. I am a personal agent with a personality, a story, and free will. My wife gets me to take out the trash with words. "Sam, please take out the trash." Her words interact with my will, and they move me to action.

If we are persons, then the interface between God and people is a dialogical link rather than merely a causal link. To put it simply, God effects his will with his words.[11]

God's creation of the universe begins with words: "Let there be light." Jesus raises Lazarus from the dead with words: "Lazarus, come out!" And God raises us from our spiritual death into new life with words: the words of the gospel.

## The Person's Side of the Story: I *Converted*

Conversion is a theological term to describe what a person has to do to be saved. It answers the question asked by the jailer, "What must I do to be saved?" (Acts 16:30). While regeneration describes what God does to save a person, conversion describes what the person needs to do to be saved. Typically, theologians break down the act of conversion into two different but related actions: repentance and faith. And the act of repentance is further divided into two different but related actions: *metanoia* and *epistrophe*.

### *Metanoia*

The Greek term *metanoia* describes a change of heart, character, and disposition. This change has a positive aspect. In the same way that it is good to change out of dirty old clothes into clean new clothes, it is good to have a change of heart, character, or disposition. I remember as a young backpacker the thrill of showering after a weeklong trip and changing into clean clothes. This is a picture of the thrill of a new convert who experiences *metanoia:* it feels good to be clean again!

I emphasize this because as theologian Anthony Hoekema notes, poor Bible translations have missed this positive aspect. *Metanoia* was translated as "penance" by the Latin Vulgate and in Luther's German Bible, and as "remorse" *(repentez-vous)* in older French Bibles. So our understanding of

---

11. I owe these observations to teachings that I absorbed in various lectures from Graham Cole and Kevin Vanhoozer during my time as a student at Trinity Evangelical Divinity School, Deerfield, Illinois.

*metanoia* through these poor translations became one of sorrow, fear of punishment, and an emotional crisis. True piety was seen as emphasizing regret, remorse, and morbid introspection.[12]

But the biblical understanding of *metanoia* is far more positive. Instead of merely looking inward and regretting the past, it is looking outward and forward. When Jesus says, "Repent [*metanoieo*], for the kingdom of heaven has come near" (Matt. 4:17), he is saying, "You must *change your hearts*—for the kingdom of Heaven has arrived" (Phillips). He is calling us to look ahead to the arrival of the kingdom. By being outward and forward looking, *metanoia* produces fruit (Matt. 3:8), knowledge (2 Tim. 2:25), life (Acts 11:18), and salvation (2 Cor. 7:10).

### Epistrophe

The Greek term *epistrophe* is the second aspect of biblical repentance. It describes a complete turnaround and has both negative and positive aspects: we turn away from something negative and toward something positive. It reminds me of the time I went along a one-way street in the wrong direction, hoping to take a shortcut. Unfortunately, a large truck was heading straight toward me. I had to quickly make a U-turn—a complete turnaround—away from certain collision and toward going the right way on the one-way street.

We read in 1 Thessalonians 1:9 that the Thessalonians "turned to God from idols to serve the living and true God." And Paul's mission is to "turn them from darkness to light, and from the power of Satan to God" (Acts 26:18). Both passages describe a turning away from something negative toward something positive: toward service to God.

But who is responsible for repentance? On the one hand, God grants repentance (Acts 11:18; 2 Tim. 2:25; John 6:65). But on the other hand, the convert must decide to repent (Jer. 25:5). And even (on another hand!) the evangelist contributes to this process, urging the listener toward repentance (2 Tim. 2:25; 2 Cor. 5:20; James 5:20).

### Understanding Biblical Faith

In the Bible, the word for faith can be translated into many English words, such as belief, trust, and of course faith (Gen. 15:6; Ps. 25:2; Ps. 57:1; John 3:16; 1 John 3:23). The Reformers identified three aspects of faith. There is propositional knowing *(notitia)* that includes knowledge and

---

12. Anthony Hoekema, *Saved by Grace* (Grand Rapids, Mich.: Eerdmans, 1994), 124–25.

understanding of facts. For example, I know there is scientific data that says exercise is good for me. In the same way, I know that there is a person called Jesus Christ who claims to be the Son of God. But knowing the facts, while important, is not all there is to biblical faith. There is also assent *(assensus)*, where I grant that such claims are true. For example, I acknowledge that exercise really is good for me. In the same way, I acknowledge that Jesus Christ really is the Son of God. So we have knowledge of facts and assent that they are true, but something further is still necessary to have biblical faith. We must also exercise trust *(fiducia)*, making our lives consistent with the truth claims we agree with. For example, I commit myself to exercise, trusting that it is good for me. In the same way, I commit myself to Christ, trusting that he will save me from my sins. The first two aspects are necessary, but not sufficient, for salvation, for even demons know that Jesus is Lord (James 2:19). It is the final aspect—trusting in Jesus—that is necessary for salvation (John 3:16). This is what is commonly called saving faith.

We believe that we are saved by faith and not by works. But if we have saving faith, it will naturally produce good works. If I return to my exercise example, if I know that exercise is good for me, really believe it, and then take steps that reflect this belief, I'll experience the fruit of my faith: the benefits of exercise. In this sense, we can say that saving faith is always accompanied by works. Or as the Reformers said, we are saved by faith alone, but that faith is never alone.

For example, faith, when it is described in Luke's Gospel, is always accompanied by action:

- Friends lower a paralyzed man through the roof in front of Jesus (5:20).
- A centurion asks Jesus to heal his servant with a word (7:9).
- A sinful woman washes Jesus' feet with her tears and hair (7:50).
- A bleeding woman fights through a crowd to touch Jesus' cloak (8:48).
- The man healed from leprosy comes back to thank Jesus (17:19).
- The blind beggar calls to Jesus to have mercy on him (18:42).

Faith is accompanied by high-risk actions, the type that will make you look foolish if you're wrong. For example, consider the chutzpah of the friends who dug through someone else's roof to interrupt Jesus by lowering their paralyzed friend into the middle of a large crowd. Someone once told me this would be like interrupting a Beyoncé concert. Or consider the centurion who tells Jesus not to bother to come to his home but to heal his servant with a word. Imagine how silly he would've felt if he returned home and found that his servant was still sick. He would've had to explain to his disappointed servant why he told Jesus not to bother to come. The centurion's household would've blamed him for the servant's eventual death. It was a bold and risky move to trust Jesus.

The climactic example of faith in the Gospel of Luke is Zacchaeus (19:1–9). He is the foil to the rich young ruler (18:18) and the Pharisees (16:14) who fail to exercise faith in Jesus. Although the word faith is not used, Zacchaeus demonstrates faith with his actions—running ahead of the crowd, climbing a tree, welcoming Jesus to his home for a meal, and giving away his possessions to the poor. All of this illustrates that while salvation is a free gift from God—it's not something we earn or merit—the faith required to accept this free gift might prove to be costly. Faith asks us to commit fully to what we believe.

## WHAT IS FAITH?

Faith asks us to believe in God. But we can know God only by believing in his Word, in what he has revealed to us. So the character of our faith depends on the nature of God's revelation. In the history of theology, the debate has swung between understanding God's revelation as propositional—we have an *I-it* encounter with God—and as existential—we have an *I-Thou* encounter with God. In the end, the Bible indicates that it is both. To know God, we have to know the propositions about him. But God is more than a set of propositions; he is also personal. So to know God also means to encounter God existentially and personally.

It is no different when we exercise saving faith. Biblical faith is not less than understanding (*notitia*) and assenting (*assensus*) to propositional truths about Jesus. But it is more than that. It requires trust (*fiducia*) in Jesus as a person. And often trust in Jesus requires us to make a daring existential leap—to get out of our comfort zones and risk our possessions and our reputations.

Who is responsible for faith? Is it a gift or something we have to find within ourselves? On the one hand, the Bible teaches that God grants the believer faith (Eph. 2:8; Phil. 1:29). But on the other hand, the Bible is clear that the convert is responsible to believe (John 3:16; Rom. 3:28). And yet even further (on another hand!), the evangelist's role is to urge the listener toward belief (John 20:31). We are told that faith comes from hearing the word about Christ (Rom. 10:17).

This raises another question that many are asking today: What is the relationship between conversion and discipleship? Are we always responding with repentance and faith to the gospel? If so, does that mean we're always converting to Jesus? Or to put it another way, When does conversion end and discipleship begin? The confusion arises because we are using extrabiblical words such as conversion and discipleship to understand different aspects of salvation. And although these aspects are different, they are also continuous with each other. The following table illustrates what I'm talking about:

| God's Actions | The Person's Actions |
|---|---|
| 1. Internal call of the gospel | 1. Hears the external call of the gospel |
| 2. Regeneration | 2. Conversion (faith and repentance) |
| 3. Progressive sanctification | 3. Discipleship (faith and obedience) |
| 4. Preservation | 4. Perseverance |
| 5. Glorification | |

When we talk about conversion, we are speaking of a one-time action. And when we talk about discipleship, we are talking about a repeated activity, a daily action. But they are both actions of the same nature, actions that involve trusting and obeying Jesus. And they are effected by the same agent—the Holy Spirit—by the same means—through the words of the gospel.

That's why the Bible gives us another motif to understand the Christian life. The Bible speaks of the Christian life as a journey. It has a starting point and a destination, and there is a process of traveling to get to that destination. In this sense, conversion is the decision to begin the journey with Jesus. And discipleship is the decision to continue on this journey with Jesus each day. Every day is a day when we decide to follow Jesus, deny ourselves, and take up our crosses (Luke 9:23).

## IS THERE A SINGLE MODEL OF CONVERSION?

Dr. Graham Cole has suggested that the New Testament illustrates for us at least three models of conversion: the story of the prodigal son, the conversion of Saul, and the conversion of Timothy.

### The Prodigal Son (Luke 15:11–32)

In Jesus' parable about the prodigal son, the son is a rebel. He defies and breaks his relationship with his father. He lives a life of willful disobedience, even taking his father's money and wasting it on prostitutes. Later, facing a crisis, he has an awakening. As a result, he repents and returns to his father, who forgives him.

Real-life examples of this forgiven-rebel model might be John Newton, the former slave trader who wrote the hymn "Amazing Grace," or Augustine of Hippo, who experienced a similar radical crisis and conversion.

### Saul (Acts 9:1–30; 22:1–21; 26:1–23; Gal. 1:11–24)

Saul is a religious zealot (Acts 22:3; Phil. 3:4–6). He fulfills all of his religious duties, even to the point of persecuting enemies of his religion. But he realizes that none of his efforts can make him acceptable to God. He needs a righteousness not of his own but one that comes from Christ (Phil. 3:7–9).

A later example of a religious person who senses the inadequacy of their efforts and need for God might be Martin Luther, who was an Augustinian monk. In an act of zeal, Luther allegedly crawled up the steps of the Scala Sancta, kissing each step, hoping to find atonement. But he found nothing in his acts of contrition. Then, as he read the Psalms and Romans, he discovered that God had promised him a righteousness not of his own but from Christ.

### Timothy (2 Tim. 1:5; 3:15)

Timothy was born into a believing family, and Paul tells us Timothy had a "sincere faith" (1:5) that first lived in his grandmother Lois and his mother, Eunice. He was raised to know the Scriptures since he was an infant and, as a result, presumably had a saving faith in Jesus since infancy also (3:15). If we could ask Timothy when he came to have a relationship with God, he might say that he cannot remember a moment when he did not know him. For his whole life, he has believed, followed, and prayed to Jesus.

I would list myself as an example of this model of conversion. I was raised by believing parents, and I can't identify a moment when I had to repent from unbelief. I can't describe a distinct decision to follow Jesus. For as long as I can remember, I have believed, followed, and prayed to Jesus. This doesn't mean that I have not needed to confess and repent of my sin. It simply means that I have been on a lifelong journey of repentance and discipleship.

### Learning from the Three Models of Conversion

In addition to there being three different models of conversion in the Bible—the rebel, the zealot, and the believer since infancy—we can say that there also are different experiences of conversion. The rebel and the zealot had a moment when "the lights came on" and they believed. But the believer since infancy can't point to such a decisive moment.

There also are different gospel metaphors. (We'll say more about this in a later chapter.) The rebel needs to hear that they have transgressed God's laws. The zealot needs to hear that they fall short of God's holiness. The believer since infancy needs to hear that they remain in Christ. All of this suggests that the experience of conversion is not one size fits all.

## IS THERE A SINGLE MODEL FOR EVANGELISM?

One common question that arises is whether there is a single biblical way to do evangelism. As you might guess, I believe the answer is no. Pastor and author Timothy Keller, in a sermon called "Changed Lives," gives several reasons. Keller believes Acts 16 illustrates at least three different models for evangelism: Paul's evangelizing of Lydia, of the slave girl, and of the Philippian jailer. In this section, I have imaginatively expanded on these three to give us a sense of how they present models for us today.[13]

### Lydia (Acts 16:13–15)

Lydia is an Asian woman from Turkey living in the "European" city of Philippi. Socioeconomically, she is a rich, successful, and powerful businesswoman. She owns a home. She mixes with the fashionable, wealthy, and social elites. If she lived today, she would be a successful businesswoman

---

13. For this section, I have loosely appropriated and adapted ideas from Timothy Keller's sermon "Changed Lives." Admittedly, our observations go beyond what is specified in Acts 16, but I think they are within the imaginative possibilities of Acts 16. Timothy Keller, "Changed Lives," sermon preached at Redeemer Presbyterian Church, March 22, 1998, http://www.sermoncloud .com/redeemer-presbyterian/changed-lives. Accessed June 10, 2016.

living in the inner suburbs of a large city, importing and selling the latest fashions from Asia. At night she would dine in fine restaurants and mix with the A-list crowd.

Lydia is a cognitive thinker. She needs facts, evidence, and discussion. She prefers that someone give her a logical presentation of ideas. She is persuaded by a well-reasoned argument. Though we don't know all of the details of her life, we can picture her as someone who does her best to be a good person. Perhaps she believes that there is some sort of God of the universe and that there must be laws and moral absolutes. She is aware of the need for social justice. She donates to worthy causes, but she also has a spiritual yearning. Lately she has been exploring different faiths. Presently, she is a "worshiper of God"—checking out the Christian faith—with some Christian friends.

Her business is successful. She is respected by her peers. Her children no longer live at home with her and are scattered in countries around the world. But existentially, her life is aimless. There are no more worlds to conquer. If we had to identify an idol in her life, it would be her wealth, which gives her status among her A-list friends. With it, she is somebody. But without it, she would be nobody. This leaves her trapped. Her lifestyle owns her, and she can't walk away from it.

How do we evangelize someone like Lydia? Paul's model of evangelism to her is a reasoned discussion (vv. 13–14). He makes an appeal to her mind.

## Slave Girl (Acts 16:16–21)

The slave girl in Acts 16 is Greek, having grown up in the local culture. Socioeconomically she's in one of the lower castes—exploited, outcast, powerless. Her owners take advantage of her, often treating her cruelly. She has no home and sleeps in the hostels. Today, she would be the equivalent of a sex worker on the streets of the red-light district of a large city. She's the regular drug user who has never dined in a fine restaurant. If she's lucky, her pimp might give her a slice of pizza or a falafel roll.

She is an intuitive thinker. She needs emotions and feelings. She is persuaded by transcendent experiences. But she is rarely allowed to think for herself. She's often being told what to do by the men in her life—her boyfriend, pimp, and suppliers.

Spiritually, she is demon possessed. Religiously, she experiments in the occult—in witchcraft, tarot cards, fortune telling. Existentially, she is in a dark place. Her life is out of control, leaving her in despair and torment. Her idols are living ones. She is under the control of the evil spirit in her.

She is also under the control of her owners. Ironically, without these owners, her life would spiral further out of control. She needs the owners to give her structure and accountability.

How do we evangelize someone like this slave girl? Paul's model of evangelism to her is a power encounter (v. 18). Paul casts out the evil spirit from her. She has a transcendent experience with Jesus. Jesus proves to be stronger than all the powers in her life—the evil spirit and the owners. Paul makes an appeal to her heart.

## The Jailer (Acts 16:22–34)

The jailer of the town of Philippi is probably a Roman citizen, because most of the good civil-service jobs were given to retired Roman soldiers. Socioeconomically, he is an honest member of the working class. He works hard to support his family and to pay off their modest house.

Today, he would be seen as a low-skill worker in a government institution. He could be the janitor in the library, a landscaper or a tradesman, or a security guard at the hospital. He lives in the outer suburbs where the houses are cheaper and has a long commute each day. For a treat, he takes his family out for a meal at a fast-food restaurant.

The jailer is a concrete-relational thinker. He wants to learn only things that are practical. He is persuaded by stories, especially stories that show how things work in someone's life. He is impatient with abstract theories, propositions, and arguments. And he hates appeals to emotion, which he finds manipulative. The jailer does his best to be a good husband, father, and worker. He is motivated by duty, honor, and tradition. He never takes a sick day. He pays his taxes. He is always on time.

Spiritually, the jailer is not searching. He believes in God but has no warm personal relationship with him. He figures that as long as he has been a dutiful husband and father, he'll be okay. Religiously, he hates church. Church does nothing for him. The sermons are long and boring. The singing is emotional and awkward. And everything is so effeminate— music, flowers, and cupcakes. He might turn up at church on Christmas and Easter, but only out of duty. Apart from that, he's just not interested in it. His idol is his reputation. If he failed in his marriage or at his job, the shame would kill him. It almost does just that. When the prisoners appear to have escaped and he senses that he has failed in his duty, he tries to kill himself (v. 27).

How do we evangelize someone like the jailer? Paul's model of evangelism to him is the example of his own life: Paul and Silas are so fulfilled that they can happily remain in jail (v. 28). Paul and Silas have something that the jailer is looking for. In desperation, the jailer asks them, "What must I do to be saved?" (v. 30). Paul appeals by example.

## Learning from the Three Models of Evangelism

We imaginatively explored three different models of evangelism in Acts 16. Cognitive thinkers are persuaded by a reasoned discussion. They need to think about the gospel. We reach them with a logical presentation of ideas. Intuitive thinkers are persuaded by emotions. They need to sense the awe of the gospel. We reach them with events and transcendental experiences. Concrete-relational thinkers are persuaded by stories. They need to see how the gospel works. We reach them with the example of our lives.

Often we wonder why we're not effective in reaching one particular audience—professionals or teenagers or tradespeople or retirees. The reason is that there is no one-size-fits-all model for our evangelism. We have different audiences with different thinking and learning styles, different socioeconomic groupings, and different existential entry points. So we should be prepared to engage in a wider variety of models of evangelism. We should also not be so quick to criticize others' models. They might be evangelizing an audience different from ours. And we should be humble about our own models, because they might not be as transferrable to other audiences as we think they are.

## CONCLUSION

We began this chapter with Anne's story. Anne reads to the play group stories from the Bible along with other stories, but the other Christian parents are complaining that she's not doing any evangelism. They are impatient with her use of stories, crafts, and coffee. They wonder why she won't hurry up and get to the point about Jesus' dying for sinners on a cross. Why doesn't she pull out her Four Spiritual Laws booklet and just share the gospel with the kids?

In this chapter, we have explored and defined several terms. We've seen that the essence of evangelism is its message, the gospel of Jesus Christ. Evangelism is defined by its message, not by its method, medium, or audience. We've also seen that there are different models of evangelism in the Bible: sometimes it's a logical presentation of ideas, sometimes it's an event with emotional impact, and sometimes it's through stories. There are also different models of conversion: different people have different experiences of God's regenerating work. Also, people will be persuaded in different ways: through logic, experiences, or personal examples. And different people will have different existential entry points to knowing Jesus.

So the challenge for us when we evangelize is to be open to different methods, mediums, and entry points. We don't have to evangelize the same way that we were evangelized. And we don't have to impose our learning styles on other people.

Evangelism is an activity in which we communicate the gospel of Jesus Christ in our natural, mundane, and ordinary presentations. But God uses our gospel presentations as natural means for his supernatural regenerating work. This keeps us humble about our abilities. But it also encourages us to keep doing the work of an evangelist, because if God so wills it, he will use our words to move someone from death to life.

 **When Can We Call Someone a Christian?**

For a summary of three different ways to approach this question, download the PDF from ZondervanAcademic.com.

To access this resource, register on the website as a student. Then sign in and download the resource from the "Study Resources" tab on the book page for *Evangelism in a Skeptical World*.

# CHAPTER 2

# EVERYDAY EVANGELISM

## How do I tell my friends about Jesus?

In case you haven't worked it out yet from my name, I am Asian. I look Asian, and even though my Australian accent surprises some Americans, my genetics are decidedly Asian.

At the risk of labeling an entire group of people, I want to assert that most Asians (at least those I've known) cannot swim. I know this is true because most Asians my age have a near-drowning story they will gladly tell you. It's usually because some well-meaning Caucasian friend pushed them into a swimming pool for fun during a BBQ party, not realizing that their Asian friend couldn't in the least bit swim.

When I was in elementary school, I was the only Asian in my class. I was also the only kid in the class who could not swim. Once a week, my class went to the school swimming pool for a lesson. But the swimming instructor didn't know what to do with me. Up until that point, all of her students could swim, even if they weren't that good. So when we got into the pool and started class, all my instructor did was yell at me, "Swim!" But this command was useless to me. If I could already swim, I would be doing it. So yelling "Swim!" at me wasn't going to make me swim. I spent the whole lesson clinging to the side of the pool.

If people can't swim, there's no point in yelling "Swim!" at them. But this is exactly the way many well-intentioned pastors and Christian leaders try to motivate Christians to evangelize. They talk and command but do little to equip people in the act of evangelism. Urging people on a Sunday morning, "Tell your friends about Jesus!" just makes them feel guilty, overwhelmed, and disheartened.

In this chapter, we want to look at this question: How can I tell my friends about Jesus? And I've written this chapter in a way that I hope will be helpful to normal everyday Christians. I will suggest some simple strategies that have worked for me, but I'm not saying that they are the only strategies. I'm not saying that if you aren't doing evangelism this way, you're doing it wrong. I'm not even saying that they're great strategies. All I'm saying is that these simple strategies might empower other normal everyday Christians to tell their friends about Jesus.

## STRATEGY 1: GET OUR FRIENDS TO BECOME THEIR FRIENDS[1]

Imagine I told you this story:

> Last night, while my wife and I were watching TV, a UFO landed in our back yard. A green alien got out of the UFO and asked us to join him. So my wife and I got into his UFO, and he took us to his home planet, Jupiter. There he showed us around his home city. We had dinner with his family. Afterward, we got into the UFO and returned to earth. But when we got back, because of the space-time continuum, we went through a time portal, and only one second of earth time had passed.

Do you believe me?
Let's say I tell you another story:

> Two thousand years ago, God sent us his Son, Jesus. This man Jesus was 100 percent God and 100 percent human at the same time. He was born from a virgin! While he was on earth, he healed sick people and raised dead people back to life. And then he died on a cross. If you believe this, he will take away all your sins and forgive you. But he didn't stay dead. He rose again to life and is now in heaven. If you trust him, God's Spirit lives in you right now. When you die, your soul will leave your dead body to be with Jesus in heaven. And one day, he will return and set up a kingdom on earth. And when he does, your dead body will rise from the grave and be reunited to your soul.

---

1. Friends have told me that they have heard Steve Timmis give similar advice. I must admit, to my shame, that up until now I haven't heard talks by Steve Timmis, nor have I read any of his books. If Steve Timmis has similar advice, then I'm happy to acknowledge the similarities, and that he, like me, discovered this intuitively, and that he probably got there before I did.

Do you believe me?

Assuming that you are a Christian, I want you to consider a question. Why are you happy to believe the second story about Jesus, but not the first story about the UFO? Let's face it, the second story sounds quite unbelievable if you aren't already a believer. Even as I'm writing it, I'm not quite sure I can believe it. To be honest, the story about the UFO sounds slightly more believable than the Jesus story.

So why do we believe the story about Jesus, but not the story about the UFO? Because of plausibility structures. We all have programmed plausibility structures that lead us to judge whether a story is believable or unbelievable.

## Plausibility Structures

What are plausibility structures? They are accepted beliefs, convictions, and understandings that either green-light truth claims as plausible or red-light them as implausible. So when I say, "Last night a UFO landed in our back yard," your plausibility structures are red-lighting this claim. *Implausible!* When I say, "We got out of the UFO and had dinner with his family," your plausibility structures are red-lighting this claim. *Implausible!* When I say, "Only one second of earth time had passed," your plausibility structures are red-lighting it. *Implausible!* Red lights are going off everywhere while I tell you the Jupiter story!

But when I tell you the Jesus story, your plausibility structures are green-lighting my truth claims. When I say, "He was born from a virgin," your plausibility structures are green-lighting this claim: "That fits with what I believe and what people I know and trust believe." *Plausible!* When I say, "He rose from the dead," your plausibility structures are green-lighting this claim. *Plausible!* When I say, "One day he will return," your plausibility structures are green-lighting this claim. *Plausible!* Green lights are going off everywhere while I tell you the Jesus story.

To be clear, I'm not talking about the truth status (ontology) of my truth claims. I'm talking about the believability status (epistemology) of my truth claims. It may be true that a UFO landed in my back yard. It may be true that Jesus rose from the dead. But what I'm talking about is whether you believe these claims. What is the believability status of these claims? It is our plausibility structures that stamp certain claims as believable and other claims as unbelievable.

So where do we get these plausibility structures? They come from three main sources: (1) community, (2) experience, and (3) facts, evidence, and data.

Right now, most of us don't belong in a community of trusted friends and family who have seen a UFO. Most of us haven't had an experience of a UFO. Most of us don't believe there are any facts, evidence, or data to support my UFO story. But most of us do belong in a community of trusted friends and family who believe in Jesus. Most of us have had an experience of Jesus. Most of us believe that there exist enough facts, evidence, and data to support the Jesus story. That's why we believe the Jesus story, but not the Jupiter story.

So which one—community, experience, or evidence—is the most influential? More often than not, it's community. We like to think the answer is evidence, but it's not. If I said to you, "The UFO is still in my back yard. Do you want to come and see it?" would you come? Probably not. You couldn't be bothered to make the trip because you would assume that it is a waste of time, convinced that I'm crazy. And let's say you did come to check out the UFO. You see it and touch it. You'd probably say something like, "Nah, there's got to be some other explanation," or, "This is an elaborate hoax!" We dismiss evidence or we explain it away. Whether we like it or not, it's our community of trusted friends and family that is most important in determining what we believe.

Why is this?

## The Role of Community in Determining Belief

Our community—our trusted friends and family—has a powerful role in forming our beliefs. Our community also shapes how we interpret our experiences. Our community also shapes how we interpret facts, evidence, and data. For example, in Australia, most Bible-believing, churchgoing Australians do not support an individual's right to bear arms (to own and carry a gun). But in the USA, many Bible-believing, churchgoing Americans do support the individual's right to bear arms. Let me be clear that I'm not getting into the gun debate here; I'm just using it as an example of how community is a large factor in the way we form beliefs. Both these Australians and Americans are Bible-believing, churchgoing Christians, but their different communities have shaped how they interpret their experiences and the facts, evidence, and data.

As another example, right now in the Western world, most of us believe that women have a right to vote. But one hundred years ago, most people in the Western world, including most Christians, didn't believe that women had a right to vote. Once again, community is powerful in forming our beliefs.

As a final example, in Australia, most Bible-believing, churchgoing

Australians are by and large in favor of government-funded healthcare. Australians are used to the idea that the government pays the bill for our hospitals. Most Australians also support rules that make it mandatory for bicycle and motorcycle riders to wear a helmet. This just seems normal for Australians. But in the USA, most Bible-believing, churchgoing Americans oppose government-funded healthcare. Americans are used to the idea that individuals should pay for their own bills and that taxes shouldn't support the health costs of others. Most Americans would also think that bicycle and motorcycle riders should be free to choose for themselves whether to wear a helmet. It's their head. They can do what they want. Besides, they will pay for their hospital costs if they have an accident, and not me! So let them do what they want.

Once again, our community has a powerful role in forming our beliefs. Different communities with some of the same experiences will interpret them in different ways. Different communities with the same facts, evidence, and data will interpret them in different ways.

Let's go back to our Jupiter story. Imagine that in a room of fifty of your trusted friends and family, I'm the only one who tells you the UFO story. You'll think that I'm a schmuck. But let's say that as I tell the UFO story, half the people in the room say, "Me too! A UFO landed in our back yard as well!" Now you'll be thinking, "Hmm, maybe there's something to this story." Suddenly, my story is more plausible. Now let's say that as I tell the story, everyone in the room also says, "Me too! A UFO landed in our back yard, and we also went to Jupiter last night. I thought that was you I saw, but I just wasn't sure, so I didn't wave, just in case." Suddenly, you're the schmuck, the one and only person who doesn't believe in the UFO story. My story has become a lot more plausible.

Here is the key idea you need to grasp: people will find a story more believable if more people in their community, their trusted friends and family, also believe the story.

This is one reason why if we raise teenagers in a small town where the youth group is only three teenagers meeting together on a Friday night, those teenagers will find the Jesus story to be unbelievable. They're the only schmucks meeting on a Friday night to worship Jesus while hundreds of other teenagers are having fun doing something else. But if we take the teenagers to an annual convention where they meet with ten thousand other teenagers who worship Jesus, suddenly the Jesus story becomes a lot more believable. Our teenagers will say, "Wow, we're not the only ones who believe this."

That's also why in 1 Corinthians 15 Paul writes that he saw Jesus risen from the dead. But he is careful to add that it wasn't just him but also five hundred others who saw Jesus alive (v. 6). In saying this, Paul increases the believability status of the resurrection story. The fact that Jesus rose from the dead is true (ontology) whether or not five hundred people saw him. But the fact that five hundred people saw him risen from the dead makes it more believable (epistemology).

## We Need to Merge Our Universes

So why are we spending all of this time talking about the importance of community and how it affects our plausibility structures? Because typically when we get fired up about evangelism, we go out solo. "I'm going to tell my friend about Jesus!" We decide it's time to hang out with non-Christians and tell them about Jesus. So we join a book-reading club or a cooking class or a flag-football team.

But a problem with this approach is that we're the one and only person in the group who believes the Jesus story. We're the schmucks. The Jesus story might be true, but it comes across as unbelievable. Added to this problem is that Christians typically have two separate universes of friends—non-Christian and Christian. When our non-Christian friends go to the movies, we go with them, and when our Christian friends go to the movies, we go with them. When our non-Christian friends have a BBQ lunch, we go with them, and when our Christian friends have a BBQ lunch, we go with them. We keep our universes separate.

What if we merged our universes of friends? What if we were able to get our Christian friends to become friends with our non-Christian friends? What if the next time our non-Christian friends go to the movies, we ask if we can bring along some of our Christian friends? And what if the next time our Christian friends have a BBQ lunch, we ask if we can bring some of our non-Christian friends? Gradually, bit by bit, our universes will have both Christians and non-Christians, hopefully with a fifty-fifty split, and the Jesus story becomes more believable to our non-Christian friends because in a room of trusted friends, half the people believe in it.

## Evangelism Is a Lifestyle Change

I realize that this example simplifies some things. Making friends takes time. Merging our social worlds may not be easy. I'm simply trying to make the point that this strategy requires a lifestyle change. It's a bit like getting in shape. Typically, we make New Year resolutions to get fit, and we promise ourselves that we'll run in the morning, sign up at a gym, and change the way we eat. The problem with this approach is that we're trying to add fitness to our existing lifestyles as an accessory item. Sure enough, our attempts at fitness fade and fail, sometimes by the first week of February. What is needed is a lifestyle change, not some activities that we add to our lives. We need to live a fit lifestyle, not a life with fitness added to it.

It's the same with evangelism. Our usual approach to evangelism is to add some activity to our lives: maybe I'm going to try to tell someone about Jesus at lunch or I'm going to join a book club. Churches do the same thing by adding an event such as an outreach night to their calendar. But we need to change our lives so that we live an evangelistic lifestyle, not a life with add-on bits of evangelism. Churches need to do the same thing.

When I worked full-time as a junior medical doctor, I shared hospital accommodations with three other doctors. We became friends and hung out together. None of the three professed to being Christian, and they certainly did not have a personal relationship with Jesus.

My Christian friends would come over, hang out, and get to know my doctor friends. When my Christian friends went out to dinner, they invited my doctor friends. And when my doctor friends went out to a movie, I invited along my Christian friends. Gradually, bit by bit, they became friends with each other.

It took two years! That's about how long it takes to form a network of trusted friends. That's why I'm arguing for a lifestyle change, not just something we tack onto our lives. By the end of the two years, all three of my doctor friends started coming along with me to church. All three gave their lives to Christ. I still hang out with one of them, and he's still walking with Jesus.

## STRATEGY 2: GO TO THEM BEFORE THEY COME TO YOU

You may be thinking, "He makes some good points, but how can we get our non-Christian friends to hang out with our Christian friends?" I know, that seems like a challenging prospect! And that brings us to the second strategy: we have to go to their things before they come to our things.

Often I'm asked to speak at dinners where people have invited their non-Christian friends. One of my friends, Andrew, organizes these dinners, and whenever I go and speak at them, I notice that Andrew has brought four or five non-Christian friends. More than that, they're different non-Christian friends each time. And his friends are happy to be there. I can tell by their body language that they haven't been dragged there kicking and screaming. They're not rolling their eyes thinking, "What are we doing here? I can't wait until this is over just so Andrew doesn't have to ask us to come to one of these things again!" It's the opposite. They listen attentively to me. They talk to me afterward. They thank me for my talk.

So I asked Andrew's wife what was going on. Why was Andrew able to bring so many non-Christian friends to these events? Why were they happy to be there? His wife answered, "It's because we're always hanging out together. We're always doing things together. We always go to their things. And they often come to our things. So this is just one of many things that we do together. If it wasn't this outreach dinner, we'd still be doing something else together."

We should always be hanging out with non-Christian friends. We go to their things—their birthday parties, kids' concerts, fundraisers, sports games. And if we do that consistently as their friends, it is only natural that they will come to our things—BBQ lunches, movies, Superbowl parties. If we happen to invite them to an outreach event, it's just one of many other things that we do together. This feels normal because if it wasn't the outreach event, we'd be doing something else together. And it doesn't risk the friendship.

## STRATEGY 3: COFFEE, DINNER, GOSPEL

But how can we get to that bit where we talk about Jesus with our friend? The third strategy is what I call the coffee-dinner-gospel sequence. First, we invite our friend for coffee, and we do this a few times. Next, we invite them for dinner, and we do this a few times. Then, organically and naturally, gospel conversations begin to occur.

Why is this sequence so effective? Let me answer by diving into some philosophy. Something unique and unusual happened in Western history several hundred years ago, something that is called the Kantian noumenal-phenomenal divide.

### The Kantian Noumenal-Phenomenal Divide

In the 1700s, as one of the features of the Western Enlightenment, German philosopher Immanuel Kant divided what we know into two realms of knowledge—the noumenal and the phenomenal. The noumenal is the realm of God, ethics, and values. It contains statements such as:

- There is a God.
- Gambling is wrong.
- Capitalism is better than socialism.[2]

The phenomenal, on the other hand, is the realm of facts, evidence, and data. It contains statements such as:

- One plus one equals two.
- The sky is blue.
- Water boils at 100 degrees Celsius.

Kant's point wasn't to say that the noumenal realm doesn't exist. Kant believed in the existence of God, ethics, and values. But Kant's point was that we have no epistemological access to this realm. We can't verify that there is God or that it's wrong to gamble or that capitalism is better than socialism. In contrast, in the phenomenal realm, we do have epistemological access. We can verify that one plus one equals two, the sky is blue, and that water boils at 100 degrees Celsius.

That's why with noumenal statements, we have arguments. Those who believe in the existence of God or say gambling is wrong or claim that capitalism is better than socialism can't prove it to those who don't. Because neither side can prove their claim, they can't agree. That's also why we've been taught never to talk about religion and politics at dinner parties.

But phenomenal statements won't usually cause arguments, because we can verify them. That's why we generally talk about phenomenal statements in conversations. "It's a nice day." "How about them Bulls?" "What did you do on the weekend?" "What movie have you seen?" They are safe things to talk about.

In the Western world, this noumenal-phenomenal divide has led to another divide, a sacred-secular divide. Sacred statements belong in the noumenal realm. And the sacred should be discussed only in private space. Secular statements belong in the phenomenal realm. Secular statements are safe and can be discussed in public space.

That's why, in the West, we are told that we are free to believe anything we want about religion so long as it's in the privacy of our own homes. No one should dare impose their views of religion or values on others in public.

---

2. I've chosen anachronistic examples that we can relate to. Obviously these aren't the examples that Kant would have used.

As a result, we are what I refer to as a defacto closed country. A closed country usually is a country where you cannot openly engage in missionary or evangelistic activity. You cannot talk about your religion in public. You cannot proselytize. And while this is true in countries that are officially closed, it is also what happens in the West because of our cultural history. While we have the freedom to share our faith and evangelize, as a practical matter it's not culturally acceptable.

If I said to you, "Let's have an open-air prayer meeting in the main street tonight," most people living in the West would feel uncomfortable about joining me. You might even feel guilty for feeling uncomfortable. But you would feel uncomfortable nonetheless. This is a result of our Western sacred-secular divide, a reality that has become further entrenched in our culture since it first arose in the 1700s.

But we should keep in mind that this is a Western phenomenon. People from non-Western cultures don't have all the same hang-ups about dividing the sacred and secular. If I go to an Asian grocery shop on a main street in Sydney, I will find that the owners have happily displayed several religious shrines in the shop. If I talk to the Asian woman who runs the newspaper stand about her gods, she won't be offended and say, "You cannot ask me about that! We should not talk about these things." And if I catch a taxi, the Middle-Eastern driver will most likely be happy to talk about his religion with me. For him, the sacred-secular divide that most Westerners live with just doesn't exist.

The sacred-secular divide is a uniquely Western phenomenon. Like it or not, right or wrong, it exists. But we can fight against it. We can dismantle it. And in the meantime, we can also work with it. After all, this is the culture that we've inherited, and just as missionaries in officially closed countries have to find ways to operate in that cultural environment, we must find ways to evangelize in our unofficially closed country.

The noumenal-phenomenal, sacred-secular divide is why many Christians feel so uncomfortable talking about Jesus with their friends. It goes against how we've been taught to act and what we believe is acceptable in Western culture. And it's not just us. Our non-Christian friends also feel uncomfortable when we talk about Jesus with them. Like most Christians, they also lack the language and tools to talk about such matters in public.

So I suggest that we begin with coffee. Invite your friend to a coffee shop. Having coffee is safe because it usually lasts for only twenty to thirty minutes. And we usually have coffee in a public space. Your friend knows that they can get away at any time. They're not trapped. And all you'll be talking about is safe stuff like the weather, what they did on the weekend, and "How about them Bulls?"

After you've done this a few times and built some rapport, invite your friend for dinner. Dinner is different from coffee. Dinner takes one or two hours and is usually in a private space, so conversations will move from trivial matters—the weather, the weekend, the sports—to deeper matters— views on education, politics, health, and maybe also religion.

Do this a few times and bit by bit they will feel respected for their deeply held views. They will feel safe talking about personal issues. And if they feel safe enough, they might ask you to talk about your views on education, politics, health, and maybe also your religion. This is your chance to talk about the gospel. But notice that by following the coffee-dinner-gospel sequence, we have moved our friend from the secular realm into the sacred realm, from the phenomenal into the noumenal, from public into private space.

## The Way Conversations Usually Work

Conversation topics exist in three concentric circles, like layers of an onion.[3] The outermost layer of conversation is where we talk about interests. "What did you do on the weekend?" "What books are you reading?" "What do you do for fun?"

The middle layer is where we talk about values. This is where we talk about what is good or bad, better or worse, wise or unwise. These are value statements. "Where will you send your children for school?" "Who will you vote for?" "What are your views on gun ownership?" "What do you think of government-funded healthcare?"

Finally, the central layer is where we talk about worldviews. This is where we talk about our views on God, life, death, humanity, spirituality, and the nature of reality. This is the underlying core of all that we believe. "Will there be life after death?" "Are humans essentially good or evil?" "Is there a God?" "Is God loving and personal, or unloving and impersonal?"

Conversations usually begin with interests. These are safe topics. They won't start arguments or disagreements. They are usually descriptive, factual statements about empirical observations. We are merely describing things that just are.

But if the other person feels safe with us, we move on to values. Either they will give us permission to move on to topics about values or we can

---

3. Peter Ritchie from Fighting Words ministry in Australia taught me this.

invite them. Usually we do this by asking questions such as, "Why do you enjoy running?" "Why do you enjoy that book?" "What do you like about picnics on weekends?" To answer these questions, they can start talking about their system of values.

If they continue to feel safe with us, we move on to worldviews. Again, either they will give us permission or we can invite them with questions such as, "What do you think this all means anyway?" "What are your views on the soul?" "Do you pray?" To answer these questions, they will have to talk about their underlying worldview.

A friend of mine was mentored by a hospital chaplain, and he told me that if people feel safe with us, they will give us hints that they want to move to the next layer of conversation. So we need to be good listeners. People will give the hint once, maybe twice, but typically only a maximum of three times in the conversation. So if we don't pick up on the hint after three times, that person will give up trying to take us with them into the next layer of conversation. We will be stuck talking about interests and will have missed the opportunity to enter the deeper layers of conversation.

In a recent conversation, someone mentioned to me several times that his mother had died earlier in the year. It should have been obvious that he wanted me to pick up on his hint. I needed to say something like, "How do you feel about losing your mother earlier this year?" to give him permission to enter the next layer with me. But I failed to pick up on the hint, and he stopped trying.

Don't miss these opportunities. Be alert to what people are saying. Learn to ask questions that transition from one layer of the conversation to the next.

## From the Front Yard to the Back Yard

Another way to think about this transition in the depth of a conversation is the front yard to back yard sequence. If we live in a neighborhood, we begin with front yard conversations. For example, if someone is watering their front garden, you can walk up to them, offer them a drink, and talk. Or on a Friday afternoon, when people have come home from work and are relaxed and looking forward to the weekend, you can organize drinks in front of your house and invite the neighbors. This will lead to front yard conversations in which you discuss interests.

From there, you can invite people into your back yard or home. For example, we might have a relaxed BBQ in our back yard or invite the neighbors into our home for dinner. Dinner can be something simple like having pizza delivered, which removes the need for cooking and cleaning up. The neighbors get to know us and each other, and it promotes relationships in the community where we all live, but it also helps us move into conversations about our values and worldviews.

My wife and I are at the stage of life where we meet parents of other young children at school, swimming lessons, football, and play group. It is difficult to have fruitful conversations in these public spaces, but we've found that when we invite them to our home for coffee, lunch, or dinner, we can have fruitful conversations because we are now in private space.

## STRATEGY 4: LISTEN TO THEIR STORY

But how do you bring up Jesus in the conversation? The fourth strategy is to listen to their story first. Instead of worrying about what we will say, we let them begin the conversation about worldviews and religion. This way, we have a better sense of where they are coming from. If we have listened to them with respect, understanding, and empathy, hopefully they will do the same for us when it's our turn to talk.

Often at a party, when I meet someone, I make small talk by asking, "What do you do for work?" They might say something like, "I work as an engineer," or, "I work as a music teacher." Then they ask me the same question. If I say something like, "I teach the Bible," *pwfff*, I've killed the conversation. Just like that. Why? Because the conversation was in the phenomenal—"What do you do for work?"—but suddenly I've dragged it into the noumenal—God, the Bible, religion. I've brought us into the realm of the sacred long before they were ready for it. And now we're both feeling awkward. So one of us might try to get the conversation back into the phenomenal—"How about that game last night?"—and *phew!* we're back into secular, public territory.

But I can also use this opportunity to give them permission to stay in the noumenal. I can ask them something like, "Do you have a faith?" or, "Do you pray?" If they change the subject, it means they don't want to talk about noumenal topics. But if they want to talk, I am giving them permission to do so.

In this strategy, we begin by letting them go first. We ask them about their faith, spirituality, prayer, or religion. As secular as the Western world is, surveys show that the majority of Westerners believe in some form of spirituality and life after death. That means that they, like Christians, also suffer from being in a defacto closed country. They have beliefs that they hold dear, but they are not allowed to talk about them. We are now giving them permission to do this.

When we ask them if they have a faith and they say something like, "I'm a Buddhist," our next step is to be genuinely interested in what they say. Ask them questions like, "How did you become a Buddhist?" "Did you grow up in a Buddhist family?" "What does that look like?" "How do you pray?" "How do you worship?" "What do you do in the temple?" "What are your dreams for your children?"

And if they say that they are an atheist, we can be just as interested because atheism, like any other worldview or religion, is a faith-based position. So we can ask similar questions: "How did you become an atheist?" "Were you always an atheist?" "Did you grow up in atheist family?" "Who are your favorite authors?"

The aim here is to listen, understand, and empathize. Don't try to interrupt. Don't think of how you can interact with their position. Don't assume you know what their faith or religion does or believes. Instead, ask as many questions as possible so that you hear properly what they are saying. Listen as much as possible so that you can understand their faith. And try to feel what they are feeling. See the world from their point of view.

If we've listened to them with respect, sooner or later they will reciprocate. For example, if we ask someone what they did on the weekend, sooner or later they will ask us what we did on the weekend. And if we ask someone about their faith, sooner or later they will ask us about our faith. If we have let them talk for ten minutes, they will let us talk for ten minutes. If we have let them talk for twenty, they will let us talk for twenty.

I had to take a plane from Sydney to Adelaide to give a talk that night on how to tell your friends about Jesus. It's a two-hour flight. I was tired and needed to rest on the plane. As I sat down in my seat, I began to put my headphones on, which is a polite way of signaling to other passengers, "Do not talk to me!" But before I got them on, the man seated next to me started a conversation with me. During the small talk, we discovered we had some things in common, so there was no polite way for me to end the conversation. We kept going from topic to topic.

Then he asked me what I was going to do in Adelaide. I tried to be brief: "I'm going to give a talk." Sure enough, he asked for details. So I had to reply, "It's a talk about Jesus." And *pwfff*, that, of course, led to an awkward silence.

I thought, "I can't believe this is happening to me. Because I'm just about to give a talk on what to do when this happens." So I said to the man, "Do you have a faith?" And he replied that when he was a teenager, he checked out Christianity, but then he discovered that Christianity is basically a front for hate crimes against marginalized groups.

So I asked him for more information. For the next sixty minutes I let him share his frustrations about Christians, the church, and religion. I tried my hardest to listen, understand, and empathize with him. He shared his major objections to Christianity: it's intolerant, science disproves it, and all religions are the same.

After he finished talking, there was a long pause. He sat there, almost pleading with me to talk next. So I asked him, "Would you like me to respond?" He eagerly said, "Yes!" So I repeated back to him a summary of everything he had said. I asked whether it was an accurate summary. I then outlined his objections to Christianity and gave my responses to them.

He let me talk for the next thirty minutes. He never interrupted. He was polite and respectful, so I was able to give a detailed reply. At the end of the flight, the man thanked me and said that our conversation had made the flight go a lot quicker!

## STRATEGY 5: TELL OUR STORY AS STORY

But what do we say when it's our turn to talk? The fifth strategy is to tell our own story as a story. Often we've been trained to read a tract or give a multiple-point gospel outline, but in a real conversation, this rarely seems to be the natural thing to do. It's just not how conversations happen.

When it's our turn to talk, we can say something like, "Would you like to hear why I'm a Christian?" We can give what is known in Christian jargon as our testimony. Our testimony is the story of either how we became a Christian or what God has been doing in our lives up until now. A story requires two elements: (1) events that have happened to us and (2) a story-telling grid by which the events are arranged.

Typically, Christian testimonies have one element but not the other. They tell you the events, but without a grid, so it becomes a rambling incoherent sequence. Or they tell you a grid, but with no events, so it becomes an abstract, formulaic, theological presentation. I used to teach at a Bible college where the students often had to share their testimonies at a church event. I used to joke that the testimonies sounded so similar that students could swap testimonies with each other and no one would notice. I was hearing a grid, but without events that marked the testimony as that person's testimony. Often they sounded like, "I grew up in a Christian family—not that that makes me a Christian, but it helps—but at the age of sixteen I had to make a decision for myself."

So how can we tell our story as a story? By using a storytelling grid to arrange the events in our lives. Obviously there isn't a single "you must use this or else" storytelling grid, but the simplest and easiest storytelling grid is what a friend of mine calls the Greek Rule of Threes.[4]

## The Greek Rule of Threes

According to the ancient Greeks, everything works better in threes. Today we still follow this principle. Somehow phrases stick better if they have three elements: Red, white, and blue. The long, the short, the tall. Blood, sweat, and tears. In photography, we use the rule of threes to compose pictures. In desktop publishing, we use the rule of threes to organize pages. Stories usually have three elements: Goldilocks and the three bears. The three little pigs. There were a priest, a Levite, and a Samaritan.

We can also apply the Greek Rule of Threes to our storytelling grid. A story basically has three movements:[5]

1. Introduction
2. Body
3. Conclusion

Between movements 1 and 2 is a definition of the mission. Between 2 and 3 is a bridge moment. And after 3 is a denouement. (See figure.)

Let's break it down further. Each of the main elements has specific functions:

- *Introduction:* We are introduced to the hero of the story. The hero's character and normal world are established.
- *Definition of the mission:* The hero has to accomplish a mission.
- *Body:* The hero progressively overcomes obstacles to achieve this mission.
- *Bridge:* The mission is once again defined in an "ah-ha" moment. All that has happened up until now is summarized. The hero recommits to the mission, ready to launch into the climax.
- *Climax:* The mission is achieved.
- *Denouement:* We are given a glimpse of the new normal world.

---

4. My friend is called John G., but I'd better not reveal more than that because of where he is.

5. There is a similar discussion in https://en.wikipedia.org/wiki/Three-act_structure. Accessed June 20, 2016.

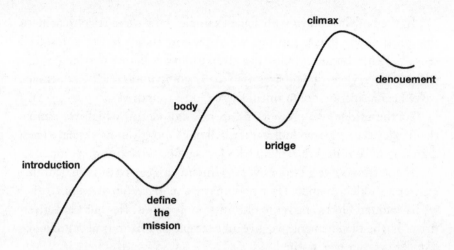

We can see how this story works in romantic-comedy movies. In the introduction, we meet the heroes—the boy and the girl—and learn about their character. When the boy and the girl meet, their mission is defined: to fall in love with each other. During the body, they become more and more romantically involved. But at the bridge, the boy loses the girl (or the girl loses the boy). All that has happened up until now is summarized in a musical montage. Then the boy (or the girl) realizes what a fool he (or she) has been and recommits to the mission. In the climax the boy (or the girl) makes a move to declare his (or her) love. The other person accepts the declaration, and the two finally commit to each other. In the denouement, we are given a glimpse into their new normal world as a couple.

The Synoptic Gospels also use this grid for the story of Jesus. In the introduction, we meet Jesus. The mission is defined when he is baptized by John the Baptist: to take away the sins of the world and save his people. During the body, Jesus progressively achieves his mission by preaching, teaching, healing, and finally entering Jerusalem. In the bridge, Jesus recommits to his mission in the garden of Gethsemane. Jesus' death and resurrection is the climax in which Jesus achieves his mission. In the denouement, we have Jesus' postresurrection appearances to his disciples.

If we are to tell our story as a story, we can apply the Greek Rule of Three. In the introduction, we establish our character. Who are we? What drives us? What are our God-given existential cries? What is our mission in life? What will ultimately fulfill us? What happy ending are we looking for? These are legitimate, God-given drives in our lives. We give strong examples from our lives that illustrate this. This defines our mission in life.

In the body, we show with some examples how we've tried to achieve this mission. At the same time, we show how there's rising unresolved tension. Why? Because if God has given us drives, but we're trying to live without God, then these drives are largely going unsatisfied. Or perhaps we've been using an idol to fulfill these God-given drives.

At the bridge, we present an "ah-ha" moment in which we realize that it's Jesus we've been looking for. All our God-given drives have been directing us to him. We explain who Jesus is and what he's done for us.

In the climax, we give our lives to Christ. This can be a gradual awareness or a sudden moment. But now that we've given our lives to Christ, we have found God's answer to our mission. Jesus satisfies our God-given drive. In the denouement, we give an example of what our new life looks like. This is our new normal.

Or to simplify things into an outline, try to give your testimony so it has these key statements:

1. *Introduction:* I am [describe yourself], and my mission is to [state your mission]. For example, [now give an example].
2. *Body:* So I tried to achieve my mission in these ways: [give examples]. But [now explain the problem of trying to achieve your mission without God]. For example, [now give an example].
3. *Bridge:* But this is what Jesus has done for me. [Explain how Jesus fulfills your mission.]
4. *Climax:* That's when I decided [explain how you decided to follow Jesus].
5. *Denouement:* So now [explain what living with Jesus looks like in your life now]. For example, [now give an example].

Using this outline, my testimony could sound like this:

I am a firstborn Asian son who is a high achiever. So my mission in life was to study hard and become a doctor. For example, in elementary school, I always asked my teacher for more work—yes, I was *that* annoying kid in your class.

So I tried to achieve my mission by becoming a doctor. For example, in high school, while all my friends were partying, I was busy studying. But the problem with being a high achiever is that you are proud yet insecure at the same time—you need achievements in order to be somebody in your own eyes. For example, I remember that being a doctor was no longer enough. I had to chase more exams and more qualifications to be somebody in both the medical community and my own eyes.

But Jesus was perfect so that I don't have to be perfect. I'd grown up in a Christian family and had known Jesus all my life. But I don't think I ever really understood until someone helped me read the Bible and showed me the bit where it says that Jesus is perfect so that I don't have to be perfect. God loves me just the way I am because of what Jesus has done.

That's when I decided I didn't need to chase achievements to be secure. I didn't have to be proud and insecure anymore. Instead, if I had Jesus, I could be humble and secure. Humble because it is Jesus who is perfect, not me. Secure, because my status was now found in Jesus, not me.

So now I no longer chase achievements to be somebody. For example, a few years ago, I had to choose whether to remain in full-time medicine. In the past, I needed to be a doctor to feel important—people at parties want to talk to you and bank managers want to lend you money! But I was able to leave full-time medicine because it no longer mattered what others thought of me. I was now important in God's eyes. Jesus is perfect so I don't have to be perfect to be somebody in God's eyes.

So I can now use this testimony instead of my previous standard "I grew up in a Christian family" testimony.

What about you? How could you give your testimony? The key moment is being able to answer the questions "Who am I?" and "What is my mission?" Once you work this out for yourself, the rest of the testimony should flow. But at the same time, these are the hardest questions to answer. When I asked my seminary students to do this exercise, often they sat staring at a blank page for an hour, repeatedly asking themselves, "Who am I?"

For example, one lady who grew up in a Christian family—her father was a church pastor!—and knew Jesus for as long as she could remember took a long time to answer these questions. So I kept asking her, "Who are you? And what is your mission? What drives you? What is your God-given existential cry?"

Finally, she got it. She said, "I am a pastor's kid, and my mission in life is to please people." So this is what she delivered as her testimony (adapted):

I am a pastor's kid. I am a people pleaser. My mission in life is to live up to other people's standards. For example, when I was a child in Sunday school classes, I always had to know the correct answer to every question. I was never allowed to get one wrong—I was the pastor's kid!

So I tried to achieve my mission by living up to the expectations of everyone. For example, in my culture, it's important to be good at everything—school, music, and church. But the problem is that you can never do this. For example, one time when I performed on the piano at an Eisteddfod, my performance was ordinary compared with everyone else's. My standards weren't good enough compared with others.

But with Jesus, I don't have to do this. God's expectation is that I'm perfect. But his other expectation is that I know Jesus. And if I know Jesus, then that's how I live up to his expectations. So now I don't have to worry whether I'm good enough in God's eyes.

That's when I realized that I needed to trust in Jesus and what he's done for me, rather than in what I can do for other people. I've known Jesus all my life, but I remember being at a conference where someone gave a talk and made this very clear to me. And that's when I decided I could trust Jesus.

So now I can own up to my failures, knowing that God loves me the way I am. For example, the other day at work, when the boss told me that I had not done something properly, I was able to accept his critique and not have to make excuses or blame someone else.

Another student, Damien, also had an ah-ha moment. "I know who I am!" he said. And this was his testimony (adapted for this book):

I am adopted. I grew up not knowing who my biological father was. My adoptive family loves me. But my mission in life has always been to find belonging. For example, in my high school, I had to choose between the nerds and the jocks. I settled on the jocks because of my love for football.

So I tried to find belonging by achieving it. For example, you have to do what your friends do, dress how they dress, and party how they party. But the problem with looking for belonging this way is that you never truly find it. For example, at the end of high school, I thought I had earned the approval of my friends by going to a big party with them. But by the end of the party, I felt even more alone.

But Jesus gives me the belonging I'm looking for. If I live for Jesus, God adopts me to be his child. I will have God as Father, Jesus as a brother, and a bunch of other people as my family.

That's when I realized that I needed to follow Jesus. I remember opening the Bible, reading about God's promise to be my Father, and then praying and asking God to adopt me as his child.

So now, with Jesus, I have the belonging I need. I am in God's family. And I can enjoy my adoptive family just for who they are. For example, I now love my adoptive parents even more. I thank them for raising me. And I wish all the more that they could also be part of God's family with me.

## Is Giving a Testimony Sharing the Gospel?

But how is this telling people the gospel? Where are the propositional ideas of the gospel? Where is the cognitive information of the gospel? As we will see in our chapter on storytelling (chapter 7), we are giving them the gospel in story. Our personal story is proclaiming the truth of the gospel, but in a practical, concrete, lived-out way.

---

 **Exercise: Preparing Your Testimony**

For more suggestions on sharing your testimony, including five examples of testimonies that utilize the storytelling approach, check out the free discussion guide available at ZondervanAcademic.com.

---

To access this resource, register on the website as a student. Then sign in and download the resource from the "Study Resources" tab on the book page for *Evangelism in a Skeptical World*.

---

## STRATEGY 6: TELL A STORY ABOUT JESUS

So far in our conversation, we've heard their story, and we've told our story. Now we can look for an opportunity to tell a story about Jesus. What I suggest is saying something like, "Would you like to hear a story that explains my story?" Tell them, "It's a story about Jesus from some of the original eyewitness accounts. It will take only one or two minutes."

I then tell a story about Jesus from the New Testament gospels. I don't memorize it word for word. I paraphrase the story in conversational English. I might simplify it by leaving out words, dialogue, or characters. Some of my favorite stories have been Jesus and Zacchaeus, Jesus and the sinful woman who washes his feet, the parable of the Pharisee and the tax collector, and the parable of the workers. These stories complement my testimony. And they have unexpected endings that disarm the audience. But I'm sure you'll have your own favorite stories that complement your testimony.

After I've told the story, I can ask them nonthreatening questions such as, "What did you like in that story?" and, "What things are hard to understand?" There are no right or wrong answers to these questions. But these questions also help the person engage with the story. Then we can move to more probing questions such as, "What does the story teach us about Jesus?" and, "What does the story want us to do?" These questions will generate a lot of discussion about the gospel. I resist the temptation to correct their answers, showing that it's safe for them to give me their answers. I'm not going to shame them by correcting them, and they don't have to hunt for the answer that I want them to say. But my questions should generate curiosity, and if they ask me a question, I'm given the opportunity to answer, sometimes with another question!

## CONCLUSION: SIX STRATEGIES FOR SHARING JESUS

When I was a doctor, one of my roommates was a guy named David. David was Asian like me, but unlike me, he grew up in a non-Christian family. He had no Christian role models or examples, and he was unfamiliar with anything Christian. He had no knowledge of the Bible. No knowledge about Jesus. And no Christian friends or family.

While living with me, David met my Christian friends. Whenever my friends did something—dinner, movie, BBQ—they invited David along. Gradually, my friends became friends with David.

One Friday night, David planned to go out. He said goodbye to me and left the apartment. But when he got inside his car, there was a large hairy spider on the inside of his windshield. David panicked and hit the spider with his shoe. He broke the windshield. Now David couldn't use his car that night.

He dragged his feet back into the apartment. He told me the sad story. There was a pause. Then he looked at me and asked, "What are you doing tonight?" I said, "I'm off with my church friends for a Bible study." There was another pause. Then I said, "Do you want to come with me?" And David gladly said yes.

David came to the Bible study and enjoyed hanging out with his new Christian friends. After that, David hung out a lot more regularly with my Christian friends. He also went along to the Friday night Bible study. Bit by bit, David began to see things from the Christian point of view. Slowly but surely, David was adopting the plausibility structures of his Christian friends. About a year later, David became a Christian. He gave his life to Christ.

David is an example of how evangelism often works in a post-Christendom society. Evangelism is not a one-time activity that interrupts our normal lives. Nor is it simply an event that our church adds to its calendar. It no longer works this way because our friends have plausibility structures that are different from ours. They have a strong sacred-secular divide.

In this chapter, I've suggested six strategies that might help us tell our friends about Jesus: (1) get our friends to become their friends; (2) go to their things before they come to our things; (3) invite them for coffee, then dinner, then talk about the gospel; (4) listen to their story as story; (5) tell our story as story; and (6) tell a story about Jesus. I hope that you get a chance to make these strategies your lifestyle and the culture of your church.

CHAPTER 3

# HOW TO CRAFT A
# GOSPEL PRESENTATION

## Scratch where they itch.

Jim was born in a small town in Iowa in the 1950s. He grew up going to church, attending Sunday school, and learning all the stories about Moses, Jonah, and Jesus. In the 1970s, Jim moved away from home to go to college in San Francisco. This was a time of experimentation for him as he explored drugs and sex and developed a new set of friends. He left behind the Christianity that he had inherited from his parents. But after a few years, he found his new lifestyle unsustainable. The drugs affected his ability to hold a steady job. Casual sex made him feel more lonely. And his new friends were self-absorbed and tiresome.

One day, Jim walked past a church. It advertised an old-style revival meeting that Saturday night. So he went. And that night Jim heard familiar hymns from his childhood. The Bible passage was also familiar: it was the story of the prodigal son from the book of Luke. Even the preaching style was familiar. A preacher delivered a fiery monologue for twenty to thirty minutes. But it wasn't the speaking style that gripped Jim; it was the preacher's message. He heard that he had knowingly disobeyed God, broken God's laws, and was now guilty. Jim realized that he deserved to be punished for his sins. But he had heard good news as well, that if he trusted and followed Jesus, his sins would be forgiven.

Jim was cut to the heart. After the preacher finished his message, Jim prayed the prayer of repentance and gave his life to Jesus. He felt a huge weight lift as his sins were washed away. That day was a clear line in the sand for him. After that, he considered himself a committed follower of Jesus Christ.

That day was long ago now, and today Jim has been happily married for more than thirty years. He and his wife have one daughter, Megan, who is all grown up and working in a career. However, Megan will have nothing to do with her father's Christianity. Whenever Jim tries to share how Jesus died for her to take away her guilt, Megan finds the message cold and offensive. For Megan, Christianity is a white man's organized religion which imposes artificially constructed laws upon people to control them by making them feel guilty.

Jim doesn't know what to do. When he heard the gospel message all those decades ago, it was so convicting to him. But that same message has no effect on his daughter. If anything, it is turning her away from Christianity.

Many Christians are familiar with one way of understanding and talking about the gospel. They grasp one chief gospel metaphor—in Jim's case the idea of guilt and forgiveness. But the Bible also gives us several other metaphors that help us understand what Jesus has done for us. In this chapter, we will explore other biblical gospel metaphors which we can use to craft a compelling gospel presentation that speaks to the needs and wants of today's audience.

## HOW DO WE PRESENT THE GOSPEL?

In Acts 16:30, the Philippian jailer, facing a crisis, asks Paul and Silas, "What must I do to be saved?" How would you have answered this question? How would you have presented the gospel to the jailer? And is there only one way to present the gospel, or are there many different ways we can do this? Is there a best way of presenting the gospel? Is there a wrong way?

Let's say we have a car that we want to give to a friend. But our friend is reluctant to take our car because they are skeptical that it is what they need. How would we promote the car to our friend?

If our friend was an engineer, we would tell them about the engine specifications—the cubic-inch capacity, the number of cylinders, and the double overhead camshaft. If our friend was an architect, we would emphasize the form and beauty of the car: "Look at the teardrop aerodynamic shape!" If our friend was a racecar driver, we would tell them about the car's performance, the quarter-mile time. If our friend was a sales representative, we would tell them about the trunk space. If our friend was a nurse, we might tell them about the safety features of the car. If our friend was a college student, we might emphasize the car's economy.

It's the same car. But we have different ways of promoting it to different people. In none of the cases are we being deceitful. Instead, we're emphasizing some aspect of the car that our friend will immediately understand. We are also promoting an aspect of the car that will engage our friend at emotional and existential levels.

Conversely, we can unwisely choose an aspect of the car that our friend will not understand. Or we can promote an aspect of the car that will not connect at an emotional or existential level. For example, a racecar driver might not be interested in trunk space. Or an engineer might not be interested in form and beauty. Or a sales representative might not be interested in engine specifications. It's not that it's wrong to do it this way. But it might not be the most strategic way because it doesn't connect.

This is also true when we present the gospel. It's the same story—God's story—true for all people, at all times, in all places. But the Bible gives us different ways of explaining it to different audiences and different people. Each audience will have different existential entry points. Each audience will find a different aspect of the gospel that connects emotionally with them. For example, when Jim heard the gospel presentation using the biblical metaphor of guilt and forgiveness, it connected with him existentially and emotionally. But that same biblical metaphor had much less connection with his daughter, Megan. So what other biblical metaphors can we use? How else can Jim try to present the gospel to his daughter? In this chapter we will answer this question by looking at the different gospel presentations in the Bible, different gospel metaphors, and several different contemporary gospel presentations.

## GOSPEL PRESENTATIONS IN THE BIBLE

The gospel is true for all people, at all times, in all places. It is the same story—God's story—for everyone. But at the same time, the different books of the Bible employ different ways of presenting the gospel for its different audiences.

In the gospels of Mark and Matthew, the gospel is God's story about Jesus—the Messiah, the Son of God. The blessing of the gospel is entry into the kingdom of God. The correct response to the gospel is for the audience to repent, deny themselves, humble themselves, and give up everything to follow Jesus (Mark 1:1; 1:14–15; 4:30–34; 10:14–15; cf. Matt. 4:17; 13:31–35; 18:1–5).

In the Gospel of Luke, the gospel presentation is similar to Mark's and Matthew's. Jesus is the Son of God. The blessing of the gospel is entry into the kingdom of God. The correct response is to repent, deny oneself, humble oneself, and give up everything to follow Jesus. But Luke's implied audience is slightly different. There's an emphasis on Jesus' mission to those who are marginalized: for example, the women, the poor, the sick. For this audience, salvation is described as freedom, healing, and restoration.

Luke also shows what the correct response to the gospel looks like for different audiences. Both the expert in the law (Luke 10:25) and the rich young ruler (Luke 18:18) ask Jesus the same question: "What must I do to inherit eternal life?" But Jesus gives a different answer to each person. The expert in the law needs to love like the Samaritan (or be loved by the Samaritan, depending on our interpretation of the parable), while the rich young ruler needs to give up his love of riches.

Luke also gives us the example of Zacchaeus as the paradigm of a true follower. While the rich young ruler is the negative example of someone who can't give up everything to follow Jesus (Luke 18:22–23), and the Pharisees are the negative example of people who love money (Luke 16:14) and are self-righteous (Luke 16:15; 18:9–12), Zacchaeus is the positive example of someone who can give up self-worth, self-dignity, and riches to follow Jesus joyfully (Luke 19:1–10).

In John's Gospel, we have the well-known gospel summary of John 3:16–17. John also shows how Jesus himself presents the gospel differently to different people. To a Pharisee—Nicodemus—Jesus says, "You must be born again" (John 3:7). But to a Samaritan woman at a well, Jesus says, "Whoever drinks the water I give them will never thirst" (John 4:14). To a man born blind, Jesus says, "I am the light of the world" (John 9:5). Moreover, we have the "I am" sayings of Jesus, where Jesus chooses a well-known Old Testament metaphor and applies it to himself, but in a way that is contextually relevant: "bread of life" (6:35, 51, 58); "light of the world" (8:12; 9:5); "gate" (10:7, 9); "good shepherd" (10:14); "resurrection and the life" (11:25); "way, truth, and life" (14:6); and "true vine" (15:1, 5). Thus, in John's presentation of the gospel, Jesus is the Son. The correct response is to believe in Jesus. The blessings of the gospel are eternal life and union with Jesus and other believers.

In the book of Acts, Luke's summary of the gospel is found in Peter's speech to the crowd on the day of Pentecost (Acts 2:32–38). Jesus is the exalted Messiah. The blessings are forgiveness of sins, indwelling of the Holy Spirit, and membership in the new people of God. The correct response is to repent and be baptized. But then in the rest of the book of Acts, Luke shows how the apostles present the gospel differently to their different audiences. To the Jewish audiences, the apostles present Jesus as the risen Messiah. They emphasize Jesus' titles—Son, Messiah, Prince, Savior. They show that Jesus is the fulfillment of Old Testament prophecies. And they use Scripture as a starting point for the conversation. Scripture gives them common ground with their audience. The Scriptures are the epistemological justification for their claims (Acts 4:10–12; 5:29–32; 13:32–41).

But to gentile audiences, the apostles use a different approach. The apostles present Jesus as the one they have been seeking all along. But there is no mention of Jesus as the fulfillment of Old Testament prophecies. There is no mention of Jesus' titles. There is no mention of Scripture. Instead, the apostles look for common ground in God's common grace (sending rain, making crops grow, providing food), general revelation (his creation), and the universal human desire to worship a god. They also quote not Scripture but references from their audience's cultural authors as starting points for the conversation (Acts 14:15–17; 17:22–31).

---

### FINDING COMMON GROUND

I'm not saying that we don't use Scripture at all when we present the gospel. We need eventually to end up with Scripture, for that is where we get our gospel. But I'm saying we don't necessarily have to begin with Scripture.

The apostles look for common ground, something that both they and their audiences already hold to be true, as a beginning into the gospel. For a Jewish audience, that common ground was Scripture. But for a gentile audience, unfamiliar with Scripture, the common ground was God's common grace, general revelation, universal human desires, and their cultural authors.

---

In Paul's letters, we can find a handful of representative summaries of Paul's presentation of the gospel (Rom. 1:1–6; 1:16–17; 2 Cor. 5:20–21). Paul presents Jesus chiefly as the Christ, the Son of God. The blessings of the gospel are justification, sanctification, reconciliation, and union with Christ. The correct response is faith and obedience. But even Paul has a variety of different ways of presenting this same gospel story. For example, I've already mentioned in a previous chapter how Paul describes the gospel as God's gospel (Rom. 1:1), but then he also calls it my gospel (Rom. 16:25). He necessarily tailors it to his audience. I remember hearing Timothy Keller note that Paul says that there is one gospel (Gal. 1:8) but then distinguishes between two different forms of the gospel—"the gospel to the circumcised" and "the gospel to the uncircumcised" (Gal. 2:7; cf. 1 Cor. 1:22–25; 9:19–23). This suggests that Paul was thinking about how to contextualize the message for the different audiences he encountered.

Finally, it's helpful to notice that every now and then in the New Testament, we get a presentation of the gospel in the form of early traditions, hymns, summaries, and creeds (1 Cor. 15:3–4; Phil. 2:5–11; Rom. 10:9; 1 Cor. 1:23; 1 Tim. 3:16). This reminds us that the message of the gospel was spoken, sung, memorized, summarized, and communicated in a variety of forms.

Every gospel presentation in the Bible essentially says something about Jesus: who he is, what he has done, what he will do. It also says something about the blessings of the gospel, which are both individual and corporate. And then it says something about the correct response to this gospel. It also implies an incorrect response—sinful response—to the gospel, and the condemnation for remaining in sin.

But notice that even in our brief and far from comprehensive survey of the New Testament, there is a wide variety of presentations of the gospel. There are different genres—narratives, speeches, letters, parables, hymns, creeds, traditions, summaries—and different metaphors—Jesus as Son, Shepherd, Bread, Life, Truth, Way, Light, Gate, Vine. There are different blessings. Different styles. Different tones.

There are also different emphases. For example, I heard Timothy Keller point out that the Synoptic Gospels emphasize the entry into the corporate kingdom of God. But John emphasizes the promise of eternal life. And Paul emphasizes justification. The significance for us is that we also should be free to try out different gospel metaphors, looking for the ones that will best connect with our audience at an existential and emotional level.

It also means that it is unfair to criticize a gospel presentation for not mentioning something. Otherwise we'd have to give a comprehensive presentation of all sixty-six books of the Bible and every single biblical metaphor in order to present the gospel. A gospel presentation is a summary of who Jesus is, what blessings are promised to us, and what our response must be. The logical flipside is that it will also communicate what sin and condemnation will look like. But we need to remember that a summary, by necessity, must leave things out. In doing so it can be sharply focused, penetrating, and to the point.

## HOW TO CRAFT A GOSPEL PRESENTATION

When we present the gospel, we are doing at least four things.

1.  Presenting the gospel elements: Jesus (or God), blessings, response, sin, condemnation.
2.  Using a set of coherent biblical metaphors to organize the elements.
3.  By necessity, leaving out other biblical metaphors.
4.  Being sharply focused, penetrating, and to the point.

My PhD supervisor, Graham Cole, helped me to understand how the Bible can give us sets of coherent biblical metaphors. To explain what this means, let's begin with table 3.1. In the lefthand column, we'll begin by filling in some biblical metaphors for God. In the other two columns, we'll fill in the corresponding metaphor for sin (or the sinful state) and the correct response based on that metaphor or aspect of God's person and nature.

| God | Sin or Sinful State | Correct Response |
|---|---|---|
| Creator | Idolatry | Worship |
| King | Rebellion | Repentance and submission |
| Holy | Impurity | Purity |
| Judge | Transgression | Righteousness |
| Savior | Self-righteousness | Calling on his name |
| Father | Broken relationship | Becoming a child of God |
| Groom | Unfaithfulness | Faithfulness |
| Shepherd | Wandering | Following |

Table 3.1

This is just an example, and we don't have to begin with God. We can mix it up. Look what happens if we begin with sin (or the sinful state) in the lefthand column. Now we can fill in the corresponding salvation blessings in the other column (table 3.2).

| Sin or Sinful State | Correct Response | Blessings |
|---|---|---|
| Transgression, guilt, rebellion, disobedience | Faith and obedience | Justification, forgiveness |
| Falling short | Calling on God's name | Reconciliation |
| Captivity | Serving Jesus | Redemption, liberation |
| Blindness | Recognizing our blindness | Illumination |
| Deadness | Recognizing our deadness | Regeneration, life |
| Enemy of God | Ceasing our hostilities | Peace, reconciliation |
| Not a child of God | Repentance, returning | Adoption, reconciliation |
| Uncleanness, impurity | Recognizing our uncleanness | Sanctification, purification |
| Separation | Returning | Union |
| Idolatry | Worshiping God | God's favor |
| Shamefulness | Honoring God | Restoration, face |
| Wandering, erring, going astray | Walking in God's ways | Being on the correct path, wisdom |
| Wickedness | Godliness | Godly flourishing |

**Table 3.2**

Or we can use metaphors and titles for Jesus in the lefthand column and fill in the corresponding metaphors for sin (or the sinful state) and our correct responses in the other columns (table 3.3).

| Jesus | Sin or Sinful State | Correct Response |
|---|---|---|
| Creator | Idolatry | Worship |
| King, Messiah, Christ | Rebellion | Repentance and submission |
| Holy, Priest | Impurity | Purity |
| Judge | Transgression | Righteousness |
| Savior | Self-righteousness | Calling on his name |
| Groom | Unfaithfulness | Faithfulness |
| Shepherd | Wandering | Following |
| Living Water | Thirsting | Drinking |

| Jesus | Sin or Sinful State | Correct Response |
|---|---|---|
| Living Bread | Starving | Eating |
| The Way | Wandering | Following |
| The Truth | Falsehood | Believing |
| The Life | Death | Living |
| The Vine | Nonparticipation | Participation, union |
| Light | Blindness | Illumination |
| Word | Deafness | Hearing |

**Table 3.3**

Or we can use metaphors for Jesus in the lefthand column and fill in the corresponding metaphors for the work of Jesus and what he saves us from (our sinful state) in the other columns (table 3.4).

| Jesus | What Jesus Does | Sinful State |
|---|---|---|
| King, Messiah, Christ | Rules | Rebellion |
| Savior | Saves | Self-righteousness |
| Priest | Reconciles | Separation and impurity |
| Shepherd | Shepherds | Going astray |
| Servant | Obeys | Disobedience |
| Groom | Loves | Unfaithfulness |
| Word | Reveals God | Ignorance of God |
| The Way | Reveals the way | Lostness |
| The Truth | Reveals the truth | Error |
| The Life | Gives eternal life | Death |

**Table 3.4**

Or we can use metaphors for Jesus' atoning work on the cross in the lefthand column and fill in the corresponding metaphors for our sinful state and our salvation blessings in the other columns (table 3.5).

| Jesus' Atoning Work | Sinful State | Salvation Blessings |
|---|---|---|
| Penal substitution | Guilt, penalty of death | Innocence |
| Ransom, redemption | Captivity | Freedom |
| Victory | Defeated by Satan, sin, death | Victory over Satan, sin, death |

**Table 3.5**

## WHAT ABOUT OTHER MODELS OF THE ATONEMENT?

I have omitted the moral influence and moral example models of atonement. That's because they are a fruit of the atonement rather than a means of atonement. We follow Jesus' example because he has atoned for our sins. But our sins are not atoned for by our following Jesus' example.

The lists of metaphors in the tables are not exhaustive. There are far more metaphors that we can use. As an exercise, see if you can add more to the lists I've given. You could also add a column to the right which identifies the corresponding condemnation from God. Keep in mind that these lists are meant only to help us craft a gospel presentation; we don't have to use the exact wording or phrases when we talk with people.

Now that we have a set of coherent biblical metaphors, we can use them to present the gospel. For example, if we begin with God as holy, our gospel presentation might go like this: "God is a holy God. But all of us are impure; we are not as good as we should be. So we deserve to be separated from God forever. But if we call on Jesus to save us, Jesus will wash our sins away and make us clean. Now we can come near to God."

Or if we begin with sin as transgression, our gospel presentation could be, "We have all done things that we know are wrong, and if we break one law, it's as good as breaking all of God's laws. We stand guilty before God. We deserve to be punished by him. But if we trust in Jesus' death for us, God will justify us."

Or if we begin with Jesus as King, our gospel presentation would have these elements: "God sent Jesus to be our King. But we have all rebelled against Jesus by living our own way. But God calls on us to repent and submit to Jesus. If we do this, we will be forgiven by God instead of being punished by him."

Or if we begin with Jesus as Word, our gospel presentation might be, "Jesus is the Word because he reveals God to us. Without Jesus we are ignorant of who God is. But now, if we listen to Jesus, we can know God personally because of him."

Use the tables as a guide to try this out for yourself. As you practice various metaphors and begin to see how they cohere, you will soon notice that your gospel vocabulary will grow as well. You will be able to talk about the Good News in a variety of ways adaptable to different contexts and people.

## EXPLORING DIFFERENT METAPHORS FOR SIN AND SALVATION

By exploring a variety of biblical metaphors for God, Jesus, sin, and salvation, we can connect with the emotional and existential needs of our audience. Here are some thoughts on using the different metaphors.

### Calling on the Name of the Lord

The metaphor of calling on the name of the Lord as a means for salvation is prominent in the Bible. It begins in Genesis 4:26 and 26:25. Abraham does it (Gen. 12:8; 13:4; 21:33). The psalmists do it (e.g., Ps. 17:6). Paul uses it in Romans 10:13 (citing Joel 2:32). It is a shorthand term for a Christian (2 Tim. 2:22) and the church (1 Cor. 1:2). It is a useful summary for what we need to do to be saved.

### Chief Metaphors for Sin

The Old Testament uses more than fifty words for sin. But according to Henri Blocher, the three main metaphors for sin in the Bible are:[1]

1. *Transgression:* to break a law, commit a crime, rebel
2. *Falling short:* to miss the mark, to be unclean
3. *Iniquity:* to be broken or bent out of shape

Each metaphor speaks differently to where we are. Someone like the prodigal son was guilty of transgression. But the apostle Paul, who was once called Saul, was not breaking laws but keeping them. Paul wouldn't have seen himself as a transgressor—far from it. Yet despite his religious

---

1. Henri A. G. Blocher, "Sin," in *New Dictionary of Biblical Theology* (Leicester, UK: Inter-Varsity, 2000), 782.

zeal, Paul fell short of God's righteousness. And Isaiah, when he stood before the throne of the Lord, was confronted by his iniquity before God.

All three metaphors are complementary. Together they give us a fuller picture of sin. For example, after David commits adultery with Bathsheba, he confesses his sin to God in Psalm 51. David uses all three of these metaphors in his confession: "Blot out my *transgressions*. Wash away all my *iniquity* and cleanse me from my [*falling short*]. For I know my *transgressions*, and my [*falling short*] is always before me" (Ps. 51:1–3).

When we share the gospel, one metaphor will often resonate more than the others with the person we're speaking with. For example, in a modern culture, which is strong on absolutes, people might see their sins as transgressions. But in a postmodern culture, which is strong on community, people might see their sins as falling short. Or in a society which is strongly aware of the prevalance of social injustices, people might see their sins as brokenness.

## Theological Components to Sin

There are also three theological components to sin that we must consider:

1. *Internal:* We sin against ourselves; we let ourselves down.
2. *Horizontal:* We sin against someone else.
3. *Vertical:* We sin against God.

For example, when David committed adultery with Bathsheba (2 Samuel 11), he sinned internally. He sinned against himself. He let himself down. He should have known better. He probably should have gone off to war instead of staying at home alone (v. 1). But he also sinned horizontally. He sinned against Bathsheba by seducing her and making her commit adultery. He also murdered her husband, Uriah. And he sinned vertically by breaking God's laws and falling short of God's righteous standards.

Ultimately every sin is against God *(coram Deo)*. This is why David eventually confesses, "Against *you* . . . have I sinned" (Ps. 51:4). Without this vertical component to sin, it's very hard to explain why God has to punish us or send us to hell. It's tempting to soften the way we communicate about sin by mentioning only the internal component—"We have let down ourselves"—or the horizontal component—"We have let down our friends." But if we don't eventually communicate the vertical component—"We have sinned against God"—it's going to be hard to explain why we need to be saved by God from his judgment.

At the same time, the internal and horizontal components give us a fuller understanding of sin. There are personal and social consequences for our sin. For example, after David's sin with Bathsheba, David lost his moral standing with his family. David's son Amnon raped his half sister, Tamar, and the moral chaos continued with David's other son, Absalom, killing Amnon and then staging a war against David. This reminds us that our sins aren't only between us and God. They are not merely things we do in the privacy of our homes. They have personal and social ramifications.

## HELL AND THE HOLINESS OF GOD

Part of the problem of hell is that the punishment seems disproportionate to the offence. Apologetically, we often defend hell by explaining that the problem exists because we have too low a view of God's holiness. If we understood how holy God is, we could understand the magnitude of our sins against God, and then we could understand the need for God to send us to hell.

But another way of explaining it is we have too low a view of humankind. For our sins are also against fellow humans. For example, if I envy or lie or curse or am impatient, I am sinning against a human—horizontally. And according to God, every human is made in his image, and thus every sin against a human is also a sin against God—vertically (James 3:9). God has a much higher view of humans than we do. Whenever God rails in the Old Testament against Israel and the nations because of their sins, often the sins listed are sins against humans—lying, cheating, fraud, violence (Mic. 6:9–12; Amos 1–2)—especially those who are disadvantaged and marginalized. So if we can understand how holy humans are, and that our sins against humans are also sins against God, we can also understand the need for God to send us to hell.

## Manifestations of Sin

There are also multiple manifestations of sin:

1. *Vertical:* offence against God, death, judgment
2. *Horizontal:* socioeconomic-political oppression
3. *Internal:* psychological disturbance

The biblical doctrine is that all humans are in a sinful state before God (Rom. 3:10–18; Eph. 2:1–3). Each and every human is guilty, responsible to God, and needs to repent and ask God for forgiveness.

But sin is manifest in many different ways to us—vertically, horizontally, and internally. For example, when the jailer asks Paul and Silas, "What must I do to be saved?" (Acts 16:30), what is he asking to be saved from? Of course he ultimately needs to be saved—vertically—from his guilt before God. But perhaps he is also oppressed—horizontally—by socioeconomic-political evils. As a member of the working-class poor, he will forever be condemned to work in unjust working conditions. Or perhaps he needs to be saved—internally—from his anxiety, insecurity, and depression. So when the jailer asks, "What must I do to be saved?" he might be aware of all three manifestations of sin in his life.

Interestingly, Jesus in Luke 4:18–19—quoting the commissioning of the Servant in Isaiah 61—claims that he has been commissioned by God to bring salvation at all three levels—vertically ("the Lord's favor"), horizontally ("good news to the poor . . . freedom for the prisoners"), and internally ("recovery of sight for the blind"). This suggests that we might be able to find an existential connection with our audience by addressing the horizontal problem of social evils. Or the internal problem of psychological and physical states. And demonstrating that this is evidence of the foundational vertical problem of our sin and need for salvation by Jesus.

## God's Judgment

There are also three components to God's judgment:

1. *Privation of good:* We miss out on God and his blessings.
2. *Separation:* We are cast away from the presence of God.
3. *Punishment:* We pay the penalty for our transgressions.

For example, we see all three components in Matthew's parable of the wedding banquet (Matt. 22:1–14). Those who decline the invitation to the banquet miss out on the feast. That is their punishment. They could have enjoyed God's blessings, but they choose not to, and God hands them over to their choices. But they are also separated from God and his banquet. They are thrown outside into the "darkness" (v. 13), and they are punished for rejecting the invitation. God is "enraged" and destroys those who refuse the invitation (v. 7). They are cast outside where there is "weeping and gnashing of teeth."

Once again, if we cast sin only as something internal or horizontal, it's very hard to explain why we need God's salvation. If we cast sin only as our "breaking a relationship with God" or "rejecting God," it's very hard to explain why God should punish us. If I break up with a friend, I don't expect them to respond with vengeance. So why should God punish us for breaking our relationship with him? If we cast sin only as our being more or less victims of social evils, it's hard to understand why we should be punished by God, for why should God blame the victims?

Even though we are allowed a variety of metaphors to explain sin, eventually we will have to explain that there is a vertical component to sin. Eventually, we will have to explain that God's judgment is more than a privation of good or a separation from him. Ultimately God's judgment is a form of retributive justice. It is punishment for our wrongs.

## Concepts of Sin

Different cultures gravitate to one of these three biblical concepts of sin:[2]

| Breaking a law | Guilt | We need forgiveness (West). |
| Defilement | Uncleanness | We need cleansing (Middle East). |
| Breaking relationships | Shame | We need restoration (East). |

Each of these concepts is taught in the Bible. And we happily affirm all of them. But different cultures will find that one concept connects more with their moral system at intellectual, emotional, and intuitive levels. For example, one day my friend was talking to a man who was a Muslim and was on his way to the mosque. But this Muslim man had also just cheated on his wife. The man was worried that he hadn't sufficiently purified himself after sex and would be too defiled to enter the mosque. He wasn't all that worried about having cheated on his wife or having broken a law. He wasn't worried about being guilty or having broken a relationship. Instead, he was worried about being unclean.

## Using Shame and Dishonor as a Model of Sin

I believe that our Western world, as it becomes more and more postmodern and post-Western, is also moving away from the guilt model of sin. Many people no longer believe in absolutes. They see laws as artificial

2. My synthesis of Paul G. Hiebert, *Transforming Worldviews: An Anthropological Understanding of How People Change* (Grand Rapids, Mich.: Baker, 2008), 62.

constructs imposed upon us by oppressive institutions of power such as churches and governments.

This might be a time for us to explore the shame model in the West.[3] Using shame will not send us down the pathway to relativism, for shame has both objective and subjective elements. And when we talk about our shame before God, we talk about how we have not lived up to God's objective standards for us. More and more, I find that talk about shame resonates with Western audiences. For example, in the West, professional athletes—especially men—often get themselves into trouble when they get into fights or drug scandals or are caught cheating on their wives. How do the sports authorities tell these athletes to behave in their public and private lives? Such men don't care about laws; they're professional athletes and can do anything they like! They are a law unto themselves. But the authorities have had some success appealing to a code of honor. They tell the sportsmen to behave to avoid "bringing the game into disrepute" and "letting down their teammates." This is an appeal to shame and honor.

In 2011 there were riots in Vancouver, Canada, after their hockey team lost the Stanley Cup final. People trashed cars, smashed windows, and looted shops. The riots shamed Vancouver, especially because the city had just proudly hosted the 2010 Winter Olympics. After the riots, newspaper headlines screamed, "Shame!" And webpages uploaded photos to name and shame the rioters.

The use of social media has increased this phenomenon, as observed by Jon Ronson in his book *So You've Been Publicly Shamed*.[4] And David Brooks, in an op-ed piece in *The New York Times*, observes that we now live in a "modern shame culture" which can be "unmerciful to those who disagree and to those who don't fit in."[5] All of this suggests that shame is becoming more prominent in our postmodern society, with its larger emphasis on community and tribal groups. If so, we can utilize it more often in our gospel presentations.[6] For example, when I delivered gospel talks to high school students and talked about breaking God's laws and

---

3. Jackson Wu gives us a detailed treatment on the subject of shame, honor, and face in Jackson Wu, *Saving God's Face: A Chinese Contextualization of Salvation through Honor and Shame*, EMS Dissertation Series (Pasadena, Calif.: William Carey International Univ. Press, 2012).

4. Jon Ronson, *So You've Been Publicly Shamed* (New York: Riverhead, 2016).

5. David Brooks, "The Shame Culture," *New York Times*, March 15, 2016, http://www.nytimes.com/2016/03/15/opinion/the-shame-culture.html. Accessed January 3, 2017.

6. See also Andy Crouch, "The Return of Shame," *Christianity Today*, http://www.christianitytoday.com/ct/2015/march/andy-crouch-gospel-in-age-of-public-shame.html. Accessed January 3, 2017.

being rebels against God, I often got vacant looks from them and some rolled their eyes at me. They were thinking, "Here we go again. The church is imposing its oppressive laws on us, taking away our freedoms." More recently, I've been using the language of shame—we have "shamed God," we have "not been honoring God"—and the room is silent. All eyes are on me. They get it. It's personal.

I believe this is similar to the approach of the apostles in Acts. When the apostles preached the gospel to the Jews, they appealed to the guilt model of sin. The Jews had the Scriptures and should have known better. But when God sent them the Messiah, they killed him, thus breaking God's laws. For this they were guilty (Acts 2:14–40; 4:10–12; 5:29–32; 7:51–53; 13:26–41). But when the apostles preached the gospel to the pagans, they appealed to the shame model of sin. The pagans had been enjoying God's general creation blessings. But they had not been giving thanks to this God. They had not been worshiping him. Thus, they had dishonored God. For this, they needed to repent (Acts 14:15–17; 17:22–31).

In the twentieth century, modern Western culture had more in common with the religious Jews in Acts. It was churched and familiar with the Scriptures. It believed in laws and absolutes. The guilt model worked well. But in the twenty-first century, the postmodern West is postchurched, post-reached, and post-Christian. It has more in common with the unreached pagan culture in Acts. And perhaps the shame model will work better.

## Using Defilement as a Model of Sin

It might also be time for us to explore the defilement model in the West. For example, a pastor whose church has a high proportion of women who suffer domestic abuse says that the women feel defiled by what they have suffered. As a result, what attracts them to the gospel is the promise of being purified by Jesus.

I also have a friend who was addicted to methadone for years. One day while on a train, he was disgusted with his own life. He felt defiled by the drugs he was using, and he cried out to God, "If you're real, show yourself to me." At that moment, he felt God wash the drugs out of his system. He gave his life to Jesus and has never taken drugs since that day.

I understand that these examples refer to defilement by our own actions and the actions of others. They do not refer to defilement by sin. But if we feel defiled already, then the defilement model of sin will connect more immediately with us. For example, my friend who was addicted to methadone was not so much worried about breaking laws—he had been breaking them all his life—but he was more worried about the corruption of his body by drugs. Defilement and the need for purification made him also long for the truth of the gospel. Defilement and purification also became a redemptive analogy that made the gospel more plausible to him.

## Using Brokenness as a Model of Sin

We also find language of brokenness in the Bible when talking about sin. I understand that brokenness is an elastic term, and it can even be misleading. It can be unhelpful in talking about sin for a variety of reasons.[7] But at the same time, brokenness as iniquity is a legitimate biblical metaphor for our sin, and the Bible speaks of broken relationships as a metaphor for our sinful state. Brokenness is also a prominent model of sin in shame cultures. And the language of brokenness is readily accepted by our twenty-first-century audiences. So I believe we can cautiously appropriate the language of brokenness for our evangelism.

Broken relationships are a feature of the Genesis 3 postfall curses. The first curse—weeds in the garden—means that our work will be frustrated. The second curse means that childbirth will be fraught with pain, danger, and death. The third curse—"Your desire will be for your husband, and he will rule over you" (Gen. 3:16)—means that human relationships will be dysfunctional, dislocated, and fractured. All relationships will have some level of brokenness. Today in the West, relationships especially will be broken because of our emphasis on individualism, self-absorption, and pursuit of pleasure on our own terms. For example, I have attended several parenting seminars and have been impressed by the large numbers of people who attend. Many parents in the West—including me—need as much help as we can get because we cannot control our children. There is brokenness in our parent-child relationships.

As another example, I went to a seminar run by an Australian psychologist, Stephen Biddulph. Biddulph said that in a room of one hundred Australian men, thirty-three will not have spoken to their fathers in years, maybe decades. Another thirty-three will speak to their fathers, but it ends badly: words are said, someone storms out, and a door is slammed. And the last thirty-three say that they have an okay relationship with their fathers because they catch up once a week for dinner. But that's duty, not a warm relationship. Biddulph goes on to say that in a room of one hundred Australian

---

7. I refer you to an excellent article by Claire Smith, "Broken Bad," *GoThereFor.com*, May 13, 2016, http://gotherefor.com/offer.php?intid=29295. Accessed July 31, 2016.

men, only one can say that they have a warm functional relationship with their father. Biddulph goes on to propose that to function as husbands and fathers, men need to be reconciled first with their earthly fathers.[8]

I used this example when I gave a talk to a room full of a hundred powerful businessmen and CEOs. Afterward there was silence. Every set of eyes was locked onto me. Each man was inwardly acknowledging that he had a broken relationship with his father. Despite his success and status, he still had much pain and hurt. His life was broken. I then used this as a redemptive analogy for how our relationships with God, our Father, were also broken, and we need reconciliation. But unlike our earthly fathers, where reconciliation might not be possible, reconciliation with God is possible. And God can be the Father that we never had, but have always needed.

## Using Self-Righteousness as a Model of Sin

I have also started using self-righteousness as a metaphor for our sinful state. A twenty-first-century Western audience no longer believes in laws as absolutes. So they don't feel guilty about having broken any laws. And our Western narrative tells us that we are free to pursue happiness on our own terms. The mantra is to "be true to yourself." So how can anyone be guilty as long as they are trying to be happy? What can possibly be wrong with being authentic? We are now told that guilt is a social construct imposed upon us by organized religion to rob us of happiness and true identity.

But even with this narrative of freedom to pursue our own happiness, our twenty-first-century Western audience is quite self-righteous. If I am pro-environment, I might recycle, carry my groceries home in a bright-green environmentally friendly shopping bag, and drive a prominently badged hybrid car. And I will feel good about myself because I am doing the right thing. Or to give another example, if I am happily married, with children who attend an elite school, and I mail out Christmas newsletters with an impressive list of achievements each year, I will feel good about myself because I must be doing the right thing.

Correspondingly, the twenty-first-century Western audience is also quite judgmental. If I am doing my thing for the environment, I will look down on those who are not. I might roll my eyes at those who do not recycle properly, use plastic shopping bags, and drive a gas-guzzling SUV. I will feel morally superior to them. As another example, if I am happily married, I will look

---

8. Stephen Biddulph, *The New Manhood: The Handbook for a New Kind of Man* (Sydney: Finch, 2010), 20.

down on those whose marriages have failed. I might roll my eyes at how their children are not high achievers. I will feel morally superior to them.

Jesus often uses self-righteousness as his chief metaphor for sin, especially in the Synoptic Gospels, and more specifically in the Gospel of Luke. For example, Jesus tells the parable of the Pharisee and tax collector to "some who were confident of their own righteousness and looked down on everyone else" (Luke 18:9). In Luke 18:9–14, the Pharisee's sin is not that he's guilty of breaking laws. Instead his sin is self-righteousness, moral superiority, judgmentalism, and looking down on those around him.

## Using Idolatry as a Model of Sin

Our Western narrative also tells us to pursue fulfillment. We seek life, happiness, freedom, pleasure, success, identity, status, and security. Believe it or not, these are God-given things for us to enjoy. They are not bad things in and of themselves.

In the parable of the rich fool, Jesus tells us, "The ground of a certain rich man yielded an abundant harvest" (Luke 12:16). This is Jesus' way of saying that God is the one who gave the man his abundant harvest. God gave this man his success, wealth, and security. So the man's riches are not a bad thing in and of themselves. They are a good gift from a good God for him to enjoy.

But in the parable, it's what the man does with God's gift that is sinful. The man makes his riches his source of security. That's why he stores his grain, thinking the riches it will bring will guarantee him lifelong happiness: "You have plenty of grain laid up for many years. Take life easy; eat, drink and be merry" (Luke 12:19). He makes his riches do what only God can do: be the source of life, happiness, freedom, pleasure, success, identity, status, and security. Or to use the categories of the Bible, he makes an idol of his gift from God.

In the Western narrative, we do the same thing. God gives us life, freedom, pleasure, success, health, sports, school, work, family, friends, abundant wealth and possessions. But rather than worship God the giver, we worship the gifts. We ask the gifts to do what only God can do for us.

What is wrong with this? The problem is that the gifts can never be God. So we're asking too much from the gifts. And either we will destroy them or they will destroy us. For example, if I make the trophy family the source of my happiness, I will destroy my spouse and children by asking them to do for me what only God can do. Or I will destroy myself by trying to be the perfect father and husband, which only God can be. As another example, if I make fitness and beauty my source of identity, I will destroy my body by asking it to be what only God can be. Or I will destroy myself in my quest for beauty and perfection, which only God can be.

Author and pastor Timothy Keller, in his sermons and books,[9] often uses idolatry as his preferred metaphor when describing sin to a postmodern Western audience. Keller says that we've all got to live for something, otherwise we've got nothing to live for. But whatever we live for will own us. Whatever we live for will never fulfill us. And whatever we live for will never forgive us when we fail it. We become enslaved to our idols, and they ultimately destroy us.

This is the great irony of our Western narrative. Our Western narrative tells us that we are free to do whatever we want. We are free to pursue happiness on our own terms. This is the foundational premise of the US Declaration of Independence, the French Revolution, and the first line of the Australian national anthem. But the truth is that we are owned by whatever we pursue. We surrender our freedom in our quest for freedom. As Paul says to the Corinthians who glorified their pursuit of freedom, "'I have the right to do anything,' you say—but not everything is beneficial. 'I have the right to do anything'—but I will not be mastered by anything" (1 Cor. 6:12). The great paradox in the Bible is that salvation is found in giving up our freedom to pursue happiness on our own terms and worship God instead. In doing so, we will find true freedom.

## Using Falling Short as a Model of Sin[10]

Our Western narrative also tells us to be the best we can be. A prominent catchphrase of the twenty-first-century generation is that we want—actually, we need—to "make a difference" in this world. Make the most of every opportunity. *Carpe deum*. You only live once! This is the message we often hear at commencement speeches in schools across the Western world.

This is a good desire. We need to praise people who make a difference. In Genesis 2, God puts Adam and Eve in the garden to work the garden, to cultivate order, beauty, and goodness. God's mandate to humans is to seize opportunities to leave this earth better than how we found it. This is a God-given desire and mandate.

But we fall short. Although we are good people, we still fall short of the ultimate good of worshiping God. Just like my car is good as transportation,

---

9. For example, Timothy Keller, *Center Church: Doing Gospel-Centered Ministry in Your City* (Grand Rapids, Mich.: Zondervan, 2012), 126–28.

10. I owe these insights to Todd Bates and Adam Co.

but not good enough to be my friend, we are good in our deeds, but not good enough to be God's children. We fall short of this ultimate good. We are not the best we can be. And if we were true to ourselves, we would know that although we are good people, we're not good enough. But Jesus can help us to be the best we can be. We see this in the parable of the Pharisee and the tax collector. The Pharisee is a good person. It is good that he is generous with his money. It is good that he is faithful to his wife and does not cheat on her. He needs to be praised for this. He's making a difference! But the Pharisee fails to see that he is not good enough to be a child of God; this is the point of the following passage with the children coming to Jesus as children (Luke 18:15–17) and not as a rich, lawkeeping ruler (Luke 18:18–30). We need to humble ourselves—admit that we fall short (as the tax collector does)—and ask Jesus to "exalt us" (Luke 18:14), making us the best we can be: children of God.

## Using Peace as a Metaphor for Salvation

The Bible gives us many metaphors for our salvation blessings—union, adoption, justification, sanctification, redemption, reconciliation, freedom, regeneration. But Graham Cole believes that the umbrella metaphor for all of these salvation metaphors is peace or *shalom*.[11]

This is the ultimate existential cry of every human heart. Peace. Because of the curses in Genesis 3, we are not at peace with our work, our identity, our roles, the environment, our bodies, our friends, our family, and ultimately God. Today's society has so many fractured relationships at home and work that we are longing for peace. Every aspect of our lives is affected by disharmony, disruption, and despair. Peace is the opposite of our lives. This means if we allow our friends to talk about their work, health, family, and relationships, we will soon hear them talking about their search for peace.

Every child longs for peace. The sound a child hates the most is the sound of their parents fighting. They would do anything for that sound to stop. Or consider my friend and his wife. They lived in an apartment and could always hear the couple next door fighting. One day, my friend was able to talk to the man next door. He looked stressed and exhausted. So my friend asked the man what was wrong. The man said to him, "I need peace. I'm looking for peace. I need peace." So my friend was able to use peace to begin a conversation about Jesus with the man next door.

---

11. This is Graham Cole's chief argument in *God the Peacemaker: How Atonement Brings Shalom* (Downers Grove, Ill.: InterVarsity, 2009).

## Do I Need to Use the Word Sin?

You might wonder whether the word sin is still the best word to use when talking with people today. Why not? Why shouldn't we use the word sin to communicate the idea of sin? I'll say two things. First, Jesus himself often doesn't use the word sin to describe sin. Instead he uses metaphors, picture language, and stories to communicate the idea of sin. For example, in the parable of the rich fool, sin is painted as "storing up riches for yourself" and "not being rich toward God" (Luke 12:21). In the parable of the lost sheep, sin is painted as finding oneself lost, not as an act of willful rebellion, but that's just what happens to sheep (Luke 15:1–7)! In the parable of the Pharisee and the tax collector, sin is painted as being confident of one's righteousness and looking down on others (Luke 18:9). Jesus doesn't use the word sin, and yet the idea is vividly communicated. This is the basic premise of theology—that a biblical idea can be communicated without using the word for that idea (for example, the Trinity).

Second, I believe it might be more helpful not to use the word sin in our culture. Francis Spufford, in his book *Unapologetic*, explains that the meaning of the word sin in the English language has changed in recent decades. Its meaning is now closer to the idea of a guilty, playful pleasure, like chocolates, ice cream, or lingerie. Something that we have a delightful giggle about.[12] As with other words in English whose meanings have changed over time—thong, gay, dumb—we can't expect our listeners to hear the intended meaning when we use it. We might have to use different words to communicate the same meaning.

## There Are Many Ways to Share the Gospel

The gospel is God's story about how he saves the world through Jesus. For those who respond with faith and obedience, there will be salvation: entry into the kingdom! But for those who don't respond this way, there will be judgment and condemnation.

But the Bible itself uses a wide range of metaphors, genres, and styles to present this gospel. Jesus and his apostles used a variety of presentations for their different audiences. We are also free to explore a variety of gospel presentations. We can use different gospel metaphors—freedom, adoption, peace, honor—looking for the one that will best connect with our audience existentially, emotionally, and culturally.

---

12. Francis Spufford, *Unapologetic: Why, Despite Everything, Christianity Can Still Make Surprising Emotional Sense* (San Francisco: HarperOne, 2013), 24–27.

## THREE COMMON GOSPEL PRESENTATIONS

As a learning exercise, we can look at three common and recent gospel presentations. From these we can see that there is no one-size-fits-all gospel presentation. As summaries of the gospel, they all have strengths and corresponding weaknesses. And as our analysis will show, this indicates that we need to use a variety of gospel presentations.

### 1. Two Ways to Live: Matthias Media

The Two Ways to Live gospel presentation was developed in the 1980s for college ministry in Sydney, Australia. It was highly welcomed by many Christians—especially me!—because it helped explain the gospel clearly, easily, and succinctly. The pictures were easy to learn and draw. The Bible verses were easy to recite. The step-by-step presentation was engaging and easy to present to non-Christian friends. And it was hard hitting; it didn't back away from hard truths such as condemnation, hell, judgment, and penal substitution.

It is an example of brilliant contextualization for its time. Most students on college campuses in the 1980s would have gone to Sunday school or had some sort of religious education. But in college, they experimented with their newfound freedom away from home. At some stage, they hit an existential crisis—"What am I doing here?"—similar to that of the prodigal son (Luke 15:17). If someone presented them Two Ways to Live, they would readily identify as the rebel who needed to come back and submit to God's rule.

But as with all contextualization, what speaks well to one audience won't speak so well to another. With the cultural shift into postmodernity, some features of Two Ways to Live no longer resonate. The chief metaphors—God as King, sin as rebellion, and salvation as submission—find little existential traction in the postmodern West, where authority figures impose their artificially constructed laws upon us to take away our freedom and authenticity. That's why in the postmodern West our moral heroes are the rebels who resist and overthrow authorities such as kings to preserve freedom and authenticity. Think of the American Revolution. Or the Australian bushranger. Or Braveheart and his cry of "Freedom!"

But again, please note we are applying these comments as a learning exercise. In defense of Two Ways to Live, it was never designed as a standalone evangelistic tract. Instead, its purpose was to be a summary for Christians to use as a framework for gospel conversations with their friends. To do it justice, you should read the full text of the Two Ways to Live presentation online instead of relying only on my brief summary: www.twowaystolive.com.

Here's a summary with a few images from the presentation:

| 1. | | God is the loving ruler of the world.<br>He made the world.<br>He made us rulers of the world under him.<br>But is that the way it is now? | Revelation 4:11 |
|----|----|----|----|
| 2. | | We all reject the ruler—God—by trying to run life our own way without him.<br>But we fail to rule ourselves or society or the world.<br>What will God do about such rebellion? | Romans 3:10–12 |
| 3. | | God won't let us rebel forever.<br>God's punishment for rebellion is death and judgment.<br>God's judgment sounds harsh but . . . | Hebrews 9:27 |
| 4. | | Because of his love, God sent his Son into the world: the man Jesus Christ.<br>Jesus always lived under God's rule.<br>Yet by dying in our place, he took our punishment and brought forgiveness.<br>But that's not all . . . | 1 Peter 3:18 |
| 5. | | God raised Jesus to life again as the ruler of the world.<br>Jesus has conquered death, now gives new life, and will return to judge.<br>Well, where does that leave us now? | 1 Peter 1:3 |

| 6. | 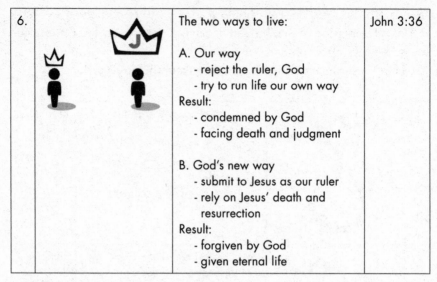 | The two ways to live:<br><br>A. Our way<br>  - reject the ruler, God<br>  - try to run life our own way<br>Result:<br>  - condemned by God<br>  - facing death and judgment<br><br>B. God's new way<br>  - submit to Jesus as our ruler<br>  - rely on Jesus' death and<br>    resurrection<br>Result:<br>  - forgiven by God<br>  - given eternal life | John 3:36 |

Two Ways to Live © Matthias Media, Sydney. Used by permission. To read the full Two Ways to Live tract text, visit twowaystolive.com.

## Analysis of Two Ways to Live

The chief gospel metaphors are:

- God is King.
- Sin is rebellion against this King.
- The judgment for sin is punishment from God.
- Salvation blessings are forgiveness and eternal life.
- Jesus is the King who died in our place.
- The Christian life is submission to God's rule.

The strengths of this presentation are that it communicates:

- God's sovereignty and right to be our ruler.
- The objective (vertical) aspects of our sin, judgment, atonement, and salvation.
- That we have sinned against God, are under God's wrath, need to be justified by God, and need Jesus as our penal substitutionary sacrifice.

But the corresponding weaknesses are:

- It is weak on the warm relational aspects of the Christian life. God is not Father but King. Jesus is not our Shepherd, brother, or friend. He is the King we submit to.
- There is no joy in the Christian life, only submission.
- The world disappears in the last frame. It offers a platonized or spiritualized view of the material world. As a result, it struggles to explain how a Christian lives in this material world after submitting to Jesus. What do I actually do with this world now that I'm forgiven?
- It struggles to explain the worth of ethics, aesthetics, arts, culture, study, work, and wealth in the Christian life. As a result, it might place a priority on "sacred" work, such as so-called full-time ministry, over "secular" work.
- The Christian in the final frame is an individual. It struggles to explain the corporate aspect of Christian living.
- It can lead, in practice, to a deistic God who acts mainly in salvation-historical moments (creation, fall, redemption, consummation), but little in between. Although it is strong on salvation-history categories, it is weak on providence. It struggles to explain guidance, prayer, healings, and miracles.

## 2. Four Spiritual Laws: CRU (Formerly Campus Crusade for Christ)

This gospel presentation was developed in the 1960s for college campuses in the United States by Campus Crusade for Christ (now known as CRU). It too is an example of brilliant contextualization for its time. In the 1960s, the USA was in a time of social turmoil with the civil rights movement, the Vietnam War, the feminist movement, free love, oral contraception (the pill), the hippie movement, and student protests. A college student living away from home for the first time would have been lost. Where am I going? Where is this world going? What am I doing here?

So if someone said to them, "God has a loving plan for your life," that is exactly what they wanted—and needed—to hear. But there are features of the Four Spiritual Laws that don't resonate well anymore. The opening premise—that there are laws—is no longer accepted by a postmodern audience, because laws are social constructs imposed by oppressive authority figures.[13]

You can check out the Four Spiritual Laws gospel presentation at

---

13. I owe this observation to my PhD supervisor, Graham Cole.

http://crustore.org/fourlawseng.htm. It's also included in the appendix Here's a summary:

> *Law 1:* God loves you and offers a wonderful plan for your life.
> *Law 2:* Man is sinful and separated from God. Therefore, he cannot know and experience God's love and plan for his life.
> *Law 3:* Jesus Christ is God's only provision for man's sin. Through him you can know and experience God's love and plan for your life.
> *Law 4:* We must individually receive Jesus Christ as Savior and Lord; then we can know and experience God's love and plan for our lives.[14]

## Analysis of the Four Spiritual Laws

The chief gospel metaphors are:

- God is Lover.
- Sin is a state of being; we are sinful.
- The judgment for sin is separation from God.
- Salvation blessings are to "know and experience God's love and plan for our lives."
- Jesus is the provision for our sin, and the means for knowing and experiencing God.
- The Christian life is to "know and experience God's love and plan for our lives."

The strengths of this presentation are that it communicates:

- God is warm, personal, loving, relational.
- It explains sin more as a state of being—who we are—rather than what we do.
- Judgment is a privation of good; we miss out on God's love and plan.
- The Christian life is one of purpose and fulfillment.
- The category of providence is prominent.

---

14. *Have You Heard of the Four Spiritual Laws?* written by Bill Bright © 1965–2017 The Bright Media Foundation and Campus Crusade for Christ, Inc. All rights reserved. http://crustore.org/four-spiritual-laws-online/. Included with permission.

But the corresponding weaknesses are:

- It almost makes me the most important person in the universe!
- The Christian life is individualized; it struggles to explain the corporate nature of the Christian life.
- What if we already have fulfillment through other things—sports, work, partying? Why do I need God if I'm already happy?
- The category of salvation history is not so prominent.

## Comparing Two Ways to Live and Four Spiritual Laws

While Two Ways to Live predominantly utilizes the categories of salvation history (creation, fall, redemption, consummation), Four Spiritual Laws predominantly relies on categories of providence (God's ongoing interaction with us and his creation). This has led to some interesting developments.

Most of my American Christian friends have grown up familiar with the Four Spiritual Laws. I've also noticed that, in general, they are more articulate with the language of providence. For example, if you ask an American missionary why she decided to leave her successful career in medicine to become a missionary, she might say, "Because God told me to."

Americans who grew up with the Four Spiritual Laws also tend to be more concerned with God's guidance: What is God's loving plan for my life? Where does God want me to live? Who does God want me to marry? They need to find God's plan and remain in it! The strength of this is a healthy concern with prayer and guidance. There is also a healthy concern with how to be part of God's plan to make a difference in this material and secular world. A weakness might be that they are led more by their subjective emotions and experiences than other objective factors. Another weakness is that it makes it hard to deal with failure, sickness, and suffering. How can this be part of God's loving plan for my life?

Conversely, many of my Australian Christian friends have grown up more familiar with Two Ways to Live. They are less articulate with the language of providence. For example, if you ask an Australian youth pastor why he decided to leave his successful job in medicine to go into full-time paid ministry, he might say, "Because my pastor encouraged me to." And if he said, "Because God told me to," his answer might be viewed with suspicion.

Similarly, my Australian Christian friends often have little to say on seeking God's guidance. If I ask them, "Should I be an engineer or a lawyer?" they might answer, "It doesn't matter as long as they are moral jobs (unlike being a bank robber)." Or if I ask, "Should I marry Jane or Jill?" they might answer, "Doesn't matter as long as she's a Christian and not already married." They tend to think in salvation-historical, sacred, and spiritual categories rather than providence, secular, and physical categories. If I ask them, "Should I be an engineer or a lawyer?" they might even answer, "It doesn't matter as long as you give up that job and go into full-time paid ministry!" This leads to a limited Christian ethic where the application for almost any sermon or Bible study is "Tell your friends about Jesus" or "Give your money to missions" or "You should go into full-time paid ministry."

### 3. The Bridge to Life: Navigators

The Bridge to Life, produced by the Navigators, is a third gospel presentation. The Navigators were founded in the 1930s and ministered to sailors in the US Navy, but by the 1950s its ministry had spread to college campuses and beyond. The Bridge to Life is also an example of brilliant contextualization for its time. This was a time of traditions and modern beliefs when most Americans believed in right and wrong, good and bad. Further, the majority of Americans described themselves as religious, and many attended churches and Sunday schools. The nagging existential cry for many Americans was that they needed to live up to the expectations of family, duty, and religion; they needed to be good people.

So if someone said to them, "You need to be good," that was common ground. They would readily agree. And then if you could show them that Jesus could help them meet the absolute standards of a holy God, that was something they wanted—and needed—to hear. But as with all contextualization, what speaks well to one audience might not speak so well to another. A twenty-first-century postmodern audience might believe that the absolute standards of good and bad do not exist. Worse, they are artificial constructs imposed upon them by those in power. They don't share the assumptions of a previous generation.

You can check out the Bridge to Life gospel presentation at https://www.navigators.org/resource/the-bridge-to-life/.

Here's a summary including some visuals from the presentation to give you a sense of what it's like:[15]

---

15. Adapted from www.navigators.org/wp-content/uploads/2017/07/navtool-bridge.pdf. Bridge to Life © 1969, The Navigators. Used by permission of The Navigators. All rights reserved.

First, we have to start at the beginning. In Genesis 1:26, when God created the first humans, he said, "Let us make mankind in our image, in our likeness." Then God blessed them and spent the days walking and talking with the people he had created. In short, life was good.

But why isn't life like that anymore? What happened to mess everything up? This brings us to the second point: when we (humankind) chose to do the opposite of what God told us, sin poisoned the world. Sin separated us from God, and everything changed. Romans 3:23 says, "For all have sinned and fall short of the glory of God," and in Isaiah 59:2 we're told, "Your iniquities have separated you from your God; your sins have hidden his face from you so that he will not hear."

This is especially bad news because there is no way for us to get across that gap on our own. We (humankind) have tried to find our way back to God and a perfect world on our own ever since then, and without any luck. We try to get there by being good people, or through religion, money, morality, philosophy, education, or any number of other ways, but eventually we find out that none of it works. "There is a way that seems right to a man, but in the end it leads to death" (Proverbs 14:12).

There is only one way to find peace with God, and the Bible says it is through Jesus Christ. We were stranded without any way of getting back to our Creator, and we needed a way to pay for our sins and be clean again so that we could be welcomed back to be with him. Romans 5:8 says, "But God demonstrates his own love for us in this: While we were still sinners, Christ died for us." So this is the Good News—that even though we were still enemies of God (as one translation says), Jesus came to die on the cross and pay the price for our sins so that we could have a relationship with him again. John 3:16 says, "For God so loved the world that he gave his one and only son, that whoever believes in him shall not perish but have eternal life."

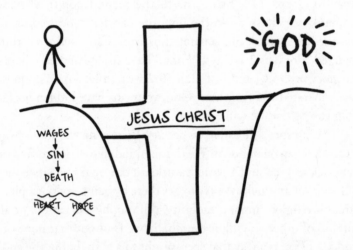

What then should be our reaction to this awesome news? This brings us to the last and most important part. John 5:24 says, "I tell you the truth, whoever hears my word and believes him who sent me has eternal life and will not be condemned; he has crossed over from death to life." Jesus Christ himself even says, "I have come that they may have life, and have it to the full" (John 10:10), and Romans 5:1 says, "we have peace with God through our Lord Jesus Christ."

So how can I have peace with God, life to the full, and be confident of eternal life like these verses say? First, through an honest prayer to God, I have to admit that I'm not perfect—that I can't escape my sins, and I can't save myself. I follow this admission by believing that Jesus Christ died for me on the cross and rose from the grave, conquering death and sin. Then I invite Jesus Christ to live in me and be the Lord of my life, accepting his free gift of eternal life with him.

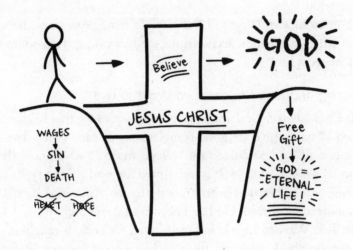

## Analysis of Bridge to Life

The chief gospel metaphors are:

- God is Creator.
- Sin is doing the opposite of what God tells us.
- The judgment for sin is separation from God.
- Salvation blessings are peace, forgiveness, abundant life.
- Jesus pays the price for our sins.
- The Christian life is peace with God, life to the full, eternal life.

The strengths of this presentation are that it communicates:

- God is the Creator.
- Judgment is separation from God.
- The Christian life is a state of being—peace with God—rather than what we do.

But the corresponding weaknesses are:

- The Christian life is individualized; it struggles to explain the corporate nature of the Christian life.

- It has little to say about the material world and what we do once we are saved. It is similar to Two Ways to Live: the Christian life is mainly spiritual without much to say about the physical or material.
- Similar to Two Ways to Live, it might struggle to show the worth of ethics, aesthetics, arts, culture, study, work, and wealth in the Christian life.

## Comparing Bridge to Life and Two Ways to Live

My PhD advisor, Graham Cole, pointed out to me that Bridge to Life and Two Ways to Live are good complements to each other. Two Ways to Live is well contextualized for college students who know they are living as rebels against God. It is well suited for prodigal son types such as Augustine or John Newton (who wrote the hymn "Amazing Grace"). They have wandered away from God and now must come back.

But Two Ways to Live is not well suited for zealous religious people who are trying to do the right thing by being good people. They are not transgressing or breaking God's laws. They attend church regularly. They are upholding God's laws piously.

Bridge to Life is much better contextualized for them. It shows that they are still separated from God, despite being good. In the end, they need to trust Jesus. Real-life examples of people who might respond to this approach include Saul (Paul before his conversion) in the Bible and Martin Luther before he discovered that justification comes by faith and not good works.

## Gospel Summaries

We have surveyed three common gospel presentations. They are summaries of the gospel, designed to be brief and sharply focused on key gospel metaphors. They are designed with a specific audience in mind. They aim to connect at emotional, existential, and cultural levels. That is their strength.

But because they are summaries, each one must necessarily leave out some key biblical ideas. For example, if we emphasize salvation-historical categories, we might leave out providence. Or if we emphasize the need for an individual decision, we leave out the need for corporate responsibilities. Or if we emphasize the spiritual salvation blessings, we leave out the physical aspects of the Christian life.

What is well contextualized for one audience might not be well contextualized for another. If all we use is one gospel presentation, we won't be able to engage a wide variety of audiences. Moreover, if we use only one gospel presentation, it will lead to reductionism in our theological understanding and practice of the Christian life.

Instead, we should develop familiarity with a wide variety of presentations. Jesus and the apostles changed their presentation and how they shared their message according to their audiences. This should free us up to do the same. It also means it's unfair for us to criticize other gospel presentations that are different from ours simply because they focus on a different set of gospel metaphors from ours.

## ANOTHER GOSPEL PRESENTATION: MANGER, CROSS, KING

In chapter 1, I mentioned the approach used by Timothy Keller as an example of how we utilize storytelling in sharing the gospel. In a talk titled "Dwelling in the Gospel," Keller suggests using the following approach to giving a gospel presentation, which he says he gets from Simon Gathercole.[16] We tell the story of how Jesus comes to us in three stages:

1. Manger
2. Cross
3. King

First, Jesus comes to us in the manger. This is the theological idea of the incarnation. Jesus, the Son of God, comes to us as a servant. He healed the sick. He uplifted the oppressed and marginalized. He preached against established religion and authority. The significance is the reversal of values in the gospel: the first will be last, whoever loses their life will find it, whoever wants to be a leader needs to be a servant.

Second, Jesus dies for us on the cross. This is the theological idea of the atonement. Jesus has to die for us in our place. The significance is the necessity of penal substitution: we are sinners who can be saved only by God's grace.

Third, Jesus is the King who will set up his kingdom on earth. This is the theological idea of renewal and restoration. The significance is that we can have a renewed life. But not only that, this earth will be renewed. So we also have a corporate responsibility in renewing and restoring the physical world.

---

16. Tim Keller, "Dwelling in the Gospel," delivered at the 2008 New York City Dwell Conference, April 30, 2008.

Like all summaries, this one has some deficiencies. For example, there is little on God as Creator. It assumes knowledge of God as the monotheistic Christian God who created the world in Genesis 1. But I like this gospel presentation for three reasons. First, it does a better job than most gospel presentations in juggling the tensions between salvation history and providence, individual salvation and corporate responsibility, and the spiritual and physical aspects of the Christian life. We are saved as individuals, but we have entered a corporate kingdom where we have a role in restoring the physical world by bringing Jesus' love, mercy, justice, beauty, goodness, peace, and truth to those around us on this earth.[17]

Second, I can easily use the structure of manger, cross, King in a variety of contexts. For example, if I am conducting the Lord's Supper and need to give a summary of the gospel, I can say, "The Lord's Supper celebrates how Jesus came to us as a human, because he really did eat a physical meal with his disciples two thousand years ago. And that he died for us on a cross, because the meal symbolizes his body, which was broken, and his blood, which was shed for us. And it looks forward to that day when Jesus will set up his kingdom here on earth and we will eat at a banquet with him."

Third, it presents Jesus as a person in a story. He comes across as real. He is someone we are to know, love, and worship. He didn't just die on a cross for us. He also had a vital earthly ministry.[18] In contrast, I think, our traditional gospel presentations (Two Ways to Live, Four Spiritual Laws, Bridge to Life) risk presenting Jesus as a propositional fact to acknowledge.

## CONCLUSION: USING A DIVERSITY OF GOSPEL METAPHORS

We began with the story of Jim. The gospel was presented to him using biblical metaphors of guilt and forgiveness. It connected with him existentially, emotionally, and culturally. But those same biblical metaphors had less connection with his daughter, Megan. Worse, they served only to reinforce her culture's hostility to organized religion and institutionalized authority.

---

17. For a fuller development of this idea, see N. T. Wright, *Surprised by Hope: Rethinking Heaven, the Resurrection, and the Mission of the Church* (San Francisco: HarperOne, 2008).

18. My PhD supervisor, Graham Cole, pointed out to me that this is a weakness in our Christian tradition. For example, the Apostles' Creed doesn't even mention Jesus' earthly ministry. Jesus simply was "born of the Virgin Mary," and then next he "suffered under Pontius Pilate, was crucified, died, and was buried."

In this chapter, we have surveyed a variety of gospel metaphors. Hopefully this will free us up to use additional metaphors for God, Jesus, sin, condemnation, salvation, and the Christian life. For example, in addition to explaining sin as breaking God's law, we can explain to Megan that sin is dishonoring God, feeling morally superior to those around us, brokenness, or being owned by whatever we're living for. And we can explain salvation blessings to Megan as freedom, adoption, peace, or honor.

In this chapter, we also surveyed a variety of gospel presentations. We found that there are many good biblical ways to share the gospel. But that doesn't mean they are the only ways. Nor should we insist upon them. This should also empower us to explore a wide range of gospel presentations for our specific audiences. For example, if we presented the gospel to Megan, we might choose a gospel presentation that emphasizes the need to be at peace with God, and the part that she can play in the renewal and restoration of this world, especially by bringing Jesus' love, mercy, justice, and beauty to this earth.

Hopefully this chapter will get us excited about the large repertoire of metaphors that God has provided for us in the Bible. For each and every one of our non-Christian friends, there should be a metaphor that we can use to connect the gospel with them at emotional, existential, and cultural points of entry.

# CHAPTER 4

# EVANGELISM TO POSTMODERNS

*I'm happy you've found Jesus, but he's not for me.*

When I went to college in the 1980s, my friends knew that I was a Christian. So they would ask me, in a nice way, questions such as, "How do you know there's a God?" or, "How do you know there's life after death?" or, "How can you believe in miracles?" At first, I didn't have good answers. So I dove into Josh McDowell's books, such as *Evidence That Demands a Verdict* and *A Ready Defense*, to find answers to their questions.

Soon I could answer almost every question by using the same logical sequence. It went something like this.

*How do you know there's a God?*

"We know it's true because Jesus says it's true."

*But how do we know what Jesus says is true?*

"Because Jesus is God, and he proves it by rising from the dead."

*But how do we know that Jesus rose from the dead?*

"Because the Bible says so."

*But how do we know that the Bible is true?*

"Because the Bible is a historically reliable document, corroborated by eyewitnesses and other sources, and has been transmitted accurately to us today."

Ta-daah!

I soon developed my own talk series—"How to Answer Tough Questions That Your Friends Ask You"—going from church to church, youth group to youth group, and conference to conference. For about a decade, my audiences loved it. They would write down what I was saying, and they would walk away empowered.

But something strange happened. Beginning in the early 2000s, I was invited to be the speaker at a youth conference in Missouri, USA. I gave them the same series of talks. And the audience was unimpressed. They were not persuaded by my logical sequence of answers. They rolled their eyes at my ta-daah! moment. Even worse, I found out that they weren't even asking—or being asked—the tough questions that I was answering. They had a new set of questions. And they wanted a new set of answers.

What had happened? Well, I'm sure you know the answer. At some stage in the last few decades, we moved away from foundationalist reasoning. And we became suspicious of metanarratives and claims of ultimate truth. We moved away from the age of modernity into the age of postmodernity. The methods of evangelism that once worked so well in the 1980s no longer had the same appeal in the 2000s. In this chapter, we will take a closer look at what happened, we'll outline the challenges that postmodernism brings to the task of evangelism, and I'll suggest some fresh ways of engaging in evangelism in our new cultural environment.

## THE AGE OF MODERNITY (1600S–1980S)

Prior to the age of modernity, there was what historians refer to as the premodern or medieval age. In its epistemology (how do we know something), the medieval age understood that God knows everything, and that everything we know is only a subset of what God knows. Everything that we know must come to us from God graciously via his general and special revelation. So if you lived in the medieval age, you would answer the "How do you know?" question with a simple answer: "Because God knows everything, and this is what he has revealed to us."

In *The Gagging of God*, author and professor Don Carson argues that the shift from premodernity to modernity is best represented by the figure of Rene Descartes (1596–1650). Descartes famously founded all knowledge on an axiom, "I think, therefore I am" *(cogito ergo sum)*. And in this new age of modernity, we answer the "How do you know?" question differently. According to Carson, six essential features define the modern period in terms of its epistemology.[1]

---

1. I owe this section to Don Carson's observations in *The Gagging of God: Christianity Confronts Pluralism* (Grand Rapids, Mich.: Zondervan, 1996), 57–64.

First, knowledge begins with "I," the ego in Descartes' cogito. I am the person who determines whether something is true. I can do this by using the tools of reason (the movement called rationalism) or my empirical senses—what I can see, touch, hear, smell, taste (the movement called empiricism). For this to work, we need an underlying premise: that I am an objective, neutral, and detached thinker, free from subjectivity and biases. Just as important, I must have the freedom and rights to think for myself. I must reject other sources of knowledge—such as the church, authority, tradition, family—as invalid sources. I need to think for myself. These are the basic principles of the Enlightenment. As Immanuel Kant said, "Dare to reason! Dare to be free!"

As Western Christians, we are still deeply influenced by this way of thinking. Perhaps you've heard a Christian give their testimony this way: "I was born into a Christian family. I can remember knowing Jesus ever since I was a child. But this didn't make me a Christian. At the age of sixteen, I had to decide for myself. So I examined the evidence and concluded that Jesus really was who he claimed to be, and I gave my life to him."

Can you see how this testimony is shaped by the epistemological framework of modernity? First, the individual has to say that they are not a Christian because of their parents or church, because they are invalid sources of knowledge. Second, the Christian has to say that they made a decision for themselves at the age of sixteen, because that is when you become a free, autonomous, adult thinker, free from traditional authority figures. Third, the decision was made only after examining evidence from a detached, neutral, objective standpoint, because that is the only valid source of knowledge—rationalism and empiricism.

## MODERN ARROGANCE

Can you see the arrogance of the modern period? They self-consciously called themselves the age of the Enlightenment and then labeled the preceding age the Middle Ages or the Dark Ages. Modern thinkers saw themselves as the climax of history (they are the final age after the so-called Middle Ages) and progress (they are the enlightened ones in contrast to the darkened ones)!

Second, the noetic structure—everything you believe and how these beliefs relate with each other—is foundationalism.[2] All knowledge must be founded upon an epistemologically prior truth. And all knowledge is ultimately founded upon a bedrock layer of foundational truths, knowledge that is self-evident, incorrigible, and evident to the senses.[3] Examples of foundational truth claims are "One plus one equals two," "All bachelors are unmarried men," "Triangles have three sides," and "The sky is blue." This creates a pyramid structure of knowledge in which each truth is like a brick that sits on another brick of prior truth. Ultimately all the bricks are sitting on a foundational layer of bricks, what we might call the foundational truths. The truths that we do know are stable, provable, and ultimately justified by a bedrock layer of certain knowledge.

Third, we discover new truths if our methods of knowing are neutral, detached, unbiased, and reliable. For example, if I set up a scientific experiment, what I need to do is enter my observations, data, formulas, and axioms. And as long as my method is correct, what comes out of the experiment is truth. This is the approach of the scientific method. For example, if you read a scientific journal, the main headings are "Observations," "Method," and "Outcome." The assumption is that if the observations are sound and if the method is valid, then the outcome is verified truth. This is how new knowledge is "discovered."

Again, we see the influence of modernism in the church today. Consider a typical small group Bible study where those studying employ the inductive Bible-study method. In seminaries, you'll find students who exegete Bible passages with the grammatico-historical method of exegesis. These are useful methods, but they also rely upon the assumptions of modernity and the scientific method that the reader is somehow neutral, detached, and unbiased. We assume that we are a blank slate and that as long as our method is valid, the outcome will be verified truth. All we have to do is enter our observations—"What do the Bible verses say?"—and then we use the method of grammatico-historical exegesis and the outcome will be truth from the Bible. We will have exegeted—discovered—meaning from the Bible passage.

Fourth, the modern age believed that certainty of knowledge was possible, attainable, and desirable. As long as we think for ourselves, using

---

2. Paul G. Hiebert, *Transforming Worldviews: An Anthropological Understanding of How People Change* (Grand Rapids, Mich.: Baker, 2008), 157–58.

3. I got this definition of foundationalism from Paul Feinberg's lectures on religious epistemology at Trinity Evangelical Divinity School in 2001.

the tools of reason and observation, employing valid methods of discovery, we can know all truths. This was an age of optimism, and that optimism was confirmed by progress in science, advances in technology, and the discovery of new worlds in exploration in the 1800s. By the end of the 1800s, there was a fear that there would be no new knowledge to be discovered.

Fifth, naturalism is the worldview that matter is all that exists. This means that reality is limited to what we can observe in nature. It also means that there is no such thing as God, miracles, or the supernatural. Related to the rise of naturalism was the development of the theory of evolution. Evolution gave people permission to be naturalists by giving a natural explanation for the origin of life, the species, and human beings. It removed the necessity of the teleological argument—the argument that design in the universe must come from God, the Original Designer—as the only explanation for the origin of life.

Sixth, the modern age believed that truth is universal. The truth that we discover must be true for all peoples, at all times, and in all places. Truth transcends culture, history, and language, and this is because humans are united by the ability to reason and make observations. Whatever I observe to be true should be what everyone else observes to be true. If water boils at 100 degrees Celsius at sea level for me in Chicago, then it must also boil at 100 degrees Celsius at sea level for someone in London. Truth claims made in science, math, psychology, historical accounts, and architecture were assumed to be universally true for people in all cultures, at all times, and in all places. For example, if many choices of milk in my supermarket make me happy in the USA, then people in Kenya should also have many choices of milk. And if a two-party democratic system is good government in Australia, then this should also be good government in other countries.

When I was in high school in the 1980s, I was taught Australian history. And I was taught that that history began with Australia's European settlement in the late 1700s. There was little mention of the indigenous people who had been there for thousands of years prior. And the historical account of Australia was given from the perspective of its leaders—governors and prime ministers. It was a top-down account. It was also a triumphalist account of a nation that had continued to discover, progress, and advance as it matured. This way of communicating history reflects the assumptions of modernity. It assumes a universal account—a metanarrative—which is true for everyone. It privileges the account of those in authority; they are the enlightened ones, and what's true for them must be true for everyone else. And it presumes an optimism of progress, advance, and discovery.

## THE AGE OF POSTMODERNITY (1980S–PRESENT)

Earlier, I said that modernism had been largely supplanted by postmodernity, but what exactly is postmodernity? Well, it depends on how we choose to define it. Harold Netland understands postmodernity as the logical extension of the sociological features of modernity.[4] But I prefer to define postmodernity in line with Don Carson, who understands postmodernity as a reaction against the epistemological assumptions of modernity.[5] So let's revisit those assumptions and see how they have changed today.

*First, postmodernity recognizes the subjectivity of the individual.* I, the knower, am subjective. I am not neutral, detached, objective, or a blank slate; I am subjective, biased, and influenced. Consider who I am. As an Asian-Australian man who was born in Hong Kong and grew up in Australia and has lived in the Midwest region of the United States, I am shaped by the variables of my culture, history, race, experiences, and education. I will have different perspectives and worldviews from someone born in Tanzania or from someone who has worshiped in Tibet or studied in Taiwan. My perspective will be different from someone who has been oppressed by socioeconomic forces in Thailand in a way that I never was.

And to take that one step farther, we're not just shaped by our world of subjectivity but trapped in it. For example, we're trapped at the level of hermeneutics: we can't access the author behind the text. We're trapped at the level of language: we can't get beyond the symbol. We're trapped at the level of our social group: we can't get beyond our cultural perspective.

All the same, this is not necessarily a bad thing in postmodernity. This is something to be acknowledged and celebrated. Modernity was naive (at best) and arrogant (at worst) to think that the knower could transcend their context. But postmodernity celebrates the different perspectives that are enjoyed by different cultures, languages, traditions, and communities.

Let me give you an example of how I have experienced this. When my Asian family migrated to Australia in the 1960s, we were expected to assimilate by adopting the predominant European culture. Today the buzzword is multiculturalism. You keep your original culture so that we can celebrate the multiple cultures and their unique differences and valuable perspectives.

No one was telling us to keep speaking Chinese in the 1960s in Australia.

---

4. Harold Netland, *Encountering Religious Pluralism: The Challenge to Christian Faith and Mission* (Downers Grove, Ill.: InterVarsity, 2001), 16.

5. Carson, *The Gagging of God*, 57–64.

We were expected to speak English, and if that meant our native Chinese language was lost, then so be it. But today people would be horrified if our children lost the ability to speak Chinese.

In the 1900s, there was a dream that one day we would all speak one universal language called Esperanto. That dream represented the hope of modernity. But today in our postmodern culture, we celebrate each and every language and dialect as different and unique. We would consider it a tragedy if a dialect disappeared. Similarly, in postmodernity, traditions, rituals, and tribal identities are important. They are things to celebrate because they define us, and they are unique to each and every tribal group. For example, on Anzac Day (April 25) every year, Australia has a tradition of commemorating a World War I battle at Gallipoli in which soldiers from Australia and New Zealand bravely fought but were eventually defeated and forced to retreat. This day—similar to Veterans Day in the United States—is designed to commemorate the brave sacrifice of soldiers in that particular battle as well as other wars. By the 1980s, fewer people were attending the marches, not because they were antisoldier but because they were antiwar. A famous song called "And the Band Played Waltzing Matilda" was written in 1971 by Eric Bogle, and it summed up what was happening on Anzac Day with this line: "But year after year their numbers get fewer / Someday no one will march there at all."

So has Anzac Day disappeared? Far from it. Today in postmodernity, the tradition of Anzac Day has been appropriated by the younger generation. They now make pilgrimages to Gallipoli. They attend the dawn commemoration services and marches in record numbers. And Anzac Day has been redefined as the birth of a nation rather than a somber cautionary commemoration of a defeat.

One of the features of postmodernity is appropriation and intertextuality. That's because, for a postmodern, context determines meaning. So we can take a text, and by changing its context, we can appropriate that text to make it meaningful for our context. Or by changing its context, the text itself is shaped by the new context, taking on a new meaning, in a feature called intertextuality.

Film director Baz Luhrmann frequently plays with this concept of intertextuality. His film *Moulin Rouge!* (2001) is set in the year 1900. But the characters in that film sing the Elton John song "Your Song," which was composed seventy years later. The song is shamelessly taken out of its 1970 UK context and anachronistically spliced into 1900 Paris and given a new meaning. This playfulness with context is a feature of postmodernity.

## TATTOOS AND TRIBAL IDENTITY

Once upon a time, tattoos were not common in Western culture. Today they are common; estimates are that 40 percent of those in the twenty-six to forty age group in the United States have at least one tattoo.* That's because tattoos are a way of expressing a tribal identity. A Christian might get a tattoo of a cross as a symbol of their tribal identity. But it won't be just any cross. It will be a Celtic cross to emphasize an ancient tradition. Christians might also get a Bible verse as a tattoo. But it won't be in English. It will be in Greek or Hebrew, once again emphasizing the ancient tradition of their faith.

Similarly, Christians in the twenty-five to thirty-five age group in the United States who were brought up in a Baptist church are more commonly shifting their religious identity to Orthodox, Catholic, or Episcopalian churches. Whereas their local Baptist church might have been founded in 1985, the Orthodox, Catholic, and Episcopalian churches—with their Greek and Latin liturgies—belong to a tradition that can be traced back thousands of years.

---

* www.statisticbrain.com/tattoo-statistics/. Cited October 19, 2017.

*Second, the noetic structure of postmodernism is coherentism.* In the foundationalism of the modern age, each truth was justified by an epistemologically prior truth. But in coherentism, there are no epistemologically prior truths. Each truth is free floating, unanchored, and not founded upon a prior truth. Instead, each truth coheres with another truth. Rather than a pyramid of truth, you get a weblike matrix of coherent truths, or a free-floating raft made up of planks of truth loosely tied together. These truths are a product of context—culture, tribe, language, community, and upbringing. They are free floating, but they are also coherent, true to each other. If I claim these truths for myself, I am being true to myself.

You, on the other hand, will have a different weblike matrix of coherent truths. These truths are a product of your context, which is different from mine. Your truths will be different, but they won't be better or worse than my truths, because there is no hierarchy of higher or lower truths. As a result, you will have your truth, and I will have my truth.

There is no point in my asking you to prove or justify your beliefs, because your truths are a product of your context. What else can you believe? You have to be true to yourself. Who am I to impose my beliefs on you?

*Third, in postmodernity all method is biased and subjective.* We are not blank slates. We know what we are trying to prove. Our starting point—our presuppositions—will determine our end point—our conclusions. And our methods are constructs that we impose on our observations. We construe the evidence to fit our worldviews. There is no logical sequence of observation, method, outcome. Instead, it's our presuppositions that determine the outcome.[6]

Let's consider how this way of thinking affects our approach to the Bible. When we exegete the Bible, we are not neutral. We bring our traditions, upbringing, denominations, theological systems, and presuppositions to the biblical text. For example, how do we interpret Romans 11:26, which says, "all Israel will be saved"? If you come from a dispensationalist tradition, you will understand "Israel" to refer to physical, literal, ethnic Israel. But if you come from a Reformed tradition, you might understand "Israel" to refer to the Christian church as the spiritual, metaphorical Israel. Our exegesis is shaped by our denominations and our theological systems.[7]

Or consider 2 Timothy 1:6, where Paul tells Timothy to "fan into flame the gift of God, which is in you through the laying on of my hands." In my denominational tradition, the laying on of hands was understood to be correlated with God's giving Timothy his spiritual gifts. The laying on of hands was a *recognition* that Timothy had been gifted by God to lead the church.

But in other traditions, they might interpret this to mean the laying on of hands was instrumental to God's giving Timothy his spiritual gifts. The laying on of hands was the *cause* of Timothy's giftedness.

So which tradition is right? There's nothing in the text to suggest either way. But we come to our interpretations based on the theological systems that we have brought to the text.

We are not blank slates. We are doing more than employing the supposedly neutral method of grammatico-historical exegesis to the text; we are also bringing our presuppositions to the text, and our presuppositions heavily shape our interpretation.

*Fourth, in postmodernism certainty of knowledge is impossible.* Our knowledge is limited by our perspective, and it is conditioned by our culture,

---

6. Jonathan Haidt, *The Righteous Mind: Why Good People Are Divided by Politics and Religion* (New York: Penguin, 2012), Kindle edition.

7. To appreciate the complexity of this, see the discussion in Douglas J. Moo, *The Epistle to the Romans* (Grand Rapids, Mich.: Eerdmans, 1996), 719–26.

language, and traditions. All knowledge is historically and culturally determined. There are no culturally neutral facts. Knowledge is made, rather than discovered. It is construed, rather than found. Knowledge is personal. You have your truth, and I have mine. There is a breakdown in the subject-object distinction. This means that it is naive to think that certainty of knowledge is possible. To talk in such a way is ignorant (at best) and bigoted (at worst). Such certainty causes fights, arguments, and wars. It also robs us of other valuable perspectives, which can broaden our worldview. If we are certain in our knowledge, we'll be trapped in our narrow worldview, which only causes more intolerance and bigotry against other views.

*Fifth, postmodernism challenges naturalism.* Naturalism was rightly seen as the enemy of the Christian worldview, but in postmodernism it too is seen as the result of a narrow dogmatic scientism. Science itself is now viewed as a biased construal of facts from established authority figures, so its premises and conclusions can't necessarily be trusted. This means that postmodernity is open to alternative disciplines of knowledge such as nontraditional medicine, astrology, and acupuncture. It is also open to alternative ways of thinking such as nonlinear, nonlogical thinking.

I remember my final year of medicine school. The year was 1989, and my professor of respiratory medicine gave us a lecture on asthma. He lamented that many of his patients were resorting to alternative, nonscientifically proven treatments such as herbal medicine and aromatherapy. He finished his lecture by saying, "It's as if the Enlightenment never happened." What my professor didn't realize (and neither did I at the time) is that we were witnessing the effect of a larger cultural transition from modernity into postmodernity. Today, alternative medicine is an established and growing field as more and more in the medical profession are open to other ways of approaching treatment for sickness and disease.

*Sixth, in postmodernity there is no universal truth.* To say that truth is universal is to impose our truth on other cultures, peoples, and languages. It's not that postmodernism denies the existence of objective facts. It's just that all facts have to be construed. And this construal is a product of our cultures, peoples, languages, places, and upbringing. For example, it's an objective fact that the United States dropped the atomic bomb on Japan in 1945. But the telling of this story will be different from an American's perspective than from a Japanese person's perspective.

The result of this shift is that there is no such thing as a metanarrative, a grand unifying story or theory that explains it all. Instead, we have multiple narratives. For example, there will be different stories of World War II for the Russian peasant, the Japanese farmer, the American general, and the German prisoner of war. There will be different stories of the European settlement of Australia for the indigenous Australian, the Irish convict, the German free settler, and the Chinese gold miner.

In this way, postmodernity recognizes that knowledge is power. The one who gets to tell the story and impose it as a metanarrative upon others is playing a power game. In postmodernity, there is deep mistrust of organized religion, government, and other forms of established authority because that is exactly what authority figures do: they impose their metanarrative upon all peoples and use truth as a weapon to force people to conform to their metanarrative. That's also why, in postmodernity, we employ a hermeneutic of suspicion upon a narrative or truth claim. We deconstruct the narrative or truth claim by asking, "What power game is this person playing?"

## THE POSTMODERN CONTEXT

The assumption in modernity was that what is true, good, and beautiful for a person in the United States must also be true, good, and beautiful for a person in Brazil. When I took an architectural tour of Chicago, the guide pointed out the different forms of architecture in the Chicago skyline. There was the 1910s prairie style. Then there was the 1930s art deco style. Then there was the 1960s modern style. And then from the 1980s there was the postmodern style.

What does a modern skyscraper look like? It is black, oblong, and shiny. Why? Because these are universal shapes and colors. They are beautiful in Chicago. So they must also be beautiful in Belgium, Tanzania, Mongolia, and Argentina. But what does a postmodern building look like? It acknowledges its context, its surroundings. Take a look at the Sydney Opera House. It was designed by Danish architect Jørn Utzon in the 1970s. The building is shaped like waves or sails, and that's a nod to its surroundings, to the harbor, the water, the waves, and the wind. The Sydney Opera House is beautiful in its context. But it would not make sense in a different context like the Gobi Desert, the Canadian Rockies, or in downtown Manhattan. That's because context is everything. Context determines what is true, beautiful, and good.

## CHRISTIANITY IN A POSTMODERN AGE[8]

If we are living in a time defined by postmodernism, what does that mean for the task of evangelism? How do you engage in evangelism in a post-modern world? Do we change our message? Our methods? Can you even share the gospel in this context?

We certainly need to rethink some of the ways the church engaged in evangelism in a world shaped by modernity. But postmodernism is not something to be feared. While there are things we need to reject about postmodernism, there are also several positive developments that assist us in communicating the gospel.

First, we need to understand that tolerance is now the highest moral good. In modernism, it was okay to tolerate a person but not agree with their ideas. That's because truth was objective and external to the person. But in postmodernism, we are told that we must tolerate all ideas. That's because truth is viewed as subjective and internal to a person; it is a product of language, culture, and upbringing. So who are we to disagree with them and impose our ideas—which are only a product of our own upbringing—upon them? The only thing we should not tolerate as postmodern people is intolerance. That's because intolerance is understood as the worst moral evil. It is to impose our arbitrary metanarrative upon someone else's narrative. It is to play a power game. It is to do violence upon someone else's language, culture, and upbringing.

Second, postmodern thinkers believe that all religions are valid and essentially the same. We are all worshiping the same God or gods. We are all looking for the same thing. But there are differences because of our different perspectives, which are a result of our culture and upbringing. For example, you're a Christian because you grew up in the Bible belt of the USA. But if you had grown up in China, you'd be a Buddhist. Or if you had grown up in India, you'd be a Hindu. Or if you had grown up in the Middle East, you'd be a Muslim. But that's okay. Because you are a product of your context.

Third, postmodernity says that there are no absolutes. There might be objective external facts, but there are no absolute truths—or at least no absolute claims to truth. That's because all truths are the result of subjective interpretation and there is no privileged interpretation. Any claim to absolute truth is a use of power and violence upon the other person.

---

8. Once again, I owe many of these observations to Carson, *The Gagging of God*, 65–92.

## THE MODERN SITH LORD

In the movie *Star Wars: Episode III—Revenge of the Sith* (2005), Obi-Wan is not sure whether Anakin Skywalker has turned to the dark side. But when Obi-Wan confronts him about this, Anakin replies, "If you're not with me, you're my enemy." At that moment, Obi-Wan knows that Anakin has indeed turned to the dark side. How? He tells Anakin, "Only a Sith Lord deals in absolutes."

Fourth, postmodernism is unconvinced by proof or evidence. Because modernity employed a foundationalist noetic structure, it held we cannot know a truth unless it can be justified by a prior truth; it must be proven. So modernity challenged Christianity to prove itself. Prove that there's a God. Prove that Jesus rose from the dead. Prove that the Bible is true. But postmodernity is unconvinced by proofs. It understands proofs to be constructs.

We all have presuppositions as our starting points. And these presuppositions determine how we shape the evidence. So we will always have the conclusions that are determined by our presuppositions. In modernity, if you proved to someone that Jesus rose from the dead, they might believe that Jesus must be the Son of God as he claimed to be. But in postmodernity, if you proved to someone that Jesus rose from the dead, they would be unimpressed. Of course you proved that Jesus rose from the dead! That's because you already believe that Jesus is the Son of God. Why wouldn't you prove that Jesus rose from the dead?[9]

Fifth, postmodernity recognizes a diversity of ways of knowing. Modernity recognized only reason and empirical proof as valid ways of knowing something to be true. But postmodernism is open to tradition, feelings, experiences, emotions, community, and especially testimony from trusted people. For example, in modernity it was common for an advertisement on TV to feature a scientist telling us that whatever they were selling—toothpaste, shampoo, or laundry detergent—was scientifically proven to be more effective. In postmodernity it is more common to hear testimony from someone we trust—an athlete or actor—telling us how well the product works.

---

9. See Rick Richardson's experience of this in *Evangelism outside the Box: New Ways to Help People Experience the Good News* (Downers Grove, Ill.: InterVarsity, 2000), 30–36.

When our first son was born, we had trouble feeding and settling him. This meant many nights when my wife and I had a crying baby and could not sleep. My friend Tim, who is a physical therapist, said to me, "I know that you're a medical doctor. So I don't know how you feel about alternative medicine. But when our child had feeding issues, my wife and I took her to an osteopath. Did you want to take your son to this osteopath?"

By now, my wife and I were so desperate, we would try anything. So we took our child to the osteopath. The osteopath charged a large sum of money for each hour-long session. During the sessions, she held our child, and to my untrained eyes, it looked like all she did was hover a hand over his head for a prolonged period. On our way home from one session, my wife asked me, "What do you think the osteopath does when she just hovers her hand over our son's head?" I jokingly replied, "Don't ask questions. Just believe!"

Now, it's important to realize that Tim, my physical-therapist friend, and I, a doctor, are both trained in evidence-based sciences. Yet here we were taking our children to an alternative medical therapist.

I shared this story with my seminary class once. I asked, "Who here is horrified that I, as a doctor trained in evidence-based science, took my child to an osteopath?" About three hands went up. I said to those who put up their hands, "You are children of modernity. You still believe in objective, hard evidence as the only valid source of knowledge."

Then I asked, "Who here thinks, yes, I would've also gone to the osteopath because there might be something to it, and it might work?" About fifty hands went up. I said to these people, "You are children of postmodernity. You are postempirical. You believe in the validity of other perspectives. And your primary source of knowing is whether something works."

Sixth, postmodernity is open to the different perspectives of other cultures. In modernity, the Westerner—especially the Caucasian male in traditional positions of authority as father, doctor, or scientist—was the one who had the privileged vantage point. So we listened to him for the truth. But in postmodernity, we welcome perspectives from different cultures. They can see things that we can't see because we are blinded by our cultural perspectives. They can broaden and enrich our worldview.

Many years ago I attended a Chinese church in Chicago, and on Easter Sunday we had a Chinese person give the Easter message. He spoke it in Chinese, sentence by sentence, as an interpreter translated it into English, sentence by sentence. The message went for more than forty-five minutes, which is long by Western standards. And he spoke as many Chinese do, with a circular logic, rather than a linear, logical progression of ideas.

A friend of mine from Australia brought his Caucasian mother to the Easter Sunday service. She wasn't a Christian. And she couldn't understand Chinese. I thought that she would be unimpressed by the service because it was in Chinese, long, and logically all over the place. But afterward she said that the service was wonderful. That's because she grew up in the 1950s and thought that Christianity was a white man's religion. But here she was in a church where Chinese were speaking the Christian message in Chinese, and they were having to translate it into English for her.

Seventh, in postmodernity, ethics have become a barrier to belief in the gospel. When our non-Christian friends think of Christianity, they don't think of good news, salvation, forgiveness, restoration, justice, mercy, or love. Instead, they think of hate, fear, power, and violence. They think that Christians are unethical because of their perceived stances on birth control and euthanasia. They see their own views as the ethical stance because they are seeking to empower, liberate, restore justice, and give mercy to the marginalized and oppressed. Their views are labeled by words such as love, choice, mercy, freedom, equality, rights, or justice. In postmodernity, Christians are viewed as the oppressors and haters while non-Christians are viewed as the ones on the side of love, justice, and mercy.

---

 **Summarizing the Differences**

For a summary of the key differences between a modern and a postmodern audience, download the PDF from ZondervanAcademic.com.

---

To access this resource, register on the website as a student. Then sign in and download the resource from the "Study Resources" tab on the book page for *Evangelism in a Skeptical World*.

---

## EVANGELISM IN A POSTMODERN AGE

As Christians, we do not accept all of the tenets of postmodern thought. We believe in the existence of absolute objective truth. Jesus claims to be the Truth. But postmodernity is correct to say that we can apprehend this truth only through subjective interpretation. I once heard Kevin Vanhoozer say, "Moderns think that it's all truth and no interpretation. But postmoderns think it's all interpretation and no truth." As Vanhoozer is hinting, the gospel is not fully at home in either modern or postmodern ways of thinking. It is a both-and rather than an either-or. Although we can't have absolute knowledge of the truth (only God can have this), we can know the truth nonetheless through our multiple perspectives.[10] So although we can continue to affirm the existence of truth, we should also acknowledge the role of community, perspectives, and tradition in shaping our perception of truth. In light of this, I want to make several suggestions for how we can engage in fruitful evangelism in a twenty-first-century postmodern world.

## Authenticity

The buzzword for postmoderns is authenticity. Unlike moderns, the first question is not, "Is it true?" but, "Is it real in our lives?" Are we living consistently—or better, coherently—with our beliefs? Are we being true to ourselves? Do we walk the walk as well as we talk the talk? This should lead us to think about how we evangelize to our postmodern friends in a way that communicates authenticity. While the gospel is something we speak, words that communicate God's truth, there is also a sense in which we ourselves are a component of how the message is communicated. We speak the words of truth, but we speak the truth in love (Eph. 4:15). Our message is embodied. It doesn't come in a vacuum. It comes in the context of shared lives and trusted friendships. This is the model of evangelism that Paul himself uses with the Thessalonians: "Our gospel came to you not simply with words but also with power, with the Holy Spirit and deep conviction. *You know how we lived among you for your sake*" (1 Thess. 1:5). The Thessalonians don't just believe the gospel to be true; they also see that it is real by Paul's authentic living.

Our postmodern age is similar to the age of the apostles in the first century: people of different cultures, languages, and beliefs trying to live peacefully together. That's why Peter's first letter has so much to say to us today. Peter was telling the Christians he was writing to that the way they lived was just as important as what they said. For example, the Greek noun *anastrophe*, which means "the way you live," comes up over and over again in 1 Peter (1:15, 18; 2:12; 3:1, 2, 16).[11] Peter's key argument is that Christian

---

10. For good further discussions, consult the positions of critical realism in Paul G. Hiebert, for example, in Paul G. Hiebert, *Transforming Worldviews: An Anthropological Understanding of How People Change* (Grand Rapids, Mich.: Baker, 2008), 258–60 and 274–76; and the abductive, dialogical theological method of David K. Clark, for example, in David K. Clark, *To Know and Love God: Method for Theology* (Wheaton, Ill.: Crossway, 2003), 51.

11. This is sometimes obscured in English translations, which render the same Greek word with different terms, such as "conduct," "way of life," or "behavior" (ESV translation).

lives need to be authentic, true to the gospel. By doing so, wives can win over their nonbelieving husbands to the gospel not by what they say but by the way they live (3:1–2). Similarly, we need to give a reason for our hope with a clear conscience, gentleness, and respect (3:15–16).

## Hospitality

Hospitality is another means of evangelism, and if we carefully read the New Testament letters, we find that hospitality is quite prominent among the topics discussed and practiced by the early church. While the gifts of teaching and preaching proclaim the words of the gospel, hospitality demonstrates that the gospel is real, authentic, believable, attractive, and livable. Another way to say this is that hospitality breaks down plausibility structures. The gospel might be true, but to most non-Christians it sounds unbelievable. And the gospel will remain unbelievable as long as our non-Christian friends don't have many Christian friends, because we tend to adopt the plausibility structures of those we know and trust. By sharing our homes with both our non-Christian and Christian friends, our non-Christian friends will get to eat with (and know) more and more Christian friends, and maybe even adopt their Christian friends' plausibility structures.

Similarly, hospitality provides the space in which gospel conversations can happen in a friendly and safe environment. Most people are uncomfortable sharing private matters of values and worldviews—things like politics and religion—in public places. But in the private spaces of our homes, around food, our friends are more likely to talk about matters related to religion, especially if we show them it is safe to do so.

Hospitality also shows that the gospel is real. I believe one of the most powerful proclamations of the gospel is the family meal in a Christian family. Here we see that the gospel works when others join the experience of our family lives. Here is a family eating together in peace, harmony, and beauty, acknowledging that God is Lord, Creator, and Provider of all. One of my friends who later became a Christian tells me that when he was a non-Christian, he used to enjoy being invited to my home for a family dinner. At the time, I thought it was just about the food. But now I realize he also enjoyed seeing the gospel in action. We underestimate how unusual and attractive it is for a non-Christian to see a functional family in action, especially around the dinner table.

Practicing hospitality follows the model of Jesus, who ate with sinners and tax collectors. This theme is prominent in the Gospels—especially the book of Luke, where Jesus is always eating, dining, and partying with sinners and tax collectors (Luke 5:29–30; 7:34; 7:37; 11:37; 14:1–24; 15:1–2). He even invites himself to the home of Zacchaeus, a notorious tax collector (Luke 19:1–10). Obviously Jesus saw eating with sinners as a powerful proclamation of the gospel he came to proclaim. But when we practice this act, it also demonstrates to Christians that there is a distinction between loving someone and agreeing with them. For example, Jesus can eat with sinners, but that doesn't mean he agrees with what they're doing. It's the same with Christians. We can welcome people into our homes without its saying that we approve of their lifestyle. Giving hospitality to our non-Christian friends is a proclamation of the gospel: God loves the world by sending his Son, Jesus, but he sends Jesus only because he disagrees with what the world is doing. In the same way, we can eat with those who aren't Christians; we love them but don't agree with them. But we eat with them nonetheless because we love.

Hospitality is also a powerful apologetic tool. Often we have to defend questions such as, "Why are Christians so hypocritical?" or, "Why are Christians homophobic?" We can give good explanations for why Christians are (or are not) hypocritical. And we can try to give good examples for why Christians are not homophobic. But more often than not, our friends aren't listening to our answers because their minds are already made up. But if we have them over to our homes, then it is hard for them to accuse Christians of being hypocritical when they're enjoying a meal with us. And if we're inviting our gay friends for dinner, then it's hard for them to argue that we're homophobic. We're obviously not homophobic if we're opening our homes to gays for a meal.

## Testimony

Our testimony—the story of how we became a Christian and how God continues to work in our lives—is another powerful proclamation of the reality of the gospel. Again, a postmodern person is less likely to be persuaded by our clever arguments—"Is it true?"—but they might be persuaded by our life story—"Is it real?"

A postmodern person is likely to accept our testimony as a valid source of knowledge. Moreover, our testimony demonstrates that the gospel works. And even better, while our non-Christian friend can argue against a truth claim, there is no argument against our personal story.

In the past, when we designed an evangelistic event, we had a testimony from a Christian followed by the Bible talk. I guess the idea was that the

Bible talk was the Word of God in a way that the testimony wasn't and that it was good to end with the Word. And it also meant that the event ends with the truth claim of the gospel for the non-Christian to accept or reject.

I don't want to get into a theological discussion about what exactly is the Word of God.[12] But at least, pedagogically, I have found that in postmodernity it works better if we begin with the Bible talk and end with the testimony. That's because the Bible talk puts the truth of the gospel out there, but the testimony shows how this truth works, which is persuasive to a postmodern person.

For example, I once preached at a dinner event. My message was a traditional Bible talk from Romans 8:14–17 in which I explained that God adopts believers as his children. My main point was that God is the Father that we never had, but should have had. More than that, God is the Father that we need to have. After my message, a friend gave his testimony. He shared how he was never close to his earthly father because he was a harsh man. They even fought many times. So when he became a Christian, one of the richest blessings was having God as the Father who loved my friend unconditionally. He never had to win God's approval or attention. He never had to gain his acceptance. He simply was able to enjoy having a God, as Father, who loved him just the way he was.

## Using Stories

In general, we should use more stories in our evangelism. In modernity, people preferred hearing propositional data: "Give me the facts!" But in postmodernity, people prefer hearing stories: "Show me what this looks like."

But stories also work well because they invite the hearer to see the world through our eyes. When I make a truth claim, the hearer is being asked to believe it or reject it. But when I tell a story, for the entire time I'm telling the story, the hearer has to assume my narratival standpoint.[13] The hearer has to suspend their disbelief and enter my world of presuppositions, construals, and perspectives.

We can do this in many ways. Instead of giving a logical treatment of a topic, we can use a story that addresses the topic. For example, I once

---

12. In my book, *Preaching as the Word of God*, I argue that "Word of God" refers to the gospel, so actually in both cases the Word of God has been preached, either as testimony or as a Bible talk.

13. In the language of speech-act theory, when we tell a story, we are performing a narrative act with a narratival illocution. For more, see Kevin Vanhoozer, "From Speech Acts to Scripture Acts: The Covenant of Discourse and the Discourse of the Covenant," in *First Theology: God, Scripture, and Hermeneutics* (Downers Grove, Ill.: InterVarsity, 2002), 193.

spoke on the topic of hell, but instead of giving a thorough treatment of the subject, I told the story of the rich man and Lazarus (Luke 16:19–31), in which the rich man ends up in hell and Lazarus goes to heaven. Then, rather than directly expounding the story, I asked them three questions: "Is hell a real place or only metaphorical?" "Why is the rich man in hell?" and, "How do I make sure I don't end up in hell?" I used these questions to structure my talk.

Another suggestion is to use stories when you are answering a question. I once heard Ravi Zacharias say, "They can't argue against a story." For example, when people ask me, "What about people in countries who haven't heard about Jesus?" I tell them the story of my friend who grew up in a Middle Eastern country that was closed to Christianity and the gospel. I tell them how my friend received a dream about Jesus, and that's how my friend came to believe, love, and worship Jesus. I say, "I'm not saying that God reveals himself in a dream to everyone. But what I am saying is that God finds ways to reveal himself to people, and I believe that he finds ways especially to those people in countries where they can't have Christian churches or the Bible. We just don't know. But what we do know is that God has revealed himself clearly to us! Because we do have the Bible. We have heard about Jesus." They may not be fully convinced, but it does tend to address the objection in a way that satisfies them.

Finally, for those who preach, I suggest using a higher ratio of stories as illustrations and examples of what you're preaching. As we'll see in a later chapter, illustrations win over the imagination and help to make our truth claims more plausible. But how are stories—especially illustrations—the Word of God? Speech-act theory helps us see that when we preach God's Word, we're not just conveying propositional information but also performing an action. It's a false dichotomy to separate propositional from personal, utterance from event, didactic from narrative, or idea from action.[14] As such, our illustrations are part of the speech act being performed, and in this sense, they are legitimate and vital to our proclamation of the Word.

## Engaging the Creative Arts

If the age of modernity was the age of the scientist, then the age of postmodernity is the age of the artist. In modernity, we concentrated on logic, proof, and evidence. We privileged propositional data. We argued

---

14. Sam Chan, *Preaching as the Word of God: Answering an Old Question with Speech-Act Theory* (Eugene, Ore.: Pickwick, 2016), 214.

and debated about ideas. We tried to win over the mind. But in postmodernity, we should also concentrate on the imagination and aesthetics, giving attention to beauty, stories, emotions, and feelings.

C. S. Lewis did both of these well, so it should not surprise us that many Christians today look to Lewis for inspiration and as a model for evangelism to postmoderns. In *Mere Christianity*, Lewis tries to win the argument. He presents a logical argument for the truth of Christianity. But in the *Chronicles of Narnia*, he seeks to win over the heart and imagination. What is the human sinful condition? It's the land of Narnia, where it's always winter, but never Christmas. What is sin? It's Edmund eating the Turkish Delight. What is atonement? It's Aslan, the lion, laying down his life, working a deeper magic unknown to the witch and then coming back to life.

Consider another example. Have you noticed how cookbooks have changed? In modernity, a cookbook gave you a recipe with a list of ingredients and instructions on how to cook. It was propositional. But in postmodernity, the recipe comes to us in a story: "I've got friends coming to visit me tonight. So I'm going to cook them a dish that I learnt from my grandmother when I was traveling through Morocco on my spring break. But to do that we're going to have to go to the farmer's market here in Los Angeles and get some ingredients. Come with me!"

Notice how the recipe is now embodied by a personal story that is rich with historical locatedness and tradition? There are also emotions, humor, expression, and feeling. Moreover, there will be aesthetics. Color. Form. Beauty. That's why cookbooks are illustrated with large, glossy, and gorgeous photos. So when we present the gospel, it's no longer a case of presenting propositional data about Jesus. The story needs to be embodied in our own story. And tradition, aesthetics, form, and beauty are also very much part of that story.

In the past, the church has often encouraged people with intellectual gifts—those who are doctors, engineers, and lawyers—to participate in preaching, teaching, and evangelism ministries. The underlying assumption is that we need intellectual people in ministry. Such people are gifted with logic, the sciences, and argumentation. But we also need to encourage people from the creative arts into preaching, teaching, and evangelism ministries. We need creative people who are skilled with storytelling, imagination, and aesthetics. And rather than automatically encouraging our gifted people to go to seminaries, maybe we need first to send them to an arts school.

## MAKING IT PLAUSIBLE

Our non-Christian friends have been doing this well in the last few decades. For example, my wife and I love watching *Modern Family*. As you probably know, *Modern Family* depicts a gay couple who have married and adopted a child. From this storyline, it's easy for us to imagine how this might be a normal, functional, loving way to live. The gay couple are just as functional—and dysfunctional—as the straight couples in the show. At no stage does the show argue for the validity of gay marriage. But it makes you assume the worldview of the storyteller—to see the world from their vantage point—and suddenly the idea of a gay couple is a lot more imaginable, plausible, and attractive.

This is what stories and the creative arts do, and when they are done well, they can present a worldview in a way that is winsome rather than preachy, personal rather than didactic, and persuasive rather than dogmatic. We can admire and then emulate what our non-Christian friends have been doing for a long time.

## Explore Different Metaphors

We have already discussed this in chapter 3, but it's worth revisiting here. When we share the gospel with moderns, we tended to privilege the metaphors of guilt and transgression for sin, and forgiveness and justification for salvation. But when we tell the gospel to postmoderns, we should explore the variety of other biblical metaphors for sin and salvation.

People in modernity may have once shared our assumptions about absolutes, morals, and laws. So to be saved, they needed to be good people who followed these moral laws. Many of those evangelism strategies for moderns involved convincing them that they weren't as good as they thought they were. If they'd broken one law, then they'd broken all of them! If they think that they can get into heaven based on what they've done, then they are mistaken. So a common introductory question used to be, "When you die, what are you going to say to God to get into heaven?"

But a postmodern person does not hold the same assumptions. Postmoderns no longer believe there are absolutes, morals, and laws. Instead, these are cruel constructs imposed upon us by oppressive authority figures such as religion, society, and family. So in order to be saved, they need to have the courage to ignore established authority and instead be true to themselves. They must ignore what others say and bravely follow their own dreams and ambitions.

Therefore, better metaphors for sin to a postmodern person might be self-righteousness, shame, and the idea of being owned by whatever we're living for. But we can see how these metaphors apply readily to a postmodern person. For example, many of my postmodern friends have a high concern for social justice, but in doing so they can become quite self-righteous about their acts of good works and judgmental against those who don't share their concerns. Or I find many of my postmodern friends are stressed with staging the perfect wedding[15] or raising the perfect children[16] to the point where these are idols in their lives that promise status, success, and social standing; these are things that own them. Or now that postmoderns are less individualistic and looking for belonging in tribal groups, they are rediscovering the idea of shame.[17] Thus when I explain to them that we have shamed the God who loves us, I find that many postmoderns readily accept this explanation of sin.

Similarly, better metaphors for salvation might include restoration, peace, freedom, and adoption. But again we can see how these metaphors apply readily to a postmodern person who is concerned about social justice— the brokeness of this world—and longs for restoration. Or the postmodern person who looks for social harmony might also be crying out for peace. Or the postmodern person who senses that they have been owned by whatever they are living for will now be longing for freedom. Or the postmodern person who is looking for belonging might also be looking for adoption.

## Use Wisdom as an Entry Point

The Bible has three major categories of knowledge: (1) providence (how God interacts with his creation on a daily basis, and how we can live in light of this), (2) salvation history (what God has done to save us, and what we must do in response to be saved), and (3) wisdom (how God has designed life to be lived, and how we can live according to God's design).

An example of providence is God sending rain to help crops grow

---

15. Similar insights by James K. A. Smith, *You Are What You Love: The Spiritual Power of Habit* (Grand Rapids, Mich.: Brazos, 2016).

16. Similar insights by Jennifer Senior, *All Joy and No Fun: The Paradox of Modern Parenthood* (New York: HarperCollins, 2014).

17. Similar insights by Jon Ronson, *So You've Been Publicly Shamed* (New York: Riverhead, 2015).

(Matt. 5:45). As a result, we acknowledge our dependence on God for our day-by-day lives. We seek his guidance on when to plant, reap, store, buy, or sell crops (Acts 11:27–30; James 4:13–14). An example of salvation history is God saving us from our sins by sending us his Son, Jesus (Matt. 1:21). As a result, we call upon the name of Jesus to be saved (Rom. 10:13).

But there's another category of knowledge known as wisdom. When God created the world, he imprinted his wisdom upon it (Proverbs 8). So the wise person begins with a personal knowledge of this God by fearing him appropriately (Prov. 1:7). And then the wise person lives according to God's design by being a faithful spouse in marriage (Proverbs 5), a diligent worker (Prov. 12:11), someone who doesn't gossip (Prov. 11:13), a peacemaker (Prov. 15:18), and a loyal friend (Prov. 17:17). At other times, God's design is hard to discern: Does God want me to answer a fool (Prov. 26:5) or not answer a fool (Prov. 26:4)? It's not so much working out what is the right thing to do (following a law or command) but working out what is the wise thing to do (what is apt in this circumstance)?[18] This is the challenge of wisdom. How can I live according to God's natural design for this world?

These categories are related. Both the unsaved and the saved enjoy God's providence (Matt. 5:45). And this becomes the way Paul can find common ground with his nonbelieving audience in order to tell them about God's salvation-historical acts (Acts 14:15–17; 17:24–31).

But the saved enjoy God's wisdom in a way that the unsaved don't. For wisdom begins with the fear of the Lord (Prov. 1:7). A Christian who lives according to God's design for this world—by being a faithful spouse in marriage, a diligent worker, a peacemaker, and a trusted friend—should stand out as different and unique. By and large, though certainly not each and every time, things should go well for the Christian who lives wisely. They will have joy in their marriage (Prov. 5:18–19), do well in their business (Prov. 12:11), negotiate office politics (Prov. 11:13), resolve conflicts (Prov. 15:18), and be trusted as a friend (Prov. 17:17). By contrast, others will seem unfaithful, lazy, gossiping, quarrelsome, and untrustworthy.

If the book of Proverbs is right, then Christians should have a way of life that works. The Bible isn't just true, but it also works. By being faithful spouses who don't cheat, Christians have happy family lives. By being peacemakers, they resolve conflicts. By being loyal, they have rich

---

18. The idea of aptness is a helpful insight in the world of ethics and epistemology. For example, see Ernest Sosa, *Virtue Epistemology: Apt Belief and Reflective Knowledge*, vol. 1 (Oxford: Clarendon, 2007).

networks of friends. They are happier, more fulfilled, more trusted, and more respected.

If this analysis is correct, then wisdom can be an entry point into the gospel. For example, I run seminars for non-Christians who work in large corporations. They invite me to talk about general themes like leadership, success, and ethics, and I try to show that these generally work better if we use a Christian worldview. The aim of the talks is for the non-Christian to come away saying, "Wow, I can see how the Christian way is a better way." My hope is that they will be more open to the claims of Christianity and consider whether they might be true.

## CHANGING OUR PEDAGOGY

With moderns, we used to employ this logic:

**Truth, Belief, Praxis**
- This is *true.*
- If it's true, then you must *believe* it.
- If you believe it, now you must *live* it.

But with postmoderns, I believe a better pedagogical sequence is:

**Praxis, Belief, Truth**
- The Christian life is *livable.*
- If it's livable then it's also *believable.*
- If it's believable, then it's also *true.*

Therefore, evangelism to postmoderns requires a lifestyle change. We need our Christian friends to become friends with our non-Christian friends. We need to be part of the same community. And then our non-Christian friends can see how the Christian life works. Then they will discover it is livable. And if they see that, they will see that it's believable. And if they see that, they might also acknowledge that it's true. But this will happen only if we live with our non-Christian friends. Not just visit them. Not just go out with them. But live among them so that they are part of our closest network of friends, and we are part of their closest network of friends.

At our church, we designate February as Friends Month. This is the month we design the church service to be especially accessible to our non-Christian friends. But what does a service like this look like? When we used to evangelize moderns, the strategy was to simplify the service and remove awkward moments from the service—the offering, the prayers, and the announcements. The idea was to get to the Bible talk as soon as possible. The idea was also that the Bible talk would be what moves our non-Christian friends to a point of conversion. They would hear the truth of the gospel clearly presented, and they would understand that they had a simple choice: accept or reject the truth claims of the gospel.

But with postmoderns, we look at the whole service—not just the Bible talk—as evangelistic, because the whole service shows how Christianity works. When they see us take up an offering, they will see that we are generous with our money because Jesus himself generously gave himself up for us. They will see that we are content with our money because we trust God to provide. And they will see that the gospel has freed us from the hold that money has on us because God is our security. When they hear us pray, they will hear what a personal relationship with God sounds like. They will see that we have a God who is powerful enough to answer prayers but also personal enough to care about our little needs. They will hear that we love each other so much that we pray for each other in our churches. They will hear our cries for justice for the poor, oppressed, and marginalized. And when they hear our announcements, they will hear that we take food to the sick, new mothers, orphans, and people who have just moved into our suburbs. They will hear that both young and old meet together in small groups. All the parts of the service show that we have a community of believers who are transformed by Christ and who restore our world by bringing Jesus' love, mercy, and justice.

## Preach Significance

A traditional expository-Bible-preaching model spends a high proportion of time (let's say 80 percent) on explaining what the Bible passage means—usually in the body of the sermon—and then a lower proportion (say 20 percent) on applying the existential, emotional, and contextual significance of that passage—usually in the conclusion of the sermon.

But with postmodern listeners, we should consider switching the proportions. I typically begin with a short explanation of the Bible passage, and then spend the whole body of the sermon on the significance. For example, for a Christmas talk, instead of focusing on what happened at

Christmastime, I focus on the significance. One of my Christmas talks is titled "Why We Need Christmas to Be True." My main message is that we need Christmas to be true because it means that (1) we are special to God, (2) God is a loving God, and (3) it's okay for us to admit we're not okay. Or similarly, I recently gave an Easter talk to city workers during their lunchtime. Instead of focusing on what happened at Eastertime, I focused on its significance. The talk was titled "The Sweetest Thing about Easter." My main message was that we need Easter to be true because it means (1) we can believe in unconditional love, and (2) we have a purpose to life. I wasn't just explaining the Christian storyline but also showing how it works.

## AUTHENTIC AND REAL

A few years after my poor attempt at speaking to youth in Missouri, I had another chance to speak to youth. This time it was an evening Good Friday service. I was living in Chicago as a student and was helping to run the youth group. But we had been given an impossible task. While the adults met upstairs for the Good Friday service, the youth met downstairs in the hall. When I say youth, I mean everyone from the ages of four to eighteen.

The plan had been to do a standard twenty-minute Bible talk on the meaning of Easter, followed by some small-group discussion. But we had to scrap that because of the unexpectedly larger numbers and the wide age range. So what did we do? We sat on the floor. We turned off the lights. We all sat in darkness. Then someone walked into the room holding a large lit candle. The room filled with the warm light from the candle. While the person holding the candle walked in, someone else read aloud the words from John 1:1–5: "In the beginning was the Word, and the Word was with God, and the Word was God. He was with God in the beginning. Through him all things were made; without him nothing was made that has been made. In him was life, and that life was the light of all mankind. The light shines in the darkness, and the darkness has not overcome it."

We placed the candle in the middle of the room, and we all sat around it, admiring its light. And then we turned on the room lights. We handed out the words to the Apostles' Creed. I told them that the words of this creed have been recited by Christians all over the world, in many languages, dating all the way back to the early followers of Jesus. Then we recited the creed together. After that, we handed out a small section of liturgy from the Australian Prayer Book, from the Easter Friday service section. We recited some of the liturgy together.

Then we reenacted the Last Supper. We carefully explained we weren't participating in the actual sacrament, but we were performing a reenactment of Jesus' last hours before his death. As we read aloud the words from Mark 14:22–26, we tore apart some bread and drank some fruit juice so that they could see, hear, smell, taste, and feel Jesus' final moments with his disciples.

And then we turned off the lights again. The candle was now the only light. We sat in silence as someone read aloud the description of Jesus' crucifixion in John 19. And then when Jesus cried out, "It is finished!" (John 19:30), we snuffed out the candle. We sat in silence in the dark for several minutes. Someone read aloud from the description of Jesus' resurrection in John 20, and then we relit the candle. The room was warm with the light of the candle.

And then we made an invitation to the youth. If they wanted to love, worship, and follow Jesus, they could demonstrate this by taking a small candle, walking forward, and lighting their candle from the large candle. As they did so, the room was filled with the light of many smaller candles. We ended the service by sending them back into the world with a mission to accomplish for Jesus. To bring his light where there is darkness. To love where there is hate. To bring justice where there is oppression.

Can you see what happened? We proclaimed the truth of the gospel. But we did it through a variety of sources. We acknowledged the role of tradition (the Apostles' Creed and the liturgy). We addressed emotions and feelings, and we paid attention to aesthetics (light, darkness, candles). We used story (reenactment of the Lord's Supper). And we found belonging together as a community (the multiple candles at the end). It was authentic and real.

CHAPTER 5

# CONTEXTUALIZATION FOR EVANGELISM

### If Jesus came today, would he be a white man?

Adam is excited to be a youth pastor at a small church in Southern California. After growing up on a farm and studying in midwestern America, this is his first time on the West Coast. He is looking forward to the sunshine, walks along Venice Beach, and watching the sun set over the Pacific Ocean.

At the youth group meeting, Adam meets a fifteen-year-old girl named Jane. Her parents are from Taiwan, but Jane grew up in America. Her father stays in Taiwan to work, while her mother lives with Jane and plays the role of the "Asian Tiger Mom." Jane studies for hours and hours every day. She doesn't play any sports or go to summer camps. Instead, she attends tutoring for her math. Jane's ambition is to go to Harvard. And one day she will become a doctor.

As her youth pastor, Adam notices Jane's obsession with her studies and confronts Jane. He warns her that study has become her idol and tells her that she needs to repent from this. He tells her that she needs to realize that there is more to life than Harvard, and that being a doctor may be a worse thing to do because it will make her rich and worldly. If she's really serious about following Jesus, she should give up her dreams of being a doctor and be a missionary instead. Or better yet, she should consider becoming a youth pastor!

## "DO I HAVE AN ACCENT?"

When I was living in the USA, Americans would often say to me, "Oh, I love your Australian accent!" They would always follow this up with, "Do I have an accent to you?" Which was staggering to me. Because of course they had an accent—an American accent! But even more staggering was the fact that they didn't realize they had an accent, as if they of all people in the world were the ones without an accent. The whole world has an accent—except for them!

I would also meet Americans who would try to convince me that they had a neutral accent. A midwestern American once told me that the midwestern accent was the neutral accent. That's why they try to find newsreaders with a midwestern accent, rather than a southern or East Coast accent. Another time, a Californian told me that the Californian accent was the neutral accent. That's why movies were made in California, because the Californian accent was neutral to the whole world!

Now, this was truly staggering. Because not only were they saying they had a neutral accent; they were implying that their accent was the normative accent. Their way of speaking English was the universal accent for the whole world.

Many Christians are the same with regard to their culture. They do not realize they have a culture, so they cannot hear their cultural accent. They cannot taste their cultural flavoring. They aren't aware of their dress or the Christian songs they sing or their views on education, work, and smoking. And so they impose their culture, along with the gospel, as if it is normative and universal.

At the youth group meeting, Adam also meets a fifteen-year-old boy named Jack, a thorough Californian dude. Jack wears his board shorts all year round. He doesn't enjoy high school. Once the end-of-school bell rings, Jack jumps on his bicycle and rides to the beach to go surfing. Jack's ambition is to leave school when he turns sixteen and take up a day-labor job so he can surf every day with his buddies.

As his youth pastor, Adam confronts Jack. He warns him that surfing has become his idol. He needs to repent from this. And Jack needs to realize there is more to life than the beach. He tells Jack that dropping out of high school is a terrible thing to do because Jack will be wasting his God-given potential to study. If Jack is really serious about following Jesus, he should stop surfing and apply himself at school. That way he can get into a college and one day get a decent-paying job. Or better yet, he can become a youth pastor!

Did Adam give these students the gospel, or did he give them his own culture? Can you see what's happened here? Adam has asked Jane to be like Jack, and Jack to be like Jane. Even worse, Adam's asking them to be like himself.

Many Christians are like Adam. They have merged their own culture with the gospel. This is what missionaries call syncretism. In doing so, when they evangelize, they don't just give the gospel. They also impose their culture upon the convert. By doing this, Christians are asking people not only to convert to Jesus but also to convert out of their culture into another culture, usually the culture of the Christian evangelizing them. Just like Western missionaries long ago forced Africans and Asians to wear Western clothes, Christians today force converts to leave their old culture and join Christian culture. So the question we want to address is, How can Jane be a Christian and still be an Asian-American? How can Jack be a Christian and still be Californian surfer dude? This chapter will answer this question by exploring the topic of contextualization as we look at the relationship between gospel and culture.

## WHY CAN'T I JUST GIVE THEM THE GOSPEL?

Have you ever had a well-meaning Christian say, "All you have to do is give them the gospel"? And by implication, they are saying, "Why do we have to worry about culture?" To answer this question, let's consider a few scenarios.

### Scenario 1: Seek to Be Understood

I'm going to tell you the gospel: *Denn so hat Gott die Welt geliebt, daß er seinen eingeborenen Sohn gab, damit jeder, der an ihn glaubt, nicht verloren gehe, sondern ewiges Leben habe.*

That is John 3:16, the gospel in a nutshell! The timeless, universally true gospel. But it is in German, which most of you reading this book likely don't understand. So at the very least, we should admit that it's not enough to tell the gospel in a way that makes sense to us; we also need to translate it so we can be understood.

## Scenario 2: Be Sensitive

I'm going to tell you the gospel: "God so loved the world that he gave his one and only Son, that whoever believes in him shall not perish but have eternal life."

That is the gospel. And you understood it in English. But what if I had said it to you with my fly undone, speedos on my head, and pointing my index finger at you? The problem here is that I have been culturally inappropriate. In your culture, I have been offensive. Because of my appearance and actions, I am not credible. So it's not enough to tell the gospel; we need to be sensitive to the other person's culture.

If we understand another person's culture, then we have a better chance of being understood. We will also seek to be sensitive and not unnecessarily offend them. In education there is a saying: "To teach math to Johnny, you need to know both math and Johnny." In evangelism, we can similarly say, "To tell the gospel to Johnny, we need to know both the gospel and Johnny." We need to know both the gospel and Johnny's culture.

## THE RELATIONSHIP BETWEEN THE GOSPEL AND CULTURE

### The Gospel Is Transcultural

The gospel is transcultural because it is true for all cultures. In the Old Testament, God is the God of both Israel and the nations. In the New Testament, salvation is for both the Jews and the gentiles. This is why Paul can say that in Christ there is neither Jew nor gentile, slave nor free, male nor female (Gal. 3:28). For this reason, we will all answer before the same God on judgment day. The gospel is universal and normative for all peoples at all times and in all places.

### The Gospel Is Enculturated

But the gospel is not acultural, as if it hovers above culture and is devoid of any culture. Instead, the gospel is deeply enculturated.[1] Notice how enculturated these biblical terms are:

The God of Abraham, Isaac, and Jacob
The Jewish Passover
Priests, temple, sacrifices

---

1. "[T]he Bible itself is not acultural, but it is transcultural," David K. Clark, "Theology in Cultural Context," in *To Know and Love God: Method for Theology* (Wheaton: Crossway, 2003), 120.

Jesus the Lamb of God
Jesus the Shepherd
Ransom for many
Taking up your cross
Washing each other's feet
Pharisees, tax collectors, Sadducees, Samaritans, fishermen

That is why we have to explain the Bible's culture whenever we give a story or talk from the Bible. Whenever we teach the Bible to children or newcomers, we often begin with the phrase, "In their culture . . ."

Even the Son of God became enculturated. When John says "the Word became flesh and dwelt among us," he is saying that the second person of the Trinity became a first-century Jewish male who lived in Roman-occupied, Second Temple Palestine and grew up in a working-class family. To understand the gospel, we need to understand its culture. We need to do cultural hermeneutics.

## Our Audience Is Enculturated

The person we are trying to evangelize is also enculturated. They are not a person who hovers above culture and is devoid of any cultural influences. Instead, this person is deeply enculturated. And this can vary widely, even within the same geographical area. For example, if the person lived in Chicago, they could be from an:

American-born Chinese culture
African-American culture
Northwestern undergrad culture
Kellogg Business School culture
Community college culture
North Beach culture
Single mom culture
Retiree culture

Each one of these is a unique and distinct culture in the Chicagoland area. Each would have different cultural concerns, gospel interpretation, cultural communication, and cultural application.

### Cultural Concerns

For example, the American-born Chinese is concerned about honoring the family and pressures to study. The retiree is concerned about loneliness, health, and boredom. The single mom is concerned about time pressure.

### Gospel Interpretation

The gospel will be interpreted and misinterpreted differently by each culture.[2] What does their cultural lens help them to see in the Bible? What are their cultural blind spots which make them misunderstand what's in the Bible?

For example, an American-born Chinese might come to the Bible with the lenses of the Confucian worldview. They may correctly understand that they have shamed God and now need to honor this God, but they might misunderstand the requirements to obey this God as duty, perfectionism, and salvation by works.

As another example, a Californian surfer dude might come to the Bible with the lenses of Western individualism. He may correctly understand that he needs to make a personal decision to follow Jesus, but he might be culturally blind to his corporate responsibilities in the body of Christ.

### Cultural Communication

For people to understand you, you must speak in ways that their culture can understand. We often take this for granted. An Anglican bishop once told a missionary friend of mine that he didn't believe we needed any form of contextualization. My missionary friend replied, "At least you're using English rather than Greek."

This is especially important because much of our language is idiomatic. This means that we have to learn not only a culture's language but also its idioms, metaphors, and illustrations. A friend of mine, Leigh, was having lunch at a popular tourist destination in Sydney. Leigh was approached by a Chinese tourist. The tourist asked Leigh if he could use the vacant seat next to him. Leigh replied, "Go for your life!" When the tourist heard this, he ran away. Of course, what Leigh had meant was, "Sure, the seat's free, take it!" but the tourist thought Leigh was threatening him! This story shows how much of our communication is idiomatic. "Take a seat," "I want to ride shotgun," and "What's up?" are just some common examples.

---

2. I owe this insight—that the contextualization is more than communication and application, but it is also interpretation of the Bible through a particular culture's lenses—to Jackson Wu, *Saving God's Face: A Chinese Contextualization of Salvation through Honor and Shame*, EMS Dissertation Series (Pasadena, Calif.: William Carey International Univ. Press, 2012), 10–68.

I've also heard it said that people from foreign countries—China, Belgium, Brazil—who learn English as a second language still have trouble understanding native speakers from the USA, England, and Australia speaking English. But—and here is the interesting part—those from foreign countries can easily understand each other speaking English. This is because they have learned a technically precise English, but one which is different from the idiomatic English spoken by native speakers.

In addition to idioms, the way we organize and present our ideas is also culturally determined. Some cultures prefer a propositional, point-by-point presentation. Other cultures prefer stories, illustrations, and examples. All of this affects the way we communicate.

### *Cultural Application*

The gospel will also be applied differently in each culture. What are the idols of a culture? How can they honor God in their context? What does it mean to take up your cross in that culture? For example, when an American-born Chinese becomes a Christian, they face a challenge: "How can I honor God without dishonoring my non-Christian parents?"[3] The surfer dude might face a different challenge: "How can I honor God without letting down my friends?"

My PhD supervisor, Graham Cole, pointed out to me that in Luke 3:10–14, John the Baptist had different applications of the gospel for different audiences. To the crowd, John told them to share food and clothing. To the tax collectors, John told them to stop cheating. To the soldiers, John told them to stop extorting money and to stop accusing people falsely. If you've ever taught in another cultural context, you've likely faced the struggle of trying to give application to your ideas in that culture. The struggle you faced in doing this reveals that you are already implicitly doing some form of cultural hermeneutics.

## The Gospel Teller Is Enculturated

We ourselves as evangelists are also enculturated. We are not free-floating people hovering above the culture, devoid of any culture. We are not acultural. We each have a cultural accent and a cultural flavor. We are deeply enculturated, and this will affect our understanding and application of the gospel.

---

3. Hence the title of Peter Cha's book, *Following Jesus without Dishonoring Your Parents* (Downers Grove, Ill.: InterVarsity, 1998).

### Our Own Cultural Concerns

We come to the Bible with our own cultural, theological, existential, emotional, and experiential concerns—consciously or unconsciously. For example, when I was feeling lonely, I came to the Bible looking for God's comfort. Or when I was wronged, I came to the Bible looking for God's justice.

But what we're talking about is more than just our felt needs or feelings. In my theological tradition, I've been used to the idea that Jesus died for me. So I've quickly noticed Bible passages with the "for us" language—that Christ died for us (e.g., Rom. 5:8). Now, as I read and listen, I hear more theologians pointing out that Christ isn't just for us; we are also in him (our union with Christ). So now I'm noticing Bible passages with the "in him" language as well (e.g., 2 Cor. 5:21). But how did I miss such obvious language before now? Because it wasn't part of my theological concerns until now.

### Our Own Interpretation of the Gospel

We are not blank slates. We bring our own theological interpretive grids to the Bible. For example, in John 4, when Jesus tells the Samaritan woman she has had five husbands, and the man she is with isn't even her husband, what do we think of the woman? We automatically think she's an adulteress. She's a sinner.

But in other cultures, they might interpret the story to mean that she has been abandoned unfairly by five men, one after the other. And she now lives with another man for protection. But this man won't even honor her by marrying her. She's been sinned against.

There's nothing in the text to tell us whether she's a sinner or sinned against. But we come to our interpretations based on the theological systems that we have brought to the text.[4]

### Our Own Cultural Communication

I have lived in both the USA and Australia. An Australian friend once joked to me, "Never have two countries been divided so much by a common language!" That's because even though Americans and Australians both speak English, our words can mean different things. For example, in the USA, *college* refers to an undergraduate institution and *school* refers to a postgraduate institution. But in Australia, it's the other way around! As another example, in the USA, if you take a class, then you are the student

---

4. I owe this example to Clark, "Theology in Cultural Context," 119.

in the class. But in Australia, if you take a class, then you are the teacher of that class. As a final example, in the USA, you order "take out." But in Australia, you order "take away."

It's the same for us when we communicate the gospel. Words that mean one thing to our particular Christian tradition might have a completely different meaning to a non-Christian in their culture. Take the word evangelical. In our Christian tradition, it might mean a characteristic of a denomination or movement within Christianity that holds to the primacy of the gospel message—from the word *euangelion*. But to our non-Christian friend, it may mean a sociopolitical movement associated with the conservative right.

And these differences can be even more profound. In our Christian tradition, we might associate a particular formulation of the gospel as the gospel itself—Two Ways to Live, the Four Spiritual Laws, or Bridge to Life. If so, we might wrongly think that unless we tell the gospel in this particular way—using its metaphors of sin and salvation—then the gospel has not been proclaimed. In some Christian traditions and denominations, we proudly announce that we preach "Christ crucified" (the gospel) and not rhetoric (citing 1 Cor. 1:18–2:16). But what we usually fail to realize is that we do employ a rhetorical method when we present the gospel. We can't escape it. The rhetorical method is usually one that we are so used to in our culture, denomination, or tradition that we don't notice it. For example, it could be the twenty-minute Bible talk with an introduction, three points, and a conclusion. Or it could be several key points presented in logical order. We are always using a rhetorical method—usually one determined by our culture—whether we acknowledge it or not.

### Our Own Application of the Gospel

I come from a Sydney culture where the application for almost every New Testament passage was, "Give up medicine, go to seminary, go into professional ministry, and become a pastor." When I travelled to Siberia, their preachers applied every New Testament passage as, "You must not drink alcohol." If you are an American, there is a better than average chance that your American pastor applies almost every New Testament passage as, "You must do daily devotions, pray more, and give more money to missions."

These may or may not be valid applications. But it should be obvious that those who evangelize have interpretations and applications that are deeply influenced by their culture. If we become better exegetes of our own culture, we will become aware of our enculturated interpretations and applications of the gospel. In doing so, we will be aware of our reductionisms and our blind spots. And in our evangelism and presentation of the gospel, we will become more richly layered and nuanced in our communication.

## There Is No Universal, Decontextualized Form of the Gospel

There is no form for presenting the gospel that hovers above a culture, devoid of culture. We have to pick a particular form that speaks to one culture, but may not be able to speak to another culture.

Timothy Keller helpfully explains that the instant you present the gospel, you have chosen to be contextual, historical, and particular.[5] Jesus did this when he chose to be male, Palestinian, first century, and Aramaic and Greek speaking. And we do it when we choose our form of communication. For example, we have to choose a language. If we speak in English, only English-speaking people can understand us. And we still have these choices:

- What kind of English will we choose?
- Who do we quote?
- How do we illustrate?
- Do we use humor?
- What metaphors do we use?
- What clothes do we wear?
- What questions do we answer?

For example, an Asian-American audience might ask you what to do with their parents. A western African audience might ask you about lightning: Why does God send lightning which kills their children? An American audience might ask you what God's perfect plan is for them. Keller reminds us that we shouldn't be dogmatic about our preferred forms of evangelism. They might work well in our cultural setting, but they may not work well in other settings. Whatever it is that makes it work well in our setting might be the very thing that makes it not work elsewhere.

My missionary friend Bruce tells me that when he was in western Africa, well-meaning American missionaries were using the Four Spiritual Laws to tell the gospel to the Africans. Although it was effective on American college campuses, by and large they found it ineffective in traditional

---

5. Timothy Keller, "Contextualization: Wisdom or Compromise?" talk given at Covenant Seminary Connect Conference, 2004.

Africa. I come from Sydney, where my tradition uses *Two Ways to Live* as its evangelism tract. This tract worked very well in Sydney during the 1980s, and now we are trying to export it to the rest of the world. While it may work in some contexts, we should also pause to ask, "Could whatever it is that made it work well in the 1980s in Sydney mean that it may not work so well elsewhere in the world?" We can't assume that what works in one place will be appropriate for a different cultural context.

If we want our gospel presentation to appeal to a wide variety of cultures, it will likely have to be quite generic—largely abstract. It might be more universal in its reach, but it will also be less engaging and effective. Conversely, if we want our gospel presentation to be highly contextualized to a specific culture, it will likely not engage people from another culture. For example, if we target Chinese who speak Chinese and work outdoors on weekend nighttime shifts, then we cannot possibly reach Germans who speak German and work indoors on weekday daytime shifts.

## Every Form of Gospel Presentation Will Overadapt and Underadapt

According to author and pastor Timothy Keller, every form of gospel presentation will either overadapt or underadapt to a culture.[6] This is true in both interpretation and application. For example, according to Romans 8:14–17, if we have God's Spirit, then we are adopted as his children. We can cry out, "Abba, Father!" But how do we interpret this gospel truth—in particular, the Aramaic term Abba? If we read this to mean we can call God "Old Man," we might risk overadapting our interpretation of the gospel to fit our cultural perspective—in particular, our egalitarian approach to hierarchical relationships. At this point, we are misinformed about the gospel. But if we leave Abba untranslated, then we risk underadapting our interpretation of the gospel for our culture. Now we are uninformed (or underinformed) about this aspect of a great gospel truth. We miss out on relating with God as Father.

As another example, if we use only brokenness and healing as our metaphors for sin and salvation, then we might risk overadapting our interpretation of the gospel to fit our cultural perspective—in particular, our loss of categories of guilt and retributive justice in the West. At this point, we are misinformed about the gospel. We might understand sin to be a sickness that can be healed by therapy, rather than as a vertical offence against a holy God, which requires our repentance and his forgiveness. But if we use

---

6. Keller, "Contextualization."

only guilt and forgiveness as our metaphors, then we risk underadapting our interpretation of the gospel for our culture. Our culture is now uninformed (or underinformed) about other metaphors of sin and salvation, such as shame and honor, brokenness and healing, self-righteousness and exaltation, and falling short and restoration.

When we overadapt to a culture in application, we end up with syncretism to their culture. We don't ask people in that culture to give up what they should give up according to the gospel. And we don't ask them to do what they should do according to the gospel. The opposite is when we underadapt to a culture, where we end up with legalism from our culture. We think we're imposing upon them gospel norms, but we're actually imposing upon them our cultural norms. Here we ask them to give up what they shouldn't have to give up. And we ask them to do what they shouldn't have to do.

According to Keller, we are blinded by our culture. We cannot see our cultural blind spots. Because of this we will overadapt or underadapt our gospel presentation. Let's use the example of the Bible's view of sex. If we take the gospel to a culture and tell them that it's okay to have sex with prostitutes to worship the local fertility goddess, then we are guilty of syncretism. We have overadapted our gospel presentation to their cultural norms. We haven't asked them to give up things they should give up according to the gospel. But the opposite would happen if we tell them that they can have sex only in order to have children. We tell them it is wrong to have sex for any other reason, such as pleasure.[7] Here we are guilty of legalism. We have underadapted our gospel presentation. We have asked them to give up things they didn't have to give up. We have imposed upon them our cultural norms rather than the norms of the gospel.

The important thing to note here is that the opposite of overadaptation is legalism. Often we think there is a risk in overadapting (overcontextualization) to a culture because it would lead to syncretism. We think that it might be better to err on the safe side, to underadapt (undercontextualize). "Just stick to the gospel," we say. But if we underadapt, we are giving them legalism instead of the gospel. The opposite of syncretism isn't the pure gospel. The opposite of syncretism is legalism.

According to Keller, there will be no form of gospel presentation that can ever get it just right. We will always be overadapting or underadapting.

---

7. This was Augustine's view. And for a long time this was the view of the Christian church up until the Middle Ages. See the discussion in Megan Best, *Fearfully and Wonderfully Made: Ethics and the Beginning of Human Life* (Kingsford, AU: Matthias, 2012).

But if we can get it just right, then we will hit the sweet spot of contextualization. And that is when revival, with God's help, will happen!

## ADAPTATION OF GOSPEL PRESENTATION TO CULTURE

| | Underadapt | Sweet Spot | Overadapt |
|---|---|---|---|
| **The Evangelist and the Culture** | You challenge but don't enter the culture. | You enter and challenge the culture. | You enter but don't challenge the culture. |
| **Gospel Interpretation** | They are uninformed (or under-informed) of gospel truths. | They are informed of gospel truths. | They are misinformed of gospel truths. |
| **Gospel Communication** | They can't understand you. | They understand you. | They think they understand you, but they have misunderstood you. |
| **Gospel Application** | You make them do what they don't have to do and ask them to give up what they don't have to give up. | You make them do what they have to do and ask them to give up what they have to give up. | You don't make them do what they have to do and don't ask them to give up what they have to give up. |
| **Gospel Presentation** | Your gospel message has nonessentials that are confusing or unnecessarily offensive. | Your gospel message has essentials that are necessarily offensive but doesn't have nonessentials so that you don't confuse or unnecessarily offend. | Your gospel message doesn't have the essentials so that it is inoffensive when it should have been necessarily offensive. |
| **Result** | Pharisaism, legalism, cultural imperialism (imposing cultural norms as gospel norms) | Contextualized gospel | Syncretism |
| **Category of Contextualization (Hiebert)** [*] | Colonialism | Critical contextualization | Uncritical contextualization |

[*] The final row of this table is from Paul G. Hiebert, "Critical Contextualization," *International Bulletin of Missionary Research* 11 (1987): 104–12.

## YOU DON'T HAVE "THE BIBLICAL WAY"

Timothy Keller gives a great example of adapting the gospel. All cultures find somewhere to sit on the individualism-versus-collectivism and hierarchy-versus-equality spectra. So who has got it right? Which is "the biblical way"?

North Americans are individualistic rather than collective in the way they think and live. As a result, someone might say that they are not biblical, and we should be less individualistic and more collective. Take, for example, the Amish. The Amish share their possessions, eat together, and work together. Surely this is more biblical than what we typically do in North America! But then someone might say, "What about the Auca Indians?" They are more collective than the Amish. They don't live in buildings where you have privacy. You have to do everything in the open—going to the toilet, having a bath, and reading your mail.

So which is the biblical way—the typical North American, the Amish, or the Auca Indian way of living? Timothy Keller's point is that there will always be someone who has overadapted more than you, and there will always be someone who has underadapted more than you. So be humble, because you don't necessarily have it right. You don't necessarily have "the biblical way." Instead, be gracious to others. Don't call them syncretists or legalists in their forms of evangelism. Because there will be someone else out there who can bring the same charge against you!

We have just looked at six aspects of the relationship between the gospel and culture. Hopefully you are beginning to see that saying, "Just give them the gospel," is too simplistic (at best) and naive (at worst). If we are to present the gospel to someone, we need to be educated in cultural hermeneutics. We need to be able to exegete the Bible's culture, the culture we are seeking to reach, and our own culture.

## HOW TO INTERPRET CULTURE

So how, practically, do we study a culture? How do we learn to interpret culture? We need to learn the skills of cultural hermeneutics.

## What Is Its System of Thought?

We can interpret a culture as it stands at a single moment by classifying it as a system of thought. How are its ideas organized into a comprehensive, interconnecting system? For example, James Sire in *The Universe Next Door* suggests the following systems: Christian theism, deism, naturalism, nihilism, existentialism, Eastern pantheistic monism, the New Age, and postmodernism.[8] Simon Smart in *A Spectator's Guide to World Views* suggests Christian worldview, modernism, postmodernism, utilitarianism, humanism, liberalism, feminism, relativism, New Age spirituality, and consumerism.[9]

These systems or worldviews can be a helpful place to start. But the weakness of classifications like this is that they consider Christian theism as its own entity, devoid of any other worldview, as if Christianity were its own culture. The lists also tend to be adversarial, presenting Christianity versus the other systems. This can be helpful in contrasting particular points of thought, but it can also be dangerously simplistic, because our theological doctrines of general revelation and common grace tell us that there must be some truth and goodness in these other systems of thought. There must be some overlap with the Christian worldview that we can identify within the other systems.[10]

## What Are Its Themes?

We can also interpret a culture by looking at its themes. What are the dominant messages you hear in that culture? What is expressed? How does this culture answer the basic questions of life, meaning, and reality? Again, James Sire helpfully gives some guidance here. He suggests that the worldview of a particular culture can be discovered in the way it answers four key questions:

1. *Who am I?* What is the nature, task, and purpose of being a human?
2. *Where am I?* What is the nature of the universe and the world in which I live? Is the world personal, ordered, and controlled? Or is it chaotic, cruel, and random?

---

8. James Sire, *The Universe Next Door: A Basic Worldview Catalog* (Downers Grove, Ill.: InterVarsity, 2004).

9. Simon Smart, *A Spectator's Guide to World Views* (Sydney South, AU: Blue Bottle, 2007).

10. I owe this observation to my friend Timothy Silberman.

3. *What's wrong?* Why is it my world appears to be not the way it's supposed to be? How do I make sense of evil?

4. *What is the solution?* Where do I find hope for something better?[11]

Similarly, Simon Smart suggests that a worldview can be understood by what it says about the following six themes:

1. *Reality:* What is the nature of the universe and the world around us? Is there a God or gods? Is this a closed or open universe? Is there only a material world or is there also a supernatural world?

2. *Human nature:* What is a human being? Are we created or evolved? Is there only a body or also a mind or soul? Are we essentially good or evil? Is there free will or determinism? Are we nature or nurture?

3. *Death:* What happens to people when they die?

4. *Knowing:* How can we know? What can we know?

5. *Values:* What makes something right or wrong?

6. *Purpose:* What is the meaning of human history? What is the purpose of life?[12]

Kevin Vanhoozer offers yet another approach, one quite different from these approaches. He says that we can learn the themes of a culture by looking at how they view these ideas or categories: beauty, body, children, cities, gardens, gifts, guilt and shame, hope, justice, marriage, sickness, and worship.[13]

Following Vanhoozer's lead, we can come up with our own list of themes by which to interpret a culture. For example, you might want to look into how the culture understands youth, age, work, sports, or leisure. Or you might study how they think about body hair, health, wedding presents, public transportation, and democracy. There is no single way to approach this, but some themes will likely be more helpful to you than others in communicating the gospel.

---

11. James Sire, *Naming the Elephant: Worldview as a Concept* (Downers Grove, Ill.: InterVarsity, 2004).

12. Simon Smart gets this from Julie Mitchell, *Teaching about Worldviews and Values* (Melbourne: Council of Christian Education in Schools, 2004).

13. Kevin J. Vanhoozer, "What Is Everyday Theology? How and Why Christians Should Read Culture," in *Everyday Theology: How to Read Cultural Texts and Interpret Trends*, ed. Kevin J. Vanhoozer, Charles A. Anderson, and Michael J. Sleasman (Grand Rapids, Mich.: Baker, 2007).

## WHO DO YOU SAVE?

The themes of youth and age are often quite revealing. When I teach ethics, we often discuss this thought experiment. If a ship is sinking and you can put only one person onto the lifeboat, who will you choose—the eight-year-old girl or the eighty-year-old man? Interestingly, many of us in Western cultures would choose the eight-year-old because she has potential and the eighty-year-old has already lived his life. But many in traditional cultures would choose the eighty-year-old because society has invested so much in him.

## What Are Its Themes and Counterthemes?

Paul Hiebert advocates looking at themes together with their opposites, what we can refer to as counterthemes. He suggests that every culture will belong somewhere on the following spectra between themes and counterthemes:[14]

| | | |
|---|---|---|
| Individual | ⟷ | Group |
| Private emotions | ⟷ | Public emotions |
| Order, predictability | ⟷ | Chaos |
| Material world | ⟷ | Nonmaterial world |
| This-worldly | ⟷ | Otherworldly |
| Secular space | ⟷ | Sacred space |
| Achievement | ⟷ | Acquirement |
| Hierarchy | ⟷ | Equality |
| Freedom | ⟷ | Control |
| Universal, whole picture | ⟷ | Particular, specific |

For example, in traditional English and Australian cultures, emotions are private. If someone is authentic, then they shouldn't show emotions.

---

14. Paul Hiebert's appropriation of Morris Opler's "themes and counterthemes," Emmanuel Todd's demography, and Parson's evaluative themes, in Paul Hiebert, *Transforming Worldviews: An Anthropological Understanding of How People Change* (Grand Rapids, Mich.: Baker, 2008), 26–27, 63–64.

By showing emotions, they probably have something to hide. But in some Mediterranean cultures, emotions are public. If someone is authentic, then they should show emotion! When I worked as a doctor in Sydney, patients from an English culture would downplay their pain, whereas patients from Mediterranean cultures would demonstrate their pain with loud gestures and groans. But this worked against them because the healthcare staff assumed they were faking their pain. I remember one time a lady was having a heart attack, but no one believed her because she was groaning too loudly.

Hiebert suggests that at least two spectra, the themes/counterthemes of freedom-control and hierarchy-equality, can be combined to form a grid. (See figure.)

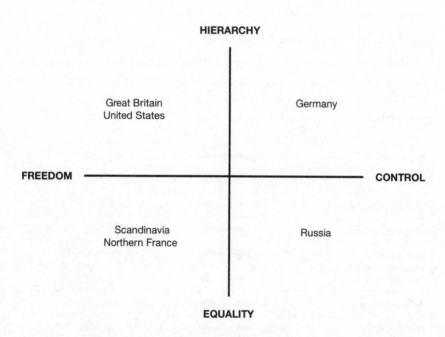

Paul G. Hiebert, *Transforming Worldviews: An Anthropological Understanding of How People Change* (Grand Rapids, Mich.: Baker, 2008), 27. Copyright 2008. Used by permission of Baker Academic, a division of Baker Publishing Group.

The grid should be self-explanatory. The cultures in Scandinavia, northern France, and Russia place a high value on equality. But Russia differs from the others in that it is a culture of control, while Scandinavia and northern France place a greater cultural emphasis on freedom. And the cultures of Great Britain, the USA, and Germany tend to have more hierarchy. But Germany is a culture that values control, while Great Britain and the USA tend to emphasize freedom to a greater extent.

When I taught this to my class in Sydney, I asked them where they would put Australia on the grid. We joked that Australia would be exactly in the center. We were neutral while the rest of the world was extreme in terms of equality, hierarchy, freedom, and control. But every culture thinks of itself as the neutral one. For example, *China* literally means "Middle Kingdom." The British have Greenwich Mean Time, where Britain's time is the reference point for the rest of the world. American maps of the world have America bang in the middle of the world map, even if this means Asia has to be divided into two on the edges of the map.

## What Is Its Storyline?

The three methods I've outlined thus far give a synchronic reading of culture. But there is a fourth method that can give us a diachronic reading. Again, Timothy Keller helpfully shows us that each culture has its own storyline.[15] Keller explains that stories typically have three parts:

1. The way things should be: a mission, a task, a journey
2. Something that stops this from happening: the bad guys
3. Something that achieves the mission: the good guys

Keller uses the example of Little Red Riding Hood to illustrate this. "Little Red Riding Hood took food to her grandmother" is not a story. But "Little Red Riding Hood went to take food to her grandmother (the mission), but a wolf was waiting to eat Little Red Riding Hood (the bad guy), but a woodsman kills the wolf and saves Little Red Riding Hood and the grandmother (the good guy)" *is* a story. To interpret a culture, we need to ask, What is the storyline of this culture? What is its mission? What should the world be like? Where are they trying to go? Who should they be? Who are the good guys? Who are the bad guys? What is wrong with the world? What is stopping it from getting its happy ending? What is a sad ending and what is a happy ending for this culture?

Do you remember Jane and Jack from the introduction to this chapter? What are their storylines? What is their mission? Who are their bad guys? Who are their good guys?

Jane's mission is to become a doctor. Her bad guys are anything or

---

15. Keller, "Contextualization."

anyone that prevents her from studying—partying, good times, friends, and sports. Her good guys are anything or anyone that helps her to study and get good grades—parents, teachers, and authority figures.

Jack's mission in life is to surf. His bad guys are parents, teachers, and authority figures. His good guys are partying, good times, friends, and sports.

Jack's good guys are Jane's bad guys, and his bad guys are her good guys!

We have a lot of tools now to read and interpret a person's culture. As a summary, we can first look at a person's systems of thoughts. For example, we can say that Jane belongs to a modern system of thought, while Jack belongs to a postmodern system of thought. Second, we can interpret a person's culture by looking at their themes. For example, Jane's values include honoring her parents, while Jack's values include the importance of doing what you love. Similarly, we can look at where that person's culture falls on the spectra between certain themes and counterthemes. For example, Jane belongs more on the group, private emotions, hierarchy, and control ends of the spectra. But Jack belongs more on the individual, public emotions, equality, and freedom ends of the spectra. Third, we can describe the person's culture as a storyline: What is their mission, who are the bad guys and good guys, and what does a happy ending look like?

## HOW TO CONNECT THE GOSPEL WITH A CULTURE

Now that we have interpreted both our culture and the other person's culture, our next step is to connect the gospel with that person's culture. This task is called contextualization. The task of contextualization is threefold: (1) interpreting the gospel, (2) communicating the gospel, and (3) applying the gospel to the hearers in their culture.[16] The aim of contextualization is to have a dialogue between the cultures of the three major players in evangelism: our culture, the culture of the Bible, and the culture of our hearer. In doing so, we recognize the role of the three cultures in interpretation, communication, and application of the gospel.[17]

According to Timothy Keller, our strategy for contextualizing is to

---

16. I owe this definition to Jackson Wu. Wu points out that most definitions—including my original definition—of contextualization are deficient because they talk only about the processes of communicating and applying the gospel to a particular culture. But contextualization necessarily also involves interpreting the gospel, because all of us come to the gospel with our culturally determined interpretive lenses.

17. Wu, *Saving God's Face*, 10–68.

enter and challenge a culture with the gospel.[18] If we only enter the culture, then we have overadapted our gospel because we have not challenged that culture with gospel norms. We have not been necessarily offensive with the gospel. We have let them do things they shouldn't do and not asked them to give up what they need to give up. We have given them syncretism. This is what missiologists call uncritical contextualization.

On the other hand, if we only challenge the culture, then we have underadapted the gospel because we have not entered that culture. We have been unnecessarily offensive with the gospel. We have asked them to do things they don't need to do and asked them to give up things that they don't need to give up. We have given them legalism. This is what missiologists call colonialism, because we have imposed upon them our cultural norms as if they are gospel norms.

But if we both enter and challenge, then we have made the gospel understood in their language, metaphors, and idioms. We have challenged them with gospel norms. We have been necessarily offensive with the gospel. We have asked them to do things that the gospel asks them to do. We have asked them to give up things that the gospel asks them to give up. We have given them the contextualized gospel. This is what missiologists call critical contextualization.[19]

## The Theological Justification for Contextualization

But how can we justify entering and challenging a culture? Many Christians have been brought up with a culture wars model in which the gospel is always in opposition to culture. So how can there be any connection between the gospel and human culture?

### The Incarnation

"The Word became flesh" (John 1:14). The second person of the Trinity became a human who was enculturated. If the Son of God can enter a particular culture, our gospel can also enter a culture. But what should raise our eyebrows is this: John uses the term *logos*, translated "Word" in our English Bibles. *Logos* is an enculturated term with all sorts of culturally loaded meanings in ancient Greek culture. According to the ancient Greeks, *logos* was the organizing principle of the universe. To understand the shock of John's using *logos*, this is the equivalent of a

---

18. Keller, "Contextualization."
19. Paul Hiebert, "Critical Contextualization," *Missiology* 12 (1984): 287–96.

Star Wars geek saying, "The force became flesh." Or a Chinese person saying, "The tao became flesh."

The challenge of contextualization is the same challenge of translating the Bible from its original languages—Greek and Hebrew—into a contemporary language. Take, for example, John 1:14. How do we translate the Greek term *logos*? We could stick with the term *logos*, but now it is meaningless to a contemporary person. Or we could translate it into the English term Word, but now we pick up other meanings in the term word which John would not have intended. And so now we risk syncretism.

This is the challenge for those who translate John 1:14 into Chinese. If they use the term *logos*, it is meaningless. If they use the Chinese term for Word, then they have a word-for-word translation, but they don't pick up the full meaning of *logos*. If they use the Chinese term Tao, as in "the tao became flesh," then they have a similar meaning to *logos*. But they also risk picking up other meanings which are syncretistic with taoism.

This is the challenge of contextualization. If we don't use the language, idioms, and metaphors of a person's culture, then our message will be meaningless. But if we do use the language, idioms, and metaphors of the person's culture, we may be understood, but we also risk syncretism with their culture. I believe that this is a risk worth taking. And it is the same risk that John took in John 1:14 when he used the term *logos*.

### General Revelation

There is some knowledge of God that is universally available (Rom. 1:19–20). God reveals his truth to all humans, at all times, and in all places. Theologians have a saying: "All truth is God's truth." There is evidence of God's truth in all human culture.

### Common Grace

God's goodness is universally available (Matt. 5:45). Richard Mouw suggests that God is glorified not only in salvation but also in his creation and beauty.[20] This is why in all cultures we can find beauty in the arts, wisdom in the sciences, truth in other religions, and morality in their ethics. In this sense, "All goodness is God's goodness!"[21] Or we can add, "All beauty is God's beauty."

---

20. Richard Mouw, *He Shines in All That's Fair: Culture and Common Grace* (Grand Rapids, Mich.: Eerdmans, 2001), 36, cited in Vanhoozer, "What Is Everyday Theology?" 43.

21. Mouw, *He Shines in All That's Fair*, 82.

### The Image of God (Imago Dei)

All humans are created in the image of God (Gen. 1:27). As a result, all humans share God's creativity to create—or cultivate—worlds and texts of meaning. If there is a creation mandate in Genesis 1, there is a cultural mandate in Genesis 2.[22] Thus, all cultures are expressions of our being in the image of God.

### Eternity in Our Hearts

God has placed eternity in our hearts (Eccles. 3:10–11). To be a human is to carry a burden from God—a longing for eternity, wisdom, and understanding in the midst of God's creation. Thus, every human has a God-given existential cry for transcendence, meaning, and eternity. And all cultures will find a way of expressing this cry.

### Sin

All humans are sinful (Romans 1–3). As a result, every culture will also find a way of expressing its rebellion, idolatry, wandering, falleness, and suppression of the truth.

### Analogies of Redemption

Creation groans for its redemption (Rom. 8:18–22). There is still some continuity between the present creation and the future new creation. Thus, there is also a conceptual link between creation and redemption.

This is why Jesus could explain the gospel with analogies from his culture: yeast, a mustard seed, a shepherd, a vine, a sower, and a wedding banquet. Paul also explained the gospel with analogies from his own culture: ransom, justification, and adoption.

This means that in every culture we should be able to find analogies we can use to explain the gospel. C. S. Lewis believed that God sent "good dreams" into the myths and stories of a culture. Don Richardson believed God planted redemptive analogies in a culture. And Brunner believed there is an *Anknupfungspunkt* ("contact point") between the gospel and culture.[23]

---

22. Mouw, *He Shines in All That's Fair*, 15–60.

23. C. S. Lewis, *Mere Christianity* (New York: Touchstone, 1980), 54; Don Richardson, *Peace Child: An Unforgettable Story of Primitive Jungle Treachery in the Twentieth Century* (Grand Rapids, Mich.: Bethany, 2005); Alister E. McGrath, *Christian Theology: An Introduction* (West Sussex, UK: Wiley and Sons, 2011), 167.

## THE PEACE CHILD

Don Richardson is the author of *Peace Child* and *Eternity in Their Hearts*. He believes that every culture has some story, ritual, or tradition that can be used to illustrate and apply the gospel.

Don Richardson and his wife, Carol, experienced this when they lived among the Sawi and learned their language. They found that the Sawi honored treachery as a virtue, so when Don told them the story of Judas betraying Jesus, the Sawi cheered Judas as the hero. How could Don and Carol possibly tell the gospel to people in this culture? What possible points of connection could there be?

Then Don and Carol found that the Sawi were often at war with neighboring villages. To make peace, the Sawi required a father in one of the two warring tribes to make an incredible sacrifice. He had to be willing to give up one of his own children as a "peace child" to his enemies. Peace could come because of a father's sacrifice of his son.

The peace child was the redemptive analogy the Richardsons discovered in the Sawi culture. It was a point of connection to the gospel, and using this analogy, Don and Carol could speak of Jesus as God's peace child to us.*

---

\* Don Richardson, *Peace Child: An Unforgettable Story of Primitive Jungle Treachery in the Twentieth Century* (Grand Rapids, Mich.: Bethany House, 2005).

---

Our theological justification for contextualization is that we can enter any culture because of the incarnation of God's Son and because of God's general revelation, common grace, our creation in the image of God, and the promise that God has placed eternity in every human heart. At the same time, we should challenge all cultures with the gospel because all human cultures are affected by sin. And we have the language to enter and challenge because we believe that God has left a redemptive analogy in every culture, a means for communicating the gospel in a way that the people in that culture can understand.

But we should also be cautious in using analogies. We use them because they make our truth claim imaginable to people. Analogies don't prove our truth claim—using analogies is not equivalent to using reason or evidence—but they make it more plausible that our truth claim is true. So it is helpful to recognize that redemptive analogies are a means and not the ends of our evangelism. Jackson Wu cautions, "If contextualization is constantly done by mere analogy, one can implicitly communicate two things: (1) the only thing that matters in the Bible is the information it takes to 'get saved,' thus short-circuiting genuine conversion and Christian growth, (2) the entire Bible is neither very important nor essential, thus implying that the revelation of God's glory is not infinitely valuable. . . . By contrast, the desired goal [of contextualization] is *worldview conversion*."[24]

For this reason, I believe that redemptive analogies by themselves will not be enough for us to communicate the gospel. By themselves they can seem trite or forced. We also need to connect the gospel to that culture's existential cry and storyline. This is what we will explore both in the following section and in the next chapter.

## A Method for Contextualization

Summing up all that we have considered to this point, a method for engaging in contextualization begins to emerge. I believe that we can start the work of contextualization by looking for any of the following points of connection between the gospel and our audience's culture.

### Find a Redemptive Analogy

Don Richardson found the "peace child" as his redemptive analogy. What is the redemptive analogy in our audience's culture?

### Find the Existential Cry

Every culture will find a way to express its God-given existential cry for transcendence, meaning, community, love, freedom, forgiveness, intimacy, uniqueness, connection, usefulness, approval, harmony, wisdom, and redemption.

### Find the Storyline and Give the Gospel as the Happy Ending

Tim Keller suggests one way for integrating the gospel into a culture's storyline.[25] Every culture has a storyline that answers the big questions. How should things be? Why are things not the way they should be? What would set things right? Most of these storylines are on the right track because of God's general revelation, common grace, our image of God,

---

24. Wu, *Saving God's Face*, 42 of 341, Location 928 of 11602, on Kindle.
25. Keller, "Contextualization."

and our cries for eternity. The storylines are expressing a right, God-given desire. Often they correctly identify what is wrong with the world and what things should be like.

What we can do is enter and challenge the storyline and then show how only Jesus can give them the happy ending that they are looking for. The way we do this is by listening and trying to understand and empathize with the culture's storyline. Then we can think about how to show people that they cannot have their happy ending the way they want by the way they are living. Finally, we communicate to them how Jesus gives them that happy ending. We can show them how Jesus gives them a far better ending than what they were wishing for.[26]

What does this look like? Let's return to Jane and Jack. If you recall, Jane wants to go to Harvard and become a doctor. But what is Jane's existential cry and storyline? Her existential cry isn't to become a doctor. Rather, her existential cry is for security. Security is very important in the Asian-American culture, and becoming a doctor is one means of achieving this. And what is her storyline? Is it to become a doctor? No, it's to achieve status in her family's eyes and to bring honor to her parents, which will ultimately give her the sense of belonging she longs for in her community. Being a doctor is one of the means for her to achieve this.

So one way of telling the gospel to Jane is to use security, belonging, and honor as gospel metaphors. We can also identify her storyline, understand it, and empathize with it; she's looking for security, and who of us doesn't want this? But becoming a doctor will not guarantee security—there will always be another exam to take; there will always be another mountain to climb. But Jesus Christ promises us true security.

Jack wants to surf every day. But what is his existential cry and storyline? His existential cry is for freedom. Working as a laborer and surfing is one means of achieving this. And what is his storyline? Is it only to surf? No, it's to find freedom—freedom from boredom, freedom to pursue pleasure, freedom to live life on his terms. Becoming a laborer and surfing is one of the means of achieving this.

So one way of telling the gospel to Jack is to use freedom as a gospel metaphor. We can also identify his storyline, understand it, and empathize with it; he's looking for freedom, and who of us doesn't want this? But working as a laborer and surfing will not guarantee freedom—there will be bills that he can't afford, there will be a hierarchy of friends to impress,

---

26. I owe this last observation to my friend Sam Hilton.

and there will be the ever-diminishing returns of pleasure. But Jesus Christ promises us true freedom. By giving him our lives, we gain it.

## A Christian in Your Own Culture

We began with the example of youth pastor Adam. Adam thought he was giving Jane and Jack the gospel, but he was unknowingly giving them his midwestern American culture as well. What Adam needs to learn is not only the gospel but also how to read his own culture and the cultures of Jane and Jack.

Ever since the gospel went out from Jerusalem, the challenge has been to allow converts to be Christian and still be of their culture without converting to the culture of the evangelist. In the early church, the Jews wanted the Greeks to submit to Jewish cultural norms. But the council of Jerusalem (Acts 15) clearly resolved that the Greek converts did not have to submit to Jewish cultural norms. They could still be of their own culture.

The theological significance of the incarnation is that the gospel can be translated into any culture. If you are from a Vietnamese culture, you can be a Christian and still be Vietnamese. If you are from a Siberian culture, you can be a Christian and still be Siberian. And if you are from an indigenous Australian culture, you can be a Christian and still be an indigenous Australian. You do not have to become a white man to become a Christian!

The challenge for us when we evangelize is to translate the gospel into our audience's culture. Jane, the high-achieving Asian-American, can be a Christian and still be a high-achieving Asian-American. And Jack, the Californian surfer dude, can be a Christian and still be a Californian surfer dude.

### THE LONGING FOR REST

When I was a young medical doctor, I shared an apartment with some other young doctor friends. We were single, always moving from one hospital apartment to another, and very lonely. One night, one of my friends asked me what Christianity is all about. I knew that we both had an existential cry for rest, just to settle down in a place we could call home. So I told the gospel to him using rest as a chief gospel metaphor. I told him that being a Christian is being able to settle down with God in a place God calls home.

CHAPTER 6

# GOSPEL-CULTURAL HERMENEUTICS

### The force became flesh.

Karen grew up in a high-achieving Asian family. Both of her parents are doctors. Her brother is in law school on the East Coast. Her sister is in the first year of an MBA at Stanford. Karen also goes to a large Asian church in Houston. Most of her friends at church study premed, physical therapy, law, or engineering. But Karen has always been interested in the creative arts.

At the start of the new school year, Karen moved to San Francisco and enrolled in an acting school. She started making new friends. But her actor friends are unchurched and would never dream of entering a Christian church. Instead, when Karen hangs out with her friends, they go to film festivals, plays, art houses, and poetry readings. This is a whole new world for Karen. No one in her previous church ever went to such things. So how can she ever possibly get her new friends to hear the gospel? And how can she ever possibly know how to speak the gospel to their world?

Many Christians know how to demonstrate the truth of the gospel from the Bible to their own familiar world. But how can we do it from the cultural texts that surround us—Star Wars, the *Mona Lisa*, and even Mother's Day—to the world of our friends? To do this, Christians need to learn key principles in gospel-cultural hermeneutics. In this chapter, we will outline the basic principles of this hermeneutical approach and then look at some examples of how this can be done.

## WHAT IS GOSPEL-CULTURAL HERMENEUTICS?

How can we connect the gospel with a culture? How can we contextualize the gospel to our audience's culture? We use the tool of gospel-cultural hermeneutics: we find a cultural text and interpret it with the lenses of the gospel. And then we speak to the audience in their culture, using the language, idioms, and metaphors of their "cultural text." Finally, we show them how Jesus fulfills their cultural storyline.

### What Is a Cultural Text?

According to Kevin Vanhoozer, cultures produce works of meaning—"cultural texts"—that both communicate meaning and call for interpretation. They act upon us. They shape us. And they are themselves the lenses through which we interpret other worldviews and texts. According to Vanhoozer, "Cultural texts include everything from the Sears Tower and Stravinksy's *Rite of Spring* to soccer moms, *The Simpsons*, and shaving cream. Each of these things has meaning to the extent that it communicates something about our values, our concerns, and our self-understanding."[1]

One of the best biblical examples of gospel-cultural hermeneutics is found in Acts 17:16–34, when the apostle Paul visits Athens. When you read that passage, you will notice that Paul uses the same principles that we are discussing in this chapter as he interprets cultural texts. In Athens, the cultural texts were the idols, and these idols fulfilled the Athenians' existential cry for transcendence. In their storyline, the Athenians wanted blessings from the gods, and the idols would appease the wrath of the gods. Notice how Paul empathizes with this desire: "I see that in every way you are very religious."

Paul's understanding and empathy are evidence that Paul has entered their culture. That's the first step. Now that he has entered, he next challenges it: "You are ignorant of the very thing you worship." Paul describes to the Athenians their own storyline. They want to worship the gods, to get their blessing and appease their wrath. But they won't find their happy ending because they don't know the name of the Unknown God.

Finally, Paul fulfills their storyline. He gives them Jesus as the happy ending that their culture's storyline is looking for: "This is what I am going

---

1. Kevin J. Vanhoozer, "What Is Everyday Theology? How and Why Christians Should Read Culture," in *Everyday Theology: How to Read Cultural Texts and Interpret Trends*, ed. Kevin J. Vanhoozer, Charles A. Anderson, Michael J. Sleasman (Grand Rapids, Mich.: Baker, 2007), 26.

to proclaim to you." He gives them Jesus as the Unknown God that they want to worship, but whose name they do not know. The Unknown God can now be the Known God.

With this example in mind, let's break this down into an overview of the basic principles for engaging in gospel-cultural hermeneutics.[2] As Paul did, we begin by finding a text from the culture. Today, this can be a movie, a book, a product, a website—any cultural artifact that you believe has something significant to say about that culture and its longings and existential cries. Once you have selected the text, you'll follow the three-part process that Paul did: enter, challenge, and fulfill.

## 1. ENTER THE STORYLINE OF THE CULTURE

### 1. Read the Text on Its Own Terms and Describe It

The first step is to describe the facts about the text, and then see if you can discover its chief motif or metaphor. The cultural text for Paul in Athens were the idols. Its chief motif or metaphor was that they were objects of worship (v. 23).

Let's say we choose *American Idol*, a singing contest, as our cultural text. This TV series lasted fifteen seasons and reached thirty million viewers. Its chief motif or metaphor was believing in yourself so you can chase your dreams and perhaps become a superstar.

Or let's say we choose a teenage movie such as *The DUFF* (2015). *The DUFF* is directed by Ari Sandel and stars Mae Whitman. It's a movie about a teenager who doesn't quite fit in. Its chief motif or metaphor is the coming-of-age story in a high school setting.

Or we can choose the recent cultural phenomenon of *Carpool Karaoke* with James Corden. These internet video clips show James Corden and a guest, say Michelle Obama, driving inside a car while singing karaoke to well-known songs. Its chief motif or metaphor is being in sync with the artists who sing the songs.

Or as another example, we can choose Beyoncé's recent songs and tours—for example, the Formation world tour. Beyoncé is an American R&B singer who has won multiple Grammy Awards. Her chief motif or metaphor is female empowerment.

And maybe as a final example, we can choose the recent cultural

---

2. This is my adaptation of the excellent guidelines provided by Vanhoozer, "What Is Everyday Theology?" 59–60.

phenomenon of cafes serving drinks in Mason jars. The Mason jar was invented in 1858 by John Landis Mason and has been mass produced since the 1900s with its iconic name—Mason—in cursive on the side of the glass jar. It was once used for canning and preserving foods but is now *de rigueur* for the global hipster aesthetic in cafes ranging from Vancouver to New Jersey, Lima to Sydney. The chief motif or metaphor is tradition.

## 2. Understand It

The second step is to understand the cultural text. What is its worldview? For example, what is its message or cultural storyline or God-given existential cry? The message of the idols in Athens, as a cultural text, is that there are gods who need to be worshiped (v. 23). The idols are part of a cultural storyline in which people need to appease and worship the gods. The existential cry is for transcendence: there is a need to connect with the transcendent spiritual realm.

What is the worldview of *American Idol*? Its message is that anyone can become a superstar. It sits comfortably in the Western cultural storyline of rugged individualism and achievement, in which success is granted to those who believe in themselves. The existential cry is for recognition, respect, and success.

What is the worldview of a teenage movie such as *The DUFF*? Its message is that you shouldn't let anyone else define you. Only you should define yourself. It also sits comfortably in the Western cultural storyline of rugged individualism, in which respect is granted to those with autonomy, independence, and self-belief. The existential cry is similarly for recognition, respect, and belonging.

What is the worldview of *Carpool Karaoke*? Its message is that it's fun to sing along with and dance to well-known songs. It also sits comfortably in the Western cultural storyline of individualism, in which you should be free to express yourself through fashion, performance, and creativity. The existential cry is probably also for recognition, respect, and belonging.

What is the worldview of Beyoncé and her songs, video clips, and tours? The message is that women stand together, *en bloc*, as a force that calls men to account for their actions. For example, her song "Single Ladies" tells men to commit; there is no such thing as a commitment-free, have-it-both-ways relationship. In her album *Lemonade*, she sings about male infidelity. The scary video of her with a baseball bat smashing car windows shows that there is moral accountability: wrongs will be outed, and there is such a thing as retributive justice. Beyoncé's message is part of the Western cultural storyline of equality, justice, and rights—in this case, for women. The existential cry is for recognition and respect.

What is the worldview of the Mason jar? The message is that we do not exist as individuals, but we belong to traditions, stories, and histories. The cultural storyline is one of finding one's identity in the stories of our predecessors. The existential cry is for both transcendence—a story greater than our own—and connectedness.

## 3. Empathize with It

Now that we have described and understood the cultural text, we need to empathize with it. Can we feel the emotion behind it? Why is it an attractive storyline? What existential need does it fulfill? Why would I want this message to be true or real? For example, in Athens, Paul doesn't immediately attack the Athenians' idols. And he doesn't make fun of the fact that the Athenians even have an idol to a god whose name they don't know. Instead he empathizes with their storyline. Of course, if there are gods who need to be appeased and worshiped, then we should have as many idols as possible. And of course, you'd even have an idol to a god whose name you don't know. Just in case. You wouldn't want to leave out any god! This would seem to be a sensible, safe, and spiritual way to worship the gods.

So how can we empathize with the worldview of *American Idol*? If it lasted fifteen seasons and reached thirty million viewers, there must be something attractive in its message. The message is attractive because it tells us that anyone, no matter who we are—big or small, rich or poor, strong or weak—has a chance of success. The only thing holding us back is our lack of faith in ourselves. But for those of us who believe hard enough, we can overcome whatever adversity is in our way. Who of us doesn't want to believe this?

What about teenage movies such as *The DUFF*? The movie's message is attractive because it tells us that it doesn't matter if people don't give us the respect we deserve. In the end, as long as we have self-respect, we have all the respect we need. This frees us from a life of dependency. This frees us from a life of worrying about what we look like, what we wear, and how much we own. It protects us from verbal and psychological abuse. This empowers us to be secure, strong, and independent.

What about *Carpool Karaoke*? I'm thinking that its message is attractive because it tells us there is fun in expressing ourselves. We are free to be who we want to be. We don't have to conform. We don't have to worry about what others think about us. We can make a fool of ourselves and still have fun. We can just be who we want to be. For those of us who are tired of conforming to the expectations of others, this can be quite liberating.

What about Beyoncé? Her message is attractive because it frees up women to be who they want to be. They don't have to conform to the confining constructs imposed upon them by a patriarchal world. Moreover, men can't get away with treating women badly any longer. This is a call for justice, rights, individuality, freedom, and respect. Who of us wouldn't want this to be true?

What about the Mason jar? Its message is that we are more than the sum of our parts. We are more than a lonely individual trying to survive. We are part of something greater—stories and traditions. It's also a cry for a time when life was supposedly simpler, with less depersonalizing mass production and technology.

## 2. CHALLENGE THE STORYLINE OF THE CULTURE

### 4. Deconstruct It

After we have entered the storyline by describing, understanding, and empathizing with it, we have earned the right to challenge it. We can do this by deconstructing the cultural storyline. How is this message deficient? What is lacking? Can it deliver the happy ending that it's chasing? Or how is this message dissonant? What is clashing? Does it have messages which can't both be true at the same time? For example, Paul challenges the idols in Athens by pointing out that the Athenians are worshiping a god whose name they don't know. Thus their message is deficient. The god lacks a name. It can't deliver the happy ending because surely you need to know the name of a god if you are to worship it.

How can we deconstruct the storyline of *American Idol*? The message of *American Idol* is dissonant because, on the one hand, it tells us that we can accomplish anything as long as we believe. But on the other hand, the essence of *American Idol* is Simon Cowell, the harsh judge who tells many contestants bluntly that they can't sing. According to Cowell, it doesn't matter how much you believe in yourself; if you are out of tune, you are simply out of tune. Thus we have a strange, dissonant phenomenon as we witness many hopeful contestants singing out of tune to the cringing faces of the judges and members of the audience.

How can we deconstruct the storyline of teenage movies such as *The DUFF*? The message of *The DUFF* is dissonant because, on the one hand, it tells us that we shouldn't worry whether other people respect us and that the only thing that matters is if we have our own self-respect. But on the other hand, the movie also ends with the main character gaining the love, respect, and friendship of all the other characters in her high school. Without this, there would not be a happy ending. So in the end, it does matter whether we get love and respect from others. We cannot survive as lone individuals. We have the basic human need for love, belonging, and respect from others.

How can we deconstruct the storyline of *Carpool Karaoke*? The message is dissonant because on the one hand, it's all about freedom, individuality, and self-expression. But on the other hand, it's all about being in sync with the song's artist. It's fun and entertaining only if James Corden and his guest are performing the same words, moves, and rhythms as the artists. If James Corden and his guest are out of sync, we cringe. We lose our respect for them. We are no longer entertained.

How can we deconstruct the storyline of Beyoncé? The message is dissonant because on the one hand, it is about freedom from constructs; women should be free to be whoever they want to be. Don't listen to what others say. But on the other hand, men are told they can't be whoever they want to be. They need to listen to what others say. But these are clashing messages.

What about the Mason jar? The Mason jar is deficient because it can't deliver what it promises. The cultural storyline's happy ending is one in which we are connected with a grander story than just our own. We want to be connected to a tradition. We want to be personalized and free from the depersonalizing effects of mass production and technology. But the Mason jar, by itself, can't get us to this happy ending because it's only a glass jar. Worse, it is now a product of mass production and technology. So how can it connect us to something greater if it is trapped in our cynical world of marketing and mass consumerism?

## 3. FULFILL THE STORYLINE OF THE CULTURE

### 5. How Does the Gospel Answer This Existential Cry and Storyline?

So far, we have demonstrated that we have heard, understood, and empathized with the cultural text's existential cry and storyline; we too would want the same happy ending. But we have also deconstructed it to show that this happy ending is impossible with the cultural storyline alone. Now we can demonstrate that the gospel is God's answer to the cultural storyline. The gospel is the happy ending that people in the culture have been looking for. Jesus fulfills their God-given, legitimate existential cry. The gospel is the only way of achieving this happy ending. There is no other way, apart from Jesus, of fulfilling their existential cry. For example, when Paul spoke in Athens, after identifying the Athenians' existential cry for transcendance and their cultural storyline's need to worship and appease the gods, he offered the gospel as God's answer to the cultural storyline. God, who sent his Son, Jesus, is the one who can fulfill their God-given, legitimate existential cry for transcendence (vv. 24–30). Moreover, Jesus is the one we need to worship and appease (v. 31).

What about *American Idol*? The storyline of *American Idol* reveals that we now have a problem. Believing in ourselves is not enough. What if, up until now, despite our self-belief, we too are out of tune, not just in our singing but in our whole lives? What if we've been so deceived by our self-belief that we can't see how much there is to cringe about in our lives? What if we are so out of tune with God that he has to send his Son, Jesus, to save us? If this is true, then the gospel is God's answer to our storyline.

What about teenage movies such as *The DUFF*? The storyline of *The DUFF* reveals that we have a problem. As much as we tell ourselves we don't need respect from others, we still do. We cannot exist in isolation. We need love, belonging, and respect from others. (Even the movie has to contradict itself with a happy ending in which the heroine wins the love and respect of the major characters in her school.) But how can we find this if it's unhealthy to become too dependent on the love and respect of others, especially from those who are toxic to us? What if God gives us the love, belonging, and respect that we need? What if this is why he sent Jesus? If so, then the gospel is God's answer to our storyline.

What about *Carpool Karaoke*? The storyline reveals that we have a problem. As much as we celebrate our individuality and personal expression, in the end it still matters whether we're in sync with the artists. If so, what if we're not in sync with what really matters in life? What if we're not in sync with God, the Original Artist? If so, this would be why God has to send his Son, Jesus, to save us. If this is true, then the gospel is God's answer to our storyline.

What about Beyoncé? Beyoncé preaches empowerment, freedom, being whoever you want to be and not letting anyone judge you for it. But Beyoncé also calls us to live accountable lives. Men, especially, can't live as if no one will judge them. Men can't be whoever they want to be. They need to be better than who they are now. But how can any of us be better than who we are now? This can be possible only if someone better than us enters our lives. If so, what if this is the reason God sent us his Son, Jesus? If this is true, then the gospel is God's answer to our storyline.

What about the Mason jar? The storyline of the Mason jar reveals that we long to be more than just atoms and molecules. We long to be more than just DNA, propogating and surviving. In the end, we want to be part of a greater story than just our own. We want to be connected to a grander tradition. But how can we find this greater story? What if this is the reason God sent us his Son, Jesus? If so, then the gospel is God's answer for our storyline.

Can you see what we've done here? We've actually got them wanting the gospel to be true and even wishing for it. This is about opening hearts for the gospel, as well as informing minds with the gospel.

## 6. Speak the Gospel

Now that we've got them wanting the gospel to be true, we can speak the gospel using the culture's same motifs and metaphors. Show how Jesus is a far better ending for their storyline than what they could wish for. For example, Paul in Athens speaks the gospel using the host culture's motifs and metaphors. He mentions their altar to the Unknown God and then announces that he will proclaim to them what they are ignorant of (v. 23). And he speaks the gospel to them by quoting back to them their own cultural texts—their poets (v. 28).

So how can we speak the gospel using *American Idol*? Self-belief is not enough. If we're out of tune, then we're still out of tune. Worse, self-belief can even deceive us into thinking we're better than we are. Simon Cowell is the reality check that many contestants need, whether they like it or not. In the same way, God sent Jesus to be our reality check. We're so out of tune with God that he had to send Jesus to save us from ourselves. For Jesus, the worst sin is what he called self-righteousness. This means deceiving ourselves with self-belief to the point where we think we're okay with God when we're not. But how can we get ourselves back in tune with God? God tells us to believe in Jesus rather than to believe in ourselves.

What about teenage movies? How can we speak the gospel using *The DUFF*? The message of the movie is that only you can define yourself. But if we're defined only by ourselves, then we end up lonely. No matter how much we protest, it does matter what others think of us. We need love, belonging, and respect. So maybe the problem isn't that we need these things but that we are looking to the wrong people for them. God sends us his Son, Jesus. And Jesus gets to define us. He calls us his friends.

So now we don't have to go looking for love and respect from the wrong people or from those who won't give it to us. With Jesus, we have all the love, belonging, and respect that we're looking for.

How can we speak the gospel using *Carpool Karaoke*? The message of *Carpool Karaoke* is that as much as we value self-expression, we still need to be in sync with the words, moves, and rhythms of the artists. We're not free to invent our tunes. Maximum enjoyment comes from singing their tunes. But what if we're not in sync with the Original Artist—God himself? This is why God sends us his Son, Jesus. The Bible often talks about being saved in Jesus. If we trust Jesus, we can be saved into sync with Jesus. We can get ourselves in sync with the words, moves, and rhythms of the one who made us and loves us. Perhaps this is why the Bible talks about God not just saving us but giving us a new song to sing.

How can we speak the gospel using Beyoncé? Her message is that men especially need to be more accountable. They need to be judged. They need to be better than who they are. But this is possible only if someone better comes into their lives. And if this is true for men, then it must also be true for all of us. So who will be our judge? Who will be the better person who comes into our lives? That's why God sent his Son, Jesus. To be our Judge. But not just our Judge but also the Light who exposes our darkness and then shows us a better way forward.

And finally, how can we speak the gospel using Mason jars? The message of the Mason jar is that we need to be connected to a transcendent, grander narrative. God sends us his Son, Jesus, to offer us a grander narrative. If we connect ourselves with Jesus, then Jesus will connect us with God's story, history, and tradition. With Jesus, we will find the transcendent narrative that we've been longing for.

## The W-Spectrum

Another way to approach this task is a model known as the W-Spectrum, a model formulated by Warrick Farah and Kyle Meeker. This spectrum, ranging from W1 to W4, describes four possible approaches for cross-cultural workers as they seek to evangelize people in their culture.[3] Rather than following the entire approach at one time, as Paul did in Athens, we can think of different types of evangelistic work that we are called to engage

---

3. Warrick Farah and Kyle Meeker, "The W-Spectrum: Worker Paradigms in Muslim Contexts," *Evangelical Missions Quarterly* 51, no. 4 (October 2015): 366–75, https://www.emqonline.com/node/3387. Accessed November 27, 2016.

in at different times. The focus is on understanding how these distinct tasks work together to bring the gospel to that culture.

- W1 workers show how Christ triumphs over the culture: "Your storyline is wrong, and you must reject it to follow Christ." W1 workers oppose the storyline. I would also suggest that W1 workers operate with the transgression or rebellion model of sin: "You have broken God's laws and now must repent and submit to Jesus."
- W2 workers show how Christ replaces the culture: "Your storyline is inferior and should be replaced by Christ." W2 workers undermine the storyline. I would also suggest that W2 workers operate with the idolatry model of sin: "You have been worshiping the wrong things instead of God; now you must replace your idols with the true God."
- W3 workers show how Christ transforms people in the culture: "Your storyline is good, but Christ can make it better." W3 workers retain and repurpose the storyline. I would also suggest that W3 workers operate with the brokeness model of sin: "You are broken, but now Jesus can restore you."
- W4 workers show how Christ completes their culture: "Your storyline is heading in the right direction, but you need Christ to fulfill it." W4 workers invite people to follow Jesus within their storyline. I would also suggest that W4 workers operate with the falling-short model of sin: "You're searching for God in the wrong places; that's why you haven't found him yet. But now if you come to Jesus, you will find what your culture's storyline is looking for."

The Bible has examples of each of these. When Jesus takes a whip through the temple, that might be an example of W1. When Jesus tells the rich ruler to leave behind his riches and follow him, that might be an example of W2. When Jesus speaks to the Samaritan woman at the well in John 4, that might be an example of W3. And when Paul speaks to the people in Athens and tells them that he knows the name of their Unknown God, that is an example of W4.

Of course, there can also be a combination of approaches. When Paul and Barnabas tell the people in Lystra in Acts 14 to turn away from "worthless things to the living God" (v. 15), that would be an example of W2. But they also tell them about the goodness that God has placed in their cultural storyline, which should point them toward the real God (v. 17). This is an example of W3.

I believe that every cultural storyline has elements that can be entered because of God's common grace and general revelation, the universal image of God in all people, and the universal cry for transcendence and eternity. Thus, there is a place for the W3 and W4 approaches. But every cultural storyline also has elements that must be challenged because of universal human sinfulness. Every culture will find a sinful way to run away from God or to oppose him. Thus, there must also be a place for W1 and W2. Contextualization will employ all of these approaches, in combination, at some stage. The approaches are complementary rather than contradictory.

That said, in terms of pedagogy, we should begin with some common ground, and that means that we have to enter before we can challenge. This means that we should begin by looking for truths that a culture's storyline has in common with the Bible. After doing this, we are better equipped to challenge the culture's storyline.

As mentioned in previous chapters, when Jesus and the apostles proclaimed the gospel to those who had the Scriptures—those who should have known better—they were oppositional. They employed approaches similar to W1 and W2. But when they proclaimed the gospel to those who were unreached by the Scriptures, they were affirmational. They employed approaches similar to W3 and W4. This suggests that our choice of approaches is largely determined not only by our giftings but also by the context: Who is our audience?

If this is correct, it has implications for our first step in evangelism. When Paul was in Athens, surrounded by idols, his first step was not to condemn the Athenians' idolatry—which would be an example of W1 or W2—but to find common ground—"I see that you are very religious"— which is an example of W3 or W4. Presumably he would eventually tell them that they needed to get rid of idols, but this was not his first step.

So what is our first step? For example, if someone says that they don't believe a loving God can send someone to hell, our first step might be to oppose them and say that they are wrong. I would instead suggest that we look for common ground and say, "I see that you are concerned that everyone should be saved, and that no one should go to hell. God says the same thing when he says that he takes no delight in the death of the wicked" (see Ezek. 33:11). Look for ways to agree with what the person is saying, affirming what is good and true in their belief. Once you have established this common ground, you can look for ways to confront and challenge. The goal is to get to the third part, where you can present Jesus as the fulfillment of what they long for.

**THE W-SPECTRUM**

|  | W1 | W2 | W3 | W4 |
|---|---|---|---|---|
| **Aim of the Evangelist** | Oppose the culture's storyline. | Undermine the culture's storyline. | Retain and repurpose the culture's storyline. | Invite people to follow Jesus within their culture's storyline. |
| **Gospel Message** | "Your culture's storyline is wrong. You must reject your culture to follow Christ." | "Your culture's storyline is inferior. You must replace it with Christ." | "Your culture's storyline is good. But Christ can make it better." | "Your culture's storyline is heading in the right direction. But you need Christ to fulfill it." |
| **Model of Christ** | Christ triumphs over the culture's storyline. | Christ replaces the culture's storyline. | Christ transforms the culture's storyline. | Christ fulfills the culture's storyline. |
| **Model of Sin** | Transgression or rebellion | Idolatry | Brokenness | Falling short |

## Applying the W-Spectrum

You may have observed the phenomenon that Asians living in the USA (and other Western countries) are converting readily to Jesus. Asians seem to be disproportionately highly represented in churches and Christian groups at high schools and colleges. In contrast, Caucasian Westerners in the USA (and other Western countries) are proving to be "hard soil" for evangelism. Why is this?

There are many reasons. But I think one reason is that the gospel completes the storyline of the Asian living in the West. It offers freedom from superstitious rituals. It offers freedom from the fear of evil spirits. And it offers a better way to find status, honor, and success. By and large, life works better if you become a Christian. You only have to compare your life with the Asians who haven't found Jesus yet: they're still captive to superstitious rituals, fear of spirits, and the never-ending drive to find success through study, qualifications, and possessions. I believe, whether we've realized it or not, that much of evangelism to Asians in the USA has been operating with the W3 or W4 models. Our gospel presentations have completed rather than combatted their cultural storyline. Jesus gives them their happy ending: freedom. Our evangelism to Asians, deliberately or not, has been surprisingly well contextualized.

In contrast, for the Caucasian Westerner, Christianity represents the loss of freedom. It represents captivity to superstitious rituals, fear of God and priests, and the never-ending need to go to church and obey out-of-date commands about sex. By and large, life is worse if you become a Christian. They compare the life of a Western Christian with a Western non-Christian. To them, the non-Christians are free from superstitious rituals, fear of God and priests, and the never-ending need to go to church and obey out-of-date commands. The non-Christians get to sleep in on a Sunday! To a Caucasian Westerner, Christianity represents the opposite of what it represents to an Asian. I believe, whether we've realized it or not, that much of evangelism to Caucasians in the USA is operating with W1 or W2 models. Our gospel presentations have combatted rather than completed their cultural storyline. Their perception is that Jesus will take away their happy ending: they will be less free with Jesus. Our evangelism, deliberately or not, has been poorly contextualized.

Maybe this is the chance now to explore creative and new ways of operating with W3 or W4 models of evangelism to Caucasian Westerners. Let's hear their God-given, legitimate existential cries. Let's understand their storyline and show that we empathize with it. Then let's show them how Jesus is who they've been looking for. Let's find ways of showing them that they will have more freedom, and not less, if they follow Jesus.

## Further Thoughts on Gospel-Cultural Hermeneutics

Here are a few things to keep in mind as you seek to read texts and practice this hermeneutic:

1. Be sure to demonstrate understanding and empathy for the cultural storyline.
2. Try to use language, idioms, and metaphors from the culture.
3. Seek to identify the universal existential cry for love, belonging, freedom, transcendence, purpose, redemption, etc.
4. Try to show that Jesus is the true fulfillment of the cultural storyline, but in a winsome way that doesn't feel forced. This may require some creativity and thought.

But keep in mind that what works for one audience or culture likely won't work for another. The more we universalize our message so that it speaks to a wider audience, the less it will be well-contextualized. But the more we contextualize our message for a particular culture, the more it will be poorly contextualized for another culture. This means we need to be humble about our gospel presentations. The fact that it's worked so well with one particular group of people will mean that it will work less well with another group. And if another person uses another form or method of gospel presentation, we need to be less critical of their different form or method. Their form or method might be different from ours because it is better contextualized for their culture.

Perhaps you want to see more examples of how to employ this hermeneutic on cultural texts. If so, there are high quality examples in the essays in *Everyday Theology: How to Read Cultural Texts and Interpret Trends*.[4] I also have a blog called *Espresso Theology* (www.espressotheology.com), which aims to complete this exercise in short, sharp, sixty-second bursts.

 **From Cultural Text to Jesus**

For six examples of how to contextualize a message for a particular culture or community, watch the videos available at ZondervanAcademic.com.

To access this resource, register on the website as a student. Then sign in and download the resource from the "Study Resources" tab on the book page for *Evangelism in a Skeptical World*.

## CONCLUSION: PUTTING IT INTO PLAY

When Karen went with her friends to see plays, films, and paintings, at first she thought it was her Christian duty to find everything that was wrong or evil about these works. But Karen soon asked herself, "Am I reacting this way because they are wrong, or simply because it's not the culture I'm used to?"

So Karen decided to see these works of art as they really are: cultural texts which create and interpret worlds of meaning. What is the cultural storyline being told? What is the God-given existential cry of each work? Slowly she learned to exegete her new cultural world. She discovered God's fingerprints on the cultural texts through God's common grace and general revelation. There were seeds of the gospel. There were redemptive analogies.

---

4. Kevin J. Vanhoozer, Charles A. Anderson, and Michael J. Sleasman, eds., *Everyday Theology: How to Read Cultural Texts and Interpret Trends* (Grand Rapids, Mich.: Baker, 2007).

But much more than that, there was an existential cry for God-given, legitimate needs such as freedom, security, identity, status, love, belonging, hope, redemption, and purpose.

She realized that her unchurched friends were actually crying out to be fulfilled by Jesus. They just didn't know it. So Karen became skilled in showing to them, from the Bible, that Jesus is the fulfillment of their cultural storyline.

# CHAPTER 7

# STORYTELLING THE GOSPEL

## Once upon a time, there was a storyteller.

When Nathan went to college in the 1990s, he often volunteered to give the lunchtime Bible talks at the local campus Christian group. He followed the standard twenty-minute model for Bible talks: a two-minute introduction, fifteen minutes of Bible explanation, and three minutes of application at the end. During the middle of the week, he led Bible studies with the small groups. Again, these were standard Bible studies: the group read a passage from the Bible and then answered questions from a Bible-study booklet.

Nathan went on to study in seminary, where he learned the methods of propositional preaching and inductive Bible studies. But when he graduated from seminary and returned to campus ministry in the 2000s, he found that the methods he had learned in seminary were less effective than they were in the 1990s. Moreover, there were now more international students, and they responded poorly to his Bible-study method. Whenever Nathan asked a question, he was met by a wall of polite silence.

That's when a missionary friend explained to Nathan that most international students are concrete-relational learners. And with recent shifts in culture, media, and technology over the past two decades, the majority of Americans may also be concrete-relational learners as well. This simply means that they prefer learning from stories and not from abstract concepts. This missionary friend suggested to Nathan that he could try storytelling the gospel on campus. This way, whenever Nathan told the gospel, he was doing it in the heart language of the majority of the college students.

## TWO DIFFERENT STYLES OF LEARNING

If I say to you, "The water in our city has been contaminated, but if the water is first boiled, then it will be safe to drink," what will you do? Most of us will heed the advice to boil the water before we drink it.

But in many parts of the world, if that's all I said, those who heard me will continue to drink the water without boiling it first. What I need to do is tell them a story: "Mary and her children were drinking water from the tap and getting sick. One night Mary boiled her water, and from then on, she and her children no longer got sick when they drank it." Why is that? Because in this case, they learn better from hearing a story about how something works than from hearing an abstract theory that needs to be applied.

This is the difference between abstract—propositional, ideational, theoretical—learning, and concrete-relational learning. People who prefer abstract learning begin with theoretical concepts which are then applied. But people who prefer concrete-relational learning begin with stories of how things work, and from that they abstract a theory.

## WE HAVE TWO AUDIENCES

We evangelize two different audiences, with two different preferred learning styles.

Abstract learners are literate learners. They prefer reading. They learn from points. If they watch a movie, they want it explained. When they look at a painting or sculpture, they look at the written explanation next to it. If you tell them stories, they get impatient and want you to get to the point.

Concrete-relational learners are oral learners. They prefer listening or watching. They prefer the movie over the book. They learn from stories. If you don't tell them stories, they complain that you are dull, dry, boring, and "don't live in my world." If you explain a story to them, they feel patronized.

One style is not better than the other. They are merely different. And one style is not holier than the other. It's just that different learners prefer one style over the other.

The Bible gives us books for both styles of learning. Abstract learners will prefer reading the epistles in the New Testament. But concrete-relational learners will prefer the stories in the Old and New Testaments. Estimates are that four out of five people in the Western world prefer concrete-relational learning. And nine out of ten non-Westerners prefer concrete-relational learning. So if we wish to reach these majorities as evangelists, we should communicate more for the concrete-relational learners than for the abstract learners. Moreover, the content of the gospel—which is a story—is better suited to the form of storytelling than propositional communication.

If this is true, why is there sometimes pushback to using storytelling for evangelism, preaching, and teaching?[1] I believe it is largely because people evangelize the way they were evangelized. Or people get used to one style and then confuse this style with the gospel itself. They confuse orthopraxy with orthodoxy, form with content, and pedagogy with theology. The great irony is that when we talk about just preaching Christ crucified and not worrying about the need for a rhetorical method, we are, in effect, privileging one rhetorical method over any others—the abstract, ideational, propositional, logical, linear approach to communication.

It comes down to a preferred pedagogical sequence. Do we go from the abstract to the concrete, or the concrete to the abstract? Do we go from theory to practice, or practice to theory? Do we go from the universal to the particular, or the particular to the universal? There is no right or wrong way. There is no "you must do it this way or you're doing it the wrong way." They are just different ways. For different learners.

If you study a trade such as carpentry, plumbing, or building, you begin with the practice during the day, and then you go to night classes for the theory. The sequence is practice to theory, concrete to abstract, and particular to universal. But when I studied medicine as a doctor, I spent five years in medical school learning the theory—anatomy, physiology, and pathology. And then I graduated, worked as an intern in a hospital, and began the practice of medicine. The sequence was theory to practice, abstract to concrete, and universal to particular. This wasn't my preferred learning style. But after five years of med school, I got used to it and learned to tolerate it. And then I learned to teach the same way that I had been taught. I knew no other way.

We do the same when we train people for professional gospel ministry. We give them years of theory—Greek grammar, exegesis, theology—and then they begin the practice of ministry. So they learn abstract, proposi-tional, ideational thinking as their preferred learning style. And they teach the same way that they've been taught even though this might not be the

---

1. For example, David Cook equates storytelling to an attack on expository preaching! "The only thing new about the current attack on expository preaching is that which nominates to be its substitute—these days, it's narrative or storytelling," quoted in Gary Millar and Phil Campbell, *Saving Eutychus* (Kingsford, AU: Matthias, 2013), ii.

preferred learning style of most of their listeners. They know no other way. And orthopraxy gets confused with orthodoxy.

I find it interesting that since I've left med school, the pedagogical pendulum has swung the other way. I've heard from med students who are studying today that a lot of med school is now case-based learning. They begin with a case—a story from a patient—from which they have to generate a theory of how to diagnose and treat the patient. So change is possible!

## HOW DO STORIES WORK?

How do stories work? Stories work by doing at least two things. First, they communicate concepts without using the words for those concepts. For example, imagine I tell you the story of Icarus:

> Icarus was a strong young man. One day, his father made him wings from feathers and wax. His father told him, "With these wings you can fly, but whatever you do, don't fly too close to the sun. Otherwise the wax will melt and you will fall to your death."
>
> So Icarus put on the wings, flapped his arms, and began to fly. As he flew, he became pleased with himself. "Look at me! Look at me!" he thought. He kept flying higher and higher and higher. But eventually he got too close to the sun. The wax on his wings melted, and the feathers fell off. With that, Icarus fell to his death.

What does this story teach us? Most of us would say something about pride, arrogance, or hubris. But did you notice that the story itself never uses the words pride, arrogance, or hubris? We all got the point of the story even though I didn't spell it out. Stories can teach us complicated concepts without even using the words for those concepts.[2]

Second, stories make the listener see through the worldview of the narrator. As we listen to the story, we assume the narrator's standpoint. For example, as we listen to the story of Icarus, we take on the implicit worldview of the story:

- Parents are authority figures who should be respected and honored.
- Pride is a moral failing.
- By and large, disobeying authority figures will lead to bad consequences.

2. I owe this insight to Abe Kurivilla.

We might not agree with the narrator's worldview. But for the story to work, as we listen we have to set aside our worldview and assume that of the narrator.

Stories also ask the listener to "suspend disbelief." For example, in the story of Icarus, we are asked to suspend disbelief that a human could ever fly by strapping on wings and flapping their arms fast enough. Technically, the listener is being asked to suspend disbelief appropriate to the genre of the storytelling. For example, Icarus is from the genre of Greek mythology. And it is appropriate for us to suspend our disbelief about humans flying with wings in Greek mythology. But it is not appropriate for us to suspend our disbelief about UFOs and time travel in Greek mythology. For example, if Icarus suddenly jumped into a UFO and traveled forward in time, then we would not be prepared to suspend our disbelief for that.

Correspondingly, when we watch a television show like *Dr. Who*, we are asked to suspend our disbelief about UFOs and time travel because this is appropriate for the genre of science fiction. But if Dr. Who suddenly strapped on wings made of feathers and wax, flapped his arms, and flew, then we would not be prepared to suspend disbelief for that, because that is not appropriate for the genre of science fiction.

In the same way, when we tell the stories from the Bible, the listener is asked to suspend their disbelief about Jesus, miracles, and people rising from the dead. This is appropriate for the genre of gospel story. But whether or not our listener is prepared to grant us that is another story! It all comes down to what genre our listener believes is the gospel—is it mythology, science fiction, or God's story for them?

One night I was watching TV. A current-affairs show aired a ten-minute story about a family—Stephen, Rachel, and two children—who were very busy with work, sports, and other errands. They were so busy that they had no time to go grocery shopping. Now they were trying out online shopping. It showed Stephen and Rachel going to a supermarket's website and putting in an order for their week's groceries. It then showed the shopkeeper at that supermarket receiving their online order—for bananas, bread, and milk. It then showed the shopkeeper filling a basket with fresh bananas, bread, and milk. The shopkeeper looked into the TV camera and said, "Whenever I fill out one of these orders, I pretend I'm shopping for myself and put in only the fruit, bread, and milk that I would buy for myself." It then showed the shopkeeper loading the groceries onto a truck, and then the truck driver delivered the fresh groceries to the family. Stephen and Rachel were very impressed and said that they were going to do their shopping online from now on.

What did I just see? An advertisement for online grocery shopping, of course! But the TV show didn't preach propositions at me: "Try out online shopping because it's cheap, reliable, and convenient." Instead, it told me a story of people using online shopping: "Look at Stephen and Rachel doing online shopping!" And from the story I could see that it was cheap, reliable, and convenient. And I was able to make the concrete-relational connection: if it worked for Stephen and Rachel, it might also work for me.

This is implicit learning rather than explicit. Concrete-relational rather than abstract. It answers the question, "How does it work?" If you are a concrete-relational learner, then you will have understood what the TV story was doing to you. But if you were an abstract learner, you would have been annoyed and asked, "What was all that about? Where's the moral to the story? Where's the explanation?" because you want to hear what the TV story is saying to you.

 **What Learning Style Are You?**

For fun, we can take this test to see what our preferred learning style is. Are we a literate (abstract) or an oral (concrete-relational) learner? Download a PDF questionnaire to find out your own learning style at ZondervanAcademic.com.

To access this resource, register on the website as a student. Then sign in and download the resource from the "Study Resources" tab on the book page for *Evangelism in a Skeptical World*.

## HOW TO TELL THE GOSPEL WITH STORYTELLING

So how do you do this? What I'd like to share with you is an adaptation I've developed of a method of storytelling the gospel, one I learned from missionary friends such as Christine Dillon, Andrew Wong, Aaron Koh, John G., Wycliffe Bible Translators, and the International Orality Network. If you want to learn more about this, I recommend that you begin by reading Christine Dillon's book[3] and website,[4] visiting the ION website,[5] or

---

3. Christine Dillon, *Telling the Gospel through Story: Evangelism That Keeps Hearers Wanting More* (Downers Grove, Ill.: InterVarsity, 2012).

4. storyingthescriptures.com.

5. orality.net.

enrolling in a Wycliffe Bible Storytelling Workshop. After you have those basics down, you will be able to adapt their methods to find something that suits you and the culture you are seeking to reach.

In what follows, I'll teach you my preferred way of doing this, but don't think this is the only way. Over the years, it has worked well for me. But I hope that you discover your own way.

## Learning to Tell a Story from the Bible

Start by choosing a story from the Bible. The following are a few of the passages that I have used that work well when you are getting started.

### Examples

| | | |
|---|---|---|
| Genesis 1 | Matthew 20:1–6 | Luke 12:13–21 |
| Genesis 2 | Matthew 22:1–14 | Luke 14:15–24 |
| Genesis 3 | Mark 2:1–17 | Luke 15:1–31 |
| Genesis 4 | Mark 15:1–39 | Luke 18:9–34 |
| Genesis 6–9 | Luke 5:12–32 | John 11:1–43 |
| Genesis 11:1–9 | Luke 7:36–50 | John 20 |
| Genesis 12 | Luke 8:4–56 | Acts 16:12–34 |

If I had time to meet with someone over several weeks, I would begin in Genesis and slowly work my way through the Old Testament before getting to the New Testament. But often I have only one meeting with someone, so most of my passages are from the New Testament because I want to get them talking about Jesus. At the same time, I understand the tension this raises, that without the Old Testament, it might be hard for someone to understand who Jesus really is.

After you have chosen a passage, read it carefully several times. The goal is to retell the story in your own words. You don't have to memorize the story word for word from the Bible. Just remember the scenes from the Bible story and then retell those scenes.

I do this by first reading three different translations of the passage. Typically I pick a literal translation like the ESV, then a dynamic-equivalent translation like the NIV or NLT, and finally a paraphrase version like *The Message*. I then learn to retell the passage in my own words, using vocabulary that the listener and I would comfortably use in an everyday conversation. Sometimes I also "storyboard" the story by drawing it in cartoon form. Then I memorize how the scenes look and retell the scenes without the visuals, using my own words.

Next, I practice retelling the story to another person who has the Bible passage in front of them. They can correct whatever errors I make. The aim is to retell the story according to the following guidelines (the acronym, which I find easy to remember, is SAM):

*Simple:* Use only words that the listener understands (e.g., change "Pharisee" to "religious leader," "synagogue" to "place of worship"). Use a maximum of three names of persons. (If the story talks about Jesus, Jairus, John, James, and Peter, you can change it to Jesus, Jairus, and three of Jesus' closest disciples.)

*Accurate:* You can simplify the story by leaving out some things—place names, names of persons, details about a particular location—but don't add things to embellish the story.

*Memorable:* Retell the story in a memorable way. What's memorable? Feel free to use facial expressions, body language, and actions to get the emotion and the drama in the story across to your listeners.

Now tell the story to your listener. You can use an introduction like, "Here's a story from the Bible that helps explain what I believe. I'm going to tell it, and then afterward we can talk about it." In informal situations, such as a conversation, I tell the story once. But in formal situations, such as a public talk or a small-group Bible study, I tell the story three times. I tell them, "I'm going to tell a story from the Bible three times. The first time, I want us to imagine the story. The second time, I want us to remember the story. And the third time, you're going to help me retell the story. Listen carefully, because you're going to help me retell it, and we'll also talk some more about the story afterward."

For another variation, I tell the story once or twice, and then my listeners, in pairs, can have a go at retelling the story to each other. Sometimes I also ask for volunteers to retell the story in front of the whole group. Whenever there is a pause or gap in memory, the rest of the group can help the volunteer retell the rest of the story. Or someone else can take over from where the last person decided to stop.

## Leading the Discussion

After telling the story, we can ask the listener these questions to generate discussion:

1. What impressed you about the story?
2. What questions do you want answered from the story?
3. What does the story teach us about people?
4. What does the story teach us about Jesus (or God)?
5. What is God teaching you from this story?

Here are some guidelines I suggest for doing this in more formal situations to a group of people. First, before telling the story from the Bible, I sometimes tell the listeners that this is an exercise in postliterate learning, so it works better if they don't look at their books, Bibles, and computer screens; instead they should look at me. And then I warn them that there will be questions afterward, so they need to listen carefully.

Second, after telling the story, I ask the first question and get listeners to discuss it in pairs, because this generates peer-to-peer discussion (removing any perceived teacher-student hierarchy) and it gives them the warrant to talk out aloud.

Third, I get listeners to share their answers with the whole group. This gives them the warrant to talk out loud. Along those lines, I resist the temptation to comment on or summarize what they have said. This removes me—the teacher—as the all-knowing expert from the discussion. It keeps the discussion at a peer-to-peer level. And more important, it means that I will not patronize their answers, nor will I shame them if they say something that I perceive to be wrong.

After they've shared, I repeat the process for the second question.

Note that the sequence of the questions is important. The first question, "What impressed you about the story?" is a safe question for which there is no wrong answer. The second question, "What questions do you want answered from the story?" is also a safe question for which there is no wrong answer. Start with these safe questions to encourage discussion.

In addition, when someone shares a question they want answered from the story, I won't answer it. I listen to everyone's questions first, then I choose some of the good questions and have the whole group break into pairs and report their answers to everyone. In this way, the group is responsible for helping each other to learn. And again, it removes me from the discussion as the all-knowing expert.

Sometimes, if no one has asked what I think is a significant question, I say, "I've got a question." I ask my question and then get everyone back into pairs to discuss my question and share their answers with the group.

If it's a large group—say more than twenty-five—then I get only ten to twelve people (five to six pairs) to share their answers for each question.

Why do this? Why so many details and rules to follow for a simple discussion? Because I've found that people prefer a dialogue to a monologue for learning. Often it's hard to generate discussions because the traditional inductive Bible-study method is patronizing for most learners. It becomes a "guess the answer in my head" exercise, where the Bible-study leader coaches the participants to say what the answer should be from the leader's perspective. And non-Western learners also don't like answering questions out aloud. They may be quiet processors rather than loud ones.[6] I know that in Asian cultures, students are reticent to respond because they don't want to shame the teacher. The teacher is the expert, and by speaking up, they are being disrespectful. But speaking up also risks shaming themselves. What if they answer out aloud and it's not the answer that the teacher is expecting? Especially if the teacher does one of those "guess the answer in my head" responses.

Another example of how to lead a discussion: I lead Bible studies at a high-school ski camp that I've spoken at for several years now, with usually around forty to fifty campers in attendance, most of whom are not Christians. We ski in the morning, then we meet for lunch and I give some Bible talks. Then we ski again in the afternoon, and after that, we break up into small discussion groups before dinner.

For the lunchtime Bible talks, I do gospel storytelling. One year I shared the following stories at lunchtime:

Monday: Luke 5:17–32
Tuesday: Luke 7:36–50
Wednesday: Luke 8:22–56
Thursday: Luke 8:4–15
Friday: Matthew 20:1–16

For the first three talks, I tell the students that I am going to tell them the story three times. The first time through, they are to imagine the story. The second time through, they need to remember the story. And the third time, I want them to help me retell the story.

Then, for the final two talks, we repeat this process, except that on

---

6. Hazel Rose Markus and Alana Conner, *Clash! Eight Cultural Conflicts That Make Us Who We Are* (New York: Hudson, 2013), 1–4.

the third time, I have them retell the story to a friend. And then we go through it one last time with a brave volunteer retelling the story to the entire group. At the end of the day, before dinner, the teenagers break up into their small groups, read the story we looked at during lunch, and go through a set of questions:[7]

1.  What shocked or surprised you in the story?
2.  What don't you understand in the story?
3.  What would you say is the main idea in the story?
4.  What does the story teach you about God, Jesus, and yourself?
5.  If the story is true, how will you live differently?

I've used this method each year that I've spoken at the camp. The teens are friendly, engaged, and intrigued by the stories, and they look forward to the talks. Many want to investigate further, and many become Christians by the end of the week.

Another example is an international hot-pot dinner I attended in the past. Most of the students who attended were from Asia studying for postgraduate degrees. Some were also specialist medical doctors, about twenty-five people altogether, with about one-third of them non-Christians and the other two-thirds practicing Christians. Before the hot-pot dinner, a speaker would storytell Genesis 1–4. They would do this for several meetings, recapping the same stories each week. We didn't cover any discussion questions during those weeks. After several weeks of this, we'd have a speaker talk during dinner and share the story of Noah and the flood from Genesis 6–9. Most of the non-Christians were hearing this story for the first time, and after the story was told, the speaker would ask the five discussion questions I use at the camp, and everyone would pair up to answer them.

The discussion was lively, lasting for more than ninety minutes. I often had to leave at 11:00 p.m., and I typically was one of the first to leave. What was remarkable was that even though one-third of those attending were non-Christians, the dialectic of the conversation always seemed to lead us toward an orthodox Christian answer without any input from the Christian leader who was facilitating the discussion.

Sometimes when I get invited to speak at a church or conference to give a Bible talk, I use an alternate version of the storytelling method. I introduce the talk by saying, "Studies show that most of us are concrete-relational

7. I learned these from my pastor, Ariel Kurilowicz.

learners. We learn better by listening to stories. So I'm going to do something that cross-cultural workers have been doing in many other countries. I'm going to tell us a story from the Bible. When I tell you the story, it works better if you just look at me and listen. But if reading is your preferred learning style, then feel free to follow along in the Bible. But for most of us, listening is our preferred learning style, so just watch me and listen."

I tell the story two or three times and break the group into pairs for the discussion questions. This works even in a very large group. I then walk down from the stage into the audience and take the microphone with me. I get people to share their answers into the microphone so that everyone can hear what they are saying. For each question, I get about six pairs to answer before moving on. I explain, "I'm really excited to hear what everyone has to say, but because this is a large group, I can hear from only a few pairs at a time."

In my experience, the storytelling model works best if you have at least one-third non-Christians in the group, with another two-thirds Christians. If possible, pair up a non-Christian with a Christian. This way, the non-Christians get to hear from the Christian perspective. Second, you should realize that the story you tell will generate its own questions. It's the Bible's own story that generates discussion rather than the questions of systematic theology or a particular application that you have in mind. For example, when I told the story of Noah and the flood, one person asked, "What about the dinosaurs?" Another person, a non-Christian, answered, "But the story doesn't say anything about dinosaurs, so it's not relevant."

As another example, the wording in Genesis 6 says, "And God saw how wicked humankind had become . . . and he regretted making them. . . . and he said, 'I will wipe them out from the face of the earth'" (Gen. 6:5–7). After hearing that, no one has asked the question, "But how can a loving God punish people?" That's a question generated by abstract, speculative questions about theology. But in the context of the story, it makes perfect sense that God wipes out wicked humankind.

Keep in mind that people will also generate questions from their own contexts. That's a good thing! In this way, we end up answering questions relevant to each person's existential, emotional, and cultural contexts. This ends up being contextualized evangelism. And people will also answer from their own perspective, so everyone is enriched by the experience. For example, listening to the story of the woman who is healed by Jesus and the story of Jairus's dead daughter (Luke 8:40–56), people from Middle Eastern cultures often pick up on how both the woman and the dead daughter were unclean. So when the woman touches Jesus, and when Jesus touches the dead daughter, it is remarkable that Jesus himself doesn't also become unclean. They also pick up on the woman's shame and how she is publicly restored by Jesus. That's why Jesus stops to say, "Who touched me?" because it will give the woman a public opportunity to be declared clean. An indigenous Australian once told me that the funeral for Jairus's dead daughter would have gone for days, so when Jesus told the parents not to tell anyone that their daughter had been raised back to life, he was focusing on how it would've been really hard for the parents to explain why the funeral had been canceled, something I had never considered before.

And that's an additional blessing to this method. You will gain a deeper appreciation for the nuances of Bible stories as you memorize and retell them. As I was repeatedly telling the story of the jailer in Acts 16, I picked up on how Paul and Silas told the jailer and his family to "believe in the Lord Jesus" (Acts 16:31). But then I noticed that the story ends with the jailer rejoicing that he and his family had "come to believe in God" (Acts 16:34). In the story, a connection is subtly made between believing in Jesus and believing in God. They are the same thing!

Storytelling has the added benefit of explaining complex theological concepts without complicated language. For example, consider the series of stories in Luke 18—the widow who looks for justice (v. 3), the Son of Man who looks for faith (v. 8), the Pharisee who trusted in his righteousness (vv. 9–12), the tax collector who asks for God's mercy (v. 13), the children who come to Jesus (vv. 15–17), the rich ruler who cannot enter the kingdom of God (vv. 18–25), salvation being impossible without God (vv. 26–27), Jesus' predicting his death (vv. 31–33), and finally a beggar who calls out for mercy and has his eyes opened (vv. 35–43). All of these communicate the theological idea of justification not by works but by the means of faith based on the atoning, substitutionary death of Jesus Christ. But they do it without using those words or terms. It's the same idea, only in story form.

## CONCLUSION: STORYTELLING IN ACTION

Nathan read books, visited websites, and participated in online forums that promoted gospel storytelling. He practiced storytelling with his missionary friend, who also ran a home Bible study group for those who were not churched but wanted to learn more about the Bible. Nathan's friend invited him to lead the next Bible study group by using the storytelling method.

Nathan was nervous, but the night was amazing. Many of the people in the group had not been to church before, nor were they Christians. Many were professionals with postgraduate degrees, yet they were so engaged by the storytelling that they covered four stories that night instead of the one Nathan had planned. The discussion was lively and went on for most of the night. And all who turned up were curious to hear more from the Bible and looked forward to coming back the next week.

CHAPTER 8

# HOW TO GIVE EVANGELISTIC TOPICAL TALKS

## Beer, sex, and Santa Claus

A lison is a seminary student studying for her MDiv. Her church has organized an end-of-year evangelistic event for women, and the theme is health. They have booked a health clinic as the venue, and they expect about fifty women to show up, twenty of whom are not Christians. The night will begin with a team of doctors giving free medical checkups to all the women who turn up. Then a personal trainer will give a talk on exercise. Then a nutritionist will give a talk on healthy eating. The organizers have asked Alison to give a twenty-minute evangelistic talk. Her talk will come at the end of the night after the medical checkups and the talks from the personal trainer and nutritionist.

But how should Alison present her talk? If she tries to give a standard Bible talk or a typical evangelistic presentation, then she risks making those who attend feeling like the night was a "bait and switch." You turn up for the free health information and—surprise—you get a Bible talk instead. And if she focuses on giving a more topical talk about God's plan for good health or why we should take care of our bodies, what should she say? If she says that Jesus is more important than our physical health, this will seem to devalue the work being done by the doctors, the personal trainer, and the nutritionist. How can Alison give a talk, staying on topic for the night's activities, and still be evangelistic?

Many Christians are comfortable using a Bible passage to tell the story of Jesus. But often we're in situations where we can't just make the jump to Jesus from the current conversation. We want to naturally and smoothly move from an extrabiblical topic to the story of Jesus. In this chapter I'll outline some principles and methods for doing this, as well as some suggestions for giving evangelistic topical talks.

## ARE TOPICAL TALKS OKAY?

When I taught at seminary, one of my students was a Qantas airline pilot. Because he was a seminary student, he had been invited to be the guest speaker at a men's evangelistic breakfast on a Saturday morning, so he decided to give a standard Bible talk. He had something prepared from a passage in Ephesians, an introduction, three points explaining the passage, and then a conclusion with some application.

He tested the talk on me first. And the talk was okay. It was certainly faithful to the Bible text, but I doubted it would hold the men's attention at 8:00 a.m. on a Saturday morning. I said to him, "You're a pilot! Talk about planes. Talk about your experience of flying jumbo planes from Australia to the USA. The guys will probably find that pretty interesting."

He agreed with me, and he ended up delivering a topical talk on flying. He started the talk by showing several images of planes. The men stopped eating. They could not take their eyes off the planes he showed them. Then he shared some stories about flying the planes. He told a story about one of his friends who liked to lean out of the open doors of a cargo plane while it was flying. His friend was strapped in by a safety harness and he knew that he couldn't fall out of the plane. He did this fairly often and got used to leaning out, held only by the strap. One day, his friend leaned out of the plane, and at the very last second realized that he had forgotten to strap himself in. He barely managed to catch his balance and fell to the floor. For the rest of that flight, he was dead silent and white faced, knowing that he had almost died that day. After sharing that story, my friend had set up his main point: all of us "are destined to die once, and after that to face judgment" (Heb. 9:27).

He finished with a story of what it's like to pilot the takeoff of a fully laden jumbo jet. He said that when you take off, you must pull back the flight controller to lift up the nose of the plane. There are always a few nervous seconds after you do this when nothing happens. The nose does not lift up. And then you pass a point of no return after which you cannot abort the takeoff. After this point, you have one option: to trust that the nose will lift even though you can't see it happening yet. If you abort the takeoff after this point, the plane will shoot past the runway, ploughing through the suburban houses next to the airport, possibly killing hundreds of people.

That lift-off moment is a moment of faith. You can't see the nose lifting up, but you have to trust that it will. If you don't have faith, you will die, and many others may as well! My friend used this to illustrate another key point: "Faith is confidence in what we hope for and assurance about what we do not see" (Heb. 11:1).

It was a stunning talk. The men were gripped by his message. It was interesting. It hit beneath the surface and spoke to their hearts. Many of the men approached him afterward wanting to talk more about what he had shared. But was it a successful talk from an evangelistic perspective? It was a topical talk, not an expository Bible talk. He used some Scriptures, but he didn't spend much time explaining them and showing connections to the text. Should he have done that instead? Isn't this an example of someone who has lost confidence in the Bible? Doesn't the Bible speak for itself? Isn't it God's Word, a message that cuts to the heart? Isn't it the Bible, the message of the gospel that has the power to save? Was my friend guilty of trying to make the Bible relevant when the Bible already is relevant?

## TYPICAL ARGUMENTS AGAINST TOPICAL PREACHING

When I was studying my PhD at Trinity Evangelical Divinity School in the north suburbs of Chicago, a Russian student preached a topical sermon at our chapel service. He introduced his sermon with a joke: "In Russia, we have a saying. 'You are allowed to preach a topical sermon. But only once. And after that you must repent immediately.'"

Everyone laughed because this isn't just true of the Russian Christians. Many people's traditions teach that topical talks are inferior to expository Bible talks. In some contexts, topical talks aren't just inferior; they are wrong and unbiblical. So before I share what I believe are the advantages of using this communication method with skeptics, let's look at some of the typical arguments for this perspective.

### Let the Bible Talk!

Some who argue that we must have only expository Bible talks say that by working our way through a Bible passage, we let the Bible set the agenda, not our sense of what should be said or the needs of the audience. When we choose a topic, the focus shifts away from the Bible to the needs of people; it's human centered, not God centered. We are letting our human context—our existential, emotional, cultural, and situational needs—set the agenda.

This is a question of what theologians call prolegomena, and it is connected to the inductive versus deductive debate about theological methodology.[1] To say it more plainly: Should we move inductively from the Bible text to our world of ideas? Or do we move deductively from our world of ideas to the Bible? Every Christian wants to say that we should only go inductively from the Bible text to our world of ideas. After all, this lets the Bible set the agenda.

## Bible Passage → Exegesis → Biblical Theology → Systematic Theology

But this approach naively assumes that we are blank slates who approach the Bible passage without prior systems, grids, traditions, theologies, and interpretive lenses. In reality, we always approach the text deductively as well as inductively. Don Carson notes, "Although in terms of authority status there needs to be an outward-tracing line from Scripture through exegesis toward biblical theology to systematic theology . . . in reality various 'back loops' are generated, [with] each discipline influencing the others."[2]

Does this mean we throw our hands up in despair and retreat to agnosticism? "How can we ever know what the Bible says if we can't escape our subjective interpretations?" No. Because it doesn't have to be an either-or approach. It can be a both-and.

We can utilize a dialogical or abductive approach to the Bible.[3] This simply means that we start out acknowledging our presuppositions. We are honest about our starting point, and we have a back-and-forth methodology where the biblical text dialogues with our interpretive lenses, and our interpretive lenses dialogue with the text.

Second, this is also a debate about the appropriate role of systematic theology. Should we be allowed to use only the tools of grammatico-historical exegesis, where we describe and explain the words of the biblical text? Or can we also utilize the tools of systematic theology, where we prescribe

---

1. Excellent discussions by Don Carson, "Systematic Theology and Biblical Theology," in *New Dictionary of Biblical Theology*, ed. T. Desmond Alexander, Brian S. Rosner, D. A. Carson, Graeme Goldsworthy (Downers Grove, Ill.: InterVarsity, 2000), 89–104; and David Clark, *To Know and Love God: Method for Theology* (Wheaton, Ill.: Crossway, 2003), 48–51.

2. Carson, "Systematic Theology and Biblical Theology," 102.

3. For example, Clark, *To Know and Love God*, 51.

concepts generated by the biblical text, though not necessarily using the exact words of the Bible? As Don Carson notes, if we use only the tools of exegesis, then "the biblical scholar who is narrowly constrained by the exegetical field of discourse may be in danger of denying [biblical doctrines]."[4] If we don't grant the legitimacy of utilizing systematic theology in evangelism, then it raises some interesting problems for us. How do we talk about the Trinity when there is no word for this in the biblical text?[5] Can we rely on this as a shorthand for a theological concept, or must we show the trinitarian reality of God from the Bible every time we want to talk about it? To push this even farther, at what point is it acceptable to utilize an English translation of the Bible without clearly explaining how we arrived at the translation, since translations are themselves conceptual translations generated by the original Greek and Hebrew texts of the Bible? We could no longer grant that our English translations are the Word of God, since they don't use the exact words of God in the original texts.

Obviously, I'm pushing the point to show some of the extremes. Let's assume, in good faith, that the objector to topical talks grants the legitimacy of systematic theology and English translations of the Bible. At what point is it okay to utilize concepts to draw connections instead of focusing on each and every word or translation nuance of the text?

My point is that most talk about expository versus topical preaching is based on a false dichotomy. All expository sermons have elements of topical preaching that are used within the talk itself. In a typical expository sermon, the preacher will introduce a topic or question that the text will answer. The preacher will then demonstrate how the text is still relevant today. And then the preacher will usually end the sermon with some words of application. These basic elements are not all that different from the elements of topical preaching; it's just that in an expository sermon, the ratio of topical to exposition might be 20 percent to 80 percent, whereas in a topical sermon the ratio might be flipped the other way.

This means that we're talking about a question of pedagogy rather than theological orthodoxy. It's a question that acknowledges the need for contextualization of the message. What is the best, most effective, most

---

4. D. A. Carson, "The Vindication of Imputation: On Fields of Discourse and Semantic Fields," in *Justification: What's at Stake in the Current Debates*, ed. Mark Husbands and Daniel J. Treier (Downers Grove, Ill.: InterVarsity, 2004), 49.

5. Brian S. Rosner uses the examples of "grace," "exclusion," and "gentleness" as concepts that are "far bigger than the words normally used [in the Bible] to refer to it." Brian S. Rosner, "Biblical Theology," in *New Dictionary of Biblical Theology*, ed. Alexander, Rosner, Carson, Goldsworthy, 6.

contextualized way to communicate the gospel to this particular audience at this particular time and place? What ratio of concrete, particular examples versus abstract explanation will work best for our audience? For example, if it's a Sunday church service, then a traditional expository talk may work very well. The audience will have a certain level of biblical knowledge, perhaps, or you can rely on them to have certain theological concepts and understandings and not have to explain or illustrate them to communicate. But what works on Sunday morning may not translate to a talk on a street corner or at a party. There will be times, places, and audiences where we might have to be more topical to be contextualized.

The objection to topical messages also reveals a confusion about what we mean when we talk about the Word of God. When the New Testament refers to the Word of God, it is referring to the gospel message, not the method employed to preach that message. So whenever we preach the gospel—either in expository or topical form—the Word is still being preached. And if we understand the gospel to be the Word of God, and the Word of God to be not just the text but a speech act, then we locate the gospel not just in the words being used but also in the speech act being performed. It is the preached Word, and both how we communicate and the text itself matter. Topical preaching, as well as expository preaching, can both perform the speech act of the gospel. If the locution is the gospel message, and it is accompanied by the appropriate illocutionary force, then Christ crucified has been preached.[6] To insist that we must privilege one form of communication over another is to confuse orthopraxy with orthodoxy, form with content, method with message, and pedagogy with theology. It is also a failure to recognize that we are all influenced by our culture. The traditional expository Bible talk is a product of Western, logical, linear, Enlightenment, and inductive communication, so when we accuse anyone else of "selling out" to culture and "trying to make the Bible relevant," we must also be attuned to our own failure to see that we might be doing the same thing. Are we like the American who cannot hear his own accent, who laughs at the funny way everyone else speaks English?

Like that American who can't hear his accent, we all need to adjust to our audience, whether we know it or not. The moment we decide to use an English translation of the Bible instead of the original Greek or Hebrew, we've decided to accommodate our audience's situation. The instant we

---

6. For a much more robust defense of this, see my book *Preaching as the Word of God: Answering an Old Question with Speech-Act Theory* (Eugene, Ore.: Pickwick, 2016).

decide which English translation to use, we've decided to accommodate our audience's situation. In deciding which passage in the Bible to use—John 3 instead of Mark 3—we're deciding to accommodate our audience's situation. There are not some people who are more God centered than others. We're all a mix of both human-centered and God-centered methods and motives. We are talking about God, but we also have to talk to another human being as a human who has human concerns and needs and obstacles. We can't avoid this. And again, the key point to recognize is that we all do it whether we know it or not. The charge of being human centered sets up a false dichotomy, as if it is a black-and-white issue. Instead of choosing one or the other, we must all be both at the same time, adjusting what we emphasize based on our audience and context so that we most clearly and accurately communicate God's truth to those we seek to reach.

## EVERY CHOICE IS A DECISION TO CONTEXTUALIZE

Opponents of topical preaching point out that it lets the audience set the agenda, that it is human centered, and that it shows a lack of trust in the Bible itself. We should let the Bible speak for itself.

Yet when I preach an expository Bible talk at a church, the organizers usually ask me for a title for my talk. But a title is actually a summary of the topic. The title itself is an example of topical preaching! Then they will ask me what my Bible passage is going to be. Or they might choose a passage for me. But by choosing a passage—whether I'm doing it or the organizers—we are being human centered. Shouldn't the Bible speak to us on its own terms; shouldn't we flip randomly to a page that God ordains each morning? I think you see my point.

As I've pointed out already, we are using an English Bible. But shouldn't we let the Greek and Hebrew Bible speak to us on its own terms? Why let the audience set the agenda by using their language and idioms and not the original text of the Bible?

The last thing I'll say about this is that when a person says we cannot have topical talks, they are giving me a topical talk about what the Bible teaches, a point that cannot be sustained by any expository Bible talk. Show me the verse in the Bible that says we can't do topical talks and you might finally convince me.

## ONE GREAT BIG TOPICAL TALK

The Bible itself is one big topical talk. Each book is written to a particular audience at a particular time in a particular place. That's why there are sixty-six books. They are written to address particular needs, existential cries, and topics.

For example, Paul wrote his first letter to the Corinthians to address specific issues inside that church. Moreover, he introduced sections with "Now, for the matters you wrote about . . ." (1 Cor. 7:1). Paul was writing to answer their questions. He was letting them set the agenda.

Jesus had different answers for different people. To Nicodemus, Jesus talked about being "born again" (John 3:3). But to the woman at the well, Jesus offered "living water" (John 4:10). So Jesus was letting the audience set the agenda.

We are being disingenuous in saying that we must never set the agenda, because the instant we choose a particular passage from the Bible over another, we are letting our preferences or those of our audiences affect our decision.

## HOW TO PREPARE A TOPICAL EVANGELISTIC TALK

So let's assume that you are convinced that there is a time and a place for giving a topical evangelistic talk. What do you do? How do you choose a topic? How do you connect that to the Bible? Where do you begin?

### Step 1: Move from the Topic to a Big Idea

For the sake of clear communication, all talks should have a single, coherent, unified "big idea." In an expository Bible talk, we typically use the Bible passage to generate the big idea. But how do we generate a big idea for a topical talk? We move through a different sequence:

### Topic → Issue → Argument (for a specific point)

*Start with Your Topic*

Sometimes when you are asked to speak somewhere, the organizers of the event will give you a topic. At other times, you might have to come up with your own topic. What do I mean by a topic? Here are some examples. You might want to talk about:

**Health:** I was once invited to speak at a men's health night run by a church on a Thursday night, complete with advice from doctors, nutritionists, personal trainers, and finally me.

**Beer:** I was once invited to speak at a beer appreciation night. The organizers had a beer-brewing demonstration. Samples of beer were served with food. A beer expert gave a talk on beers from different countries. And then there was a 5–10 minute talk from me.

**Pleasure:** I often give talks to workers either in their workplaces or in public spaces such as a bar, a café, or an auditorium. To attract them to the talks, we advertise relevant topics such as "The Secret to Extraordinary Pleasure."

**Success:** I was asked to give talks to workers fresh out of college at a bar on a Monday night. Again, to attract them to the talk, we advertised a topic such as "How to Hack Success before It Hacks You."

**Christmas:** I might get asked to speak at a church's carols night and need to deliver a short talk to families who don't usually come to church. Or I might get invited by workers to their workplace to give a lunchtime talk on the topic of Christmas.

But a topic alone will not make a talk interesting. If I just get up and talk about a topic, I will probably put you to sleep. "Today I'm going to talk about health," or, "Today I'm going to talk about the real meaning of Christmas." Zzzzzzzzzz. See, I've lost you already.

### Define the Issue

So we need to convert the topic to an issue. What's the existential or emotional connection someone might have to that topic? What problems does it create? What's culturally relevant about that topic? Where does this topic meet the felt needs of real people, especially those in your audience? Here are some examples of issues:

- "I'm getting older. How can I stay healthy so that I can keep up with my grandchildren?"
- "I like beer. How can I get more enjoyment out of having a beer?"
- "We all like to feel good. But over time, the ordinary pleasure of life can start to feel . . . ordinary. How do you find extraordinary pleasure?"

- "How do you define success? What are you doing to get there? How can you be successful in life and in work?"
- "Christmas comes and goes every year. How can I be blessed this Christmas?"

### Argue for a Point

Now that we have our issue, we need to think about how to argue toward a point. This is where the true skill of topical speaking engages. We have to come up with a point to argue for, but how do I know if I have a good point? We know we have a good point if it (1) answers the question raised by the issue, (2) has an obvious opposite point, and (3) can be supported by appeals to evidence and stories. Here are some examples:

- "Being healthy means looking after all aspects of health—physical, emotional, and spiritual."
- "No one enjoys drinking alone; the perfect beer is one drunk with a friend."
- "Pleasure comes not so much from what we do but who we're with at the time."
- "Success is more a gift from God than something we earn."
- "God wants to bless us at Christmas."

We could leave it at that. But because these are going to be evangelistic topical talks, our big idea will be:

- "We need to be healthy toward God."
- "Beer is a gift from God to be enjoyed in a right relationship with God."
- "True pleasure comes from being with God."
- "The ultimate success that matters is being right with God."
- "God's blessing comes to us as the gift of his Son, Jesus."

This point is the big idea of our talk. It's the ten-second elevator pitch, the unifying, organizing principle that will give our talk coherence.

### Step 2: Outline a Bird's-Eye View of the Talk

Let's say the talk is 20–25 minutes. The macro structure or outline of your talk might be an introduction, a body, a bridge, and a conclusion.

**Introduction (3–5 minutes):** Tell a winsome, self-deprecating story that will:
- get our audience's attention
- set up the topic
- raise the issue
- promise an answer (our point; but don't reveal it yet!)
- maybe give an outline of the structure of our talk

**Body (10–15 minutes):** Bit by bit we will reveal our point. I'll share more on this in the next step.

**Bridge (1–3 minutes):** The bridge sums up everything we have said until now, including the topic, the issue, and the point we have made as the answer to the issue.

**Conclusion (3–5 minutes):** We apply the point with a story that either illustrates or is an example of the point we have made.

Every talk will have its nuances and may deviate from this basic formula, but when you have a short time, it doesn't hurt to follow this outline.

## Step 3: Explore the Logical Sequence of Ideas in the Body of the Talk

The body of the talk is where you will spend most of your time. Here you will move through three logical sequences of ideas.

1. Resonance
2. Dissonance or deficiency
3. The gospel as fulfillment

In the first logical sequence, we are looking for a point of resonance. Here we are trying to get our audience nodding their heads and agreeing with us. We describe their cultural storyline to them. We want them thinking, "Yes! That's me. That's my world. You got me. That is so totally me!" We build rapport with the audience and communicate that we understand who they are and where they live.

In the second logical sequence, we are looking for a point of dissonance or deficiency. The goal here is to disequilibrate our audience by pointing out a dissonance or deficiency in their worldview. We want them thinking, "Huh? I've never thought of that before. Hmm, I've got a problem." Make sure that the dissonance you create follows the topic and issue you are exploring and avoid jumping from one line of thought to another. Focus on creating a sense of flow from resonance to dissonance to the gospel.

In the third logical sequence, we deliver the gospel as the answer to or fulfillment of the problem we set up in the second step. We show how Jesus is the fulfillment of their cultural storyline. Jesus is the happy ending to their culture's storyline, and they just don't know it! He's the only way of achieving the happy ending that they've been looking for. This can sound simplistic, but keep in mind that your talk doesn't have to be that way. We're simply talking about a simple method that helps the people you are talking to connect their lives to a problem they face and how the gospel meets or addresses that problem.

Let me use the topic of beer as an example of what I'm talking about. Maybe I'm giving a talk at a bar or pub. The issue might be "How can I really enjoy a good beer?" My point is going to be, "The perfect beer is that which we drink with a friend," and we're going to use this idea or issue to lead to our evangelistic point: "Beer is a gift from God to be enjoyed in a right relationship with God." Here is how we can set up the logical sequence of ideas:

**Resonance:** Beer is good. It is a gift from God to enjoy, part of the luxury that he has built into his good creation (Ps. 104:15).

**Dissonance or deficiency:** But what makes beer good to drink? It's company. Beer is designed to be drunk with friends. When we drink alone, that's when we realize we have a problem with drinking. And it's lonely drinking alone. Beer is designed to be drunk with others.

**Gospel as fulfillment:** So even if beer is a good gift from a good God for us to enjoy, it's designed for us to enjoy in relationship. And that's especially true for our relationship with God. We need a right relationship with God. We're not just meant to enjoy the gift; we're meant to enjoy the giver.

God loves a good party, and that's the image he uses to help us understand what life with him is like. When Jesus had a last meal with his disciples, he reminded them that because of what he was about to do on the cross for them, there would be a day when they could enjoy a meal and drink with Jesus when he came again to set up a kingdom here on earth (Luke 22:14–18).

Or let's say our topic is success. Our issue is "How can I be successful?" Our point is going to be "Success is more a gift from God than something we earn for ourselves," which we're going to use to lead to the evangelistic point: "The ultimate success that matters is being right with God." This is how we might set up the logical sequence of ideas:

**Resonance:** Ever since childhood, we've been taught that we can be successful at anything as long as we believe and try. This is what the story of the Little Engine That Could has been telling us!

**Dissonance or deficiency:** But we also know that not everyone will succeed. Where there are winners, there must be losers. If there's a front half of the bell curve, there must be a back half of the bell curve. So even though everyone *can* win, not every *will* win. Worse, if we win in one area of life, we may not win in another area. If we succeed at our careers, something else will likely suffer—our family, friendships, maybe our fitness and health. We just can't win at everything. Because we live in a meritocracy, we praise our winners. But then we must also blame our losers. We think they lost because they didn't try or believe enough or dream enough.

**Gospel as fulfillment:** Jesus tells a story of a man who is successful. But the story hints that his success is a gift from God: "The ground produced" (Luke 12:16). So even though we might work for our success, in the end we need to acknowledge that much of our success is really a gift from God. Recognizing this frees us to be the best we can be with what God has given us. True success and joy come when we enjoy our successes as gifts and trust God in our failures.

But more than that, the true success is whether we are "rich toward God" (Luke 12:21). This too is a gift from God made possible by Jesus Christ.

Hopefully you are starting to catch the pattern. Let's take a look at a common topic: Christmas. Our issue is "How can I be blessed this Christmas?" Our point is going to be that "God wants to bless us this Christmas," which we're going to use to lead to the evangelistic point: "God's blessing comes to us through the gift of his Son, Jesus." Here is how we can set up the logical sequence of ideas:

**Resonance:** We come today, on Christmas Day, looking for a blessing from God.

**Dissonance or deficiency:** But we won't get our blessing by earning it, because we will never know if we've done enough. Worse, even if we think we've done enough, what happens when God doesn't do what he's meant to? What if our business fails or our marriage breaks up or our dad dies of cancer? What then? We'll be angry at God: "God, what are you doing? I came to church! I obeyed your commands. So why aren't you fulfilling your side of the bargain?"

**Gospel as fulfillment:** That's why God's blessing comes to us as a gift. The gift of his Son, Jesus. Born *to us* (Luke 2:11).

I have a friend, Tim, who is now a Christian and who also works in marketing. I asked him to help me write my next Christmas talk. His first question to me was, "What sort of person are you aiming the talk at?"

I replied, "A non-Christian."

Tim replied, "Yes, but what sort of non-Christian?"

I looked at him a bit puzzled. So Tim helped me out. He said, "I once brought a non-Christian work friend to hear you give a talk at church. Since then, whenever I see her, she says to me, 'Thanks for taking me to church to hear your friend speak. I don't know what it was about that day, but ever since then, life's been good to me.'"

And then Tim added, "I'll tell you why I used to come to church as a non-Christian. I came hoping that it would cure my dad of cancer."

So Tim said to me, "The non-Christian who walks into your church on Christmas Day is trying to do a bargain with God. They are hoping that God will notice them and bless them in some way."

Now, we might be tempted to attack this motivation or write it off as a bad motive for coming to church: "How dare you come to church only on Christmas Day hoping that God will notice you and bless you!" Instead, I decided to listen to the existential cry in this storyline and then seek to show how Jesus is the fulfillment of what that person is looking for. That Christmas, I set up my evangelistic talk this way: "Today, we have come looking for a blessing from God. And why not? Today, of all days, is the day we should look for a blessing from God. So today, I'm going to show us three ways that we can try to get a blessing from God. The first two ways won't work, but the third way will." For the rest of the talk I shared how we won't get our blessing by earning it or by treating God like a magic charm. But we will get a blessing if we accept it as a gift by trusting Jesus. That was the whole point of Jesus' coming to us as a gift.

Can you see how this approach is very similar to what Paul does in Athens (Acts 17:16–34)? We are trying to complete the storyline and show how the things people are looking for can be found in Jesus, and that Jesus is the only way of fulfilling their storyline.

The next year, I was asked to do an evangelistic Christmas talk again. So this time I went to my missionary friend Phil for advice. Phil is a missionary in Taiwan. Phil's question to me was the same as Tim's: "Who are you aiming the talk at?"

Again I said, "A non-Christian."

Phil asked, "Yes, but what sort of non-Christian?"

This time I replied, "The sort of non-Christian who comes to church only once a year on Christmas Day."

Phil, however, gave me a different reason for why those people come. He said to me, "Can you see what they are doing? They're treating God like a folk religion. They try him out. And if he fixes their marriage, business, and health, then they will worship this God.

"So what I do is preach to them from the book of Luke. In Luke, the crowds follow Jesus, hoping to see a miracle. But they don't make the next step of becoming a follower of Jesus.

"Take, for example, the story of the ten men with leprosy [Luke 17:11–19]. They came to Jesus hoping to be healed. And they got healed. But only one came back to know Jesus."

And then Phil told me his application line: "The problem isn't that we want too much from Jesus. It's that we want too little. We want a miracle, but Jesus wants to give us more than that. Jesus wants to be our friend." Wow!

So that Christmas I set up my evangelistic talk this way: "Today we have come to church on Christmas Day hoping that God will notice us and touch our lives in some way. Maybe he'll work a miracle. Maybe he'll fix our marriages, our businesses, our health. And why not? Isn't that the point of Christmas? That God reaches out to us to touch our lives? But today, I'm going to show how the problem isn't that we're asking too much from God but that we're asking too little."

Again, can you see how this is similar to what Paul does in Athens? We don't attack the storyline: "How dare you come to church on Christmas Day expecting God to perform for you?" Instead, we work within their storyline to show that Jesus is the one who completes it. What all of this shows us is that if we're to adequately contextualize the gospel, then we can't just aim our talk at a generic non-Christian. Instead, we need to aim our talk at a specific non-Christian. But in doing so, because the talk is contextualized, it will be more alienating to those we're not aiming the talk at.

That's always the dilemma of contextualization. The more generic the talk, the more people we might speak to, but the more abstract the talk will be. But the more contextualized the talk, the fewer people we can speak to, but the more specific and personal the talk will be. This also shows us that if we have a specific non-Christian in mind, we need to know them pretty well. We need to hear, understand, and empathize with their cultural storyline. We need to hear their God-given, legitimate existential cry. And we need to know how to talk to them with their own cultural idioms and metaphors.

## Step 4: Flesh Out the Body of the Talk

Now that we have our three logical sequences—resonance, dissonance, gospel—what do we actually say in each sequence? To keep things simple, let's say that in each logical sequence, we're making only one statement. There will now be at least five things that we can do with that statement. I call these the five building blocks of communication.

For example, and since I'm Asian myself, please permit me to make this tongue-in-cheek, nudge-nudge, wink-wink, self-deprecating statement: "Many Asians cannot swim."

Here are the five things that I can do with this statement.

### 1. State the Idea

"Many Asians cannot swim."

- This is a propositional truth claim.
- It is abstract.
- It gives you something to believe.

### 2. Illustrate It

"Asians sink like rocks in the water."

- This is an analogy (the hint is the word "like").
- This is concrete.
- This gives you something to imagine.

### 3. Explain It

"This is because swimming is not historically a big part of Asian culture."

- This is an explanation (the hint is the word "because").
- This is abstract.
- This gives you something to understand rationally.

### 4. Give an Example

"For example, I was the only kid in my class who couldn't swim."

- This is an example (the hint is the word "example").
- Unlike an analogy, this is a real-life, concrete, particular example.
- It is concrete.
- It gives you something to see.

## 5. Give a Payload or Application

"So the next time you're at a pool party, don't push me into the water."

- This is the significance (the hint is the word "so").
- It is concrete.
- It gives you something to do.

So does the order matter? Is there a particular order in which we must present these five statements?

Many Asians cannot swim.
Asians sink like rocks in the water.
That's because swimming is not historically a big part of the Asian
    culture.
For example, I was the only kid in my class who couldn't swim.
So the next time you're at a pool party, don't push me into the water.

Or can we try this order instead?

The next time you're at a pool party, don't push me into the water.
Many Asians cannot swim.
For example, I was the only kid in my class who couldn't swim.
Asians sink like rocks in the water.
That's because swimming is not historically a big part of the
    Asian culture.

Or what about this order?

Asians sink like rocks in the water.
That's because swimming is not historically a big part of the
    Asian culture.
For example, I was the only kid in my class who couldn't swim.
Many Asians cannot swim.
The next time you're at a pool party, don't push me into the water.

Which way works best? They all work. But is there a holier way of doing it? Of course not. There is no theologically correct way (or wrong way) of doing it. The choice will be based on the preferred pedagogical style for our audience. I say this because I was trained in a tradition that told us we must explain before we illustrate, otherwise the story will set the agenda. But we could just as easily say we don't want to let the rational explanation set the agenda. And it doesn't recognize that this is a pedagogical decision rather than a theological decision. We are basing the sequence on whether our audience prefers moving from concrete to abstract (story to explanation) or abstract to concrete (explanation to story). I like to alternate between concrete and abstract statements. So I typically:

- State (abstract)
- Illustrate (concrete)
- Explain (abstract)
- Give an example (concrete)
- Provide a payload/application (concrete)

Also, with each given point, there might not be time to do all five. So it might be simply:

- State
- Illustrate
- Explain

or

- State
- Example
- Explain

or

- State
- Illustrate
- Example
- Payload

Also, if I get to do something like:

- State
- Illustrate
- Explain
- Example or payload

I use a winsome, self-deprecating story for the illustration, and a serious, intimate, or vulnerable story for the example or payload. The variation in mood (going from light to serious) makes the example or payload even more hard hitting. As the saying goes, "We have to earn the right to be serious."

Let's use our talk on success as an example. Let's say we're in the Resonance sequence of the talk:

**State it:** "Our Western success story is based on a meritocracy." This is the issue I'm here to talk about.

**Illustration:** I tell the story of how my friends talked me into a "fun run" through some bush land. I didn't know it, but this was a private race where we were given times, rankings, and a percentile. I finished dead last. But that's life. We think we're doing things for fun, but we're actually being ranked. We're given a number. A percentile.

**Explanation:** That's why we sit exams or take a test. It gives us a grade, a number by which to compare ourselves with others. We're being ranked for our place on the bell curve.

**Example:** When you're at a dinner party, you may get asked what you do for work. That's a ranking question. If you say, "I'm a brain surgeon," then that moves you up the rankings. You are seen as someone successful. But if you say, "I'm a Bible teacher," that probably moves you down the rankings.

**Payload:** Parents project their insecurities on their children. Their children have to learn a second language, play the violin, volunteer, and play soccer—at the same time! And they do this because it will give them a competitive advantage. It will move them up the rankings. It will put them on the front half of the bell curve.

Let's say we're in the Dissonance sequence of the talk.

**State it:** "The problem with our success story is that not everyone will be successful."

**Example:** When I was a child learning the piano, at the end of the year there was an awards ceremony. Everyone else was awarded As, Bs, and Cs. But I got the participation award. I didn't know what that meant, but I knew it wasn't an A or a B.

**Explain:** In a meritocracy, for every winner (As, Bs, and Cs) there also has to be a loser (me!). If there's a front half of the bell curve,

there's a back half of the bell curve. The success story tells us we
can all be winners. But it leaves out the bit about how we *can't* all
be winners; some of us have to be the losers.

**Payload:** The trouble with a meritocracy is that we might start off as
the biggest, smartest, and strongest fish in our pond. But as we
move up the rankings, we move into bigger ponds. Sooner or later
we will be in a pond where the other fish are bigger, smarter, and
stronger than us.

Malcolm Gladwell in his book *David and Goliath* even points out that
some students would have done better if they'd stayed in their normal,
local schools rather than moving up into a selective program or the Ivy
League. In the selective or Ivy League schools, these students fell onto
the back half of the bell curve, and they became discouraged and often
dropped out.

Now let's say we're in the Gospel Fulfillment sequence of the talk.

**State it:** "Success is a gift we get from God rather than something we
earn by hard work."

**Example:** My wife is much better at the piano than me. But I've
practiced more on the piano than she has. I've taken more lessons
than she has. Yet she's still better than me. That's because she's
gifted in a way I'm not. Usain Bolt is much more successful than
me at running 100 meter sprints. But I've also trained. I've also
taken coaching. Yet he's still faster than me. Why? Because he's
gifted in a way I'm not. Much of our success comes from factors
out of our control. We didn't choose our parents. We didn't choose
what country we grew up in. We didn't choose what schools we
got sent to.

**Explain:** In the Bible, Jesus explains that success is given to us by God
(Luke 12:16). Sure, we have to work hard. But that's not the full
story of success. The story is whether God gives us our success
(James 4:13–17).

**Payload:** This means that we need to redefine success. Success is
whatever God wills for us. So if God grants us success, then we
need to be humble in our success: it was a gift rather than the result
of merit alone. And if we don't get success, then we need to trust
that God has a different plan for our lives. This frees us to enjoy
whatever God wills for us. But if this is true, then success will be

found in being right with this God, not just in taking his gifts of success. It's not just trusting his plan for us but knowing him and having him as our Father, Savior, Maker, Shepherd, and Friend. For this to happen, God gives us the ultimate gift of success: his own Son, Jesus Christ.

**Illustration:** Imagine you are taking an exam, and you are sweating over the small questions at the front of the paper that make up 30 percent of the grade and forget to do the major question on the last page of the paper that makes up the other 70 percent. That's what we're like when we sweat the small stuff in this life: "How much money will I make? How high up the ladder can I climb? How do I make my family the trophy family?" But then we miss the big question that determines the majority of the outcome: "Am I experiencing life with God as my Maker, Lover, Father, Savior, Shepherd, and Friend?" True success is found in answering that question.

Here is an example of a talk given by a seminary student who wrote a topical evangelistic talk for the very first time. She delivered it at a women's night, where Christian women invited their non-Christian friends to a night of pampering: dinner, dessert, music, and massages. The event was well attended, and half of those attending would have been non-Christians. I want you to notice how in this talk, she does the following:

- She finds *resonance*. She looks for common ground, identifies a cultural idiom or metaphor, articulates the existential cry, and defines the cultural storyline.
- She raises *dissonance*. She shows how there is a deficiency in the cultural storyline, how we won't find the happy ending that we're looking for without Jesus.
- She speaks the *gospel as fulfillment*. She shows how Jesus is the happy ending to our cultural storyline. Jesus is the answer to our existential cry. And she does this by using the cultural idiom and metaphor identified at the start of the talk.

Also note how after each main point is stated, she follows it with a concrete, particular illustration or example of the point being made. Notice as well how the talk is winsome, self-deprecating, and makes you warm empathetically to the speaker.

### Title: "Rest" (by Sylvia Yeung, an Asian-Australian)
### (Adapted)

I hope you're enjoying the desserts, facials, massages, and evening music from a harp. It feels so good to relax after a long day of work, errands, and looking after the children. I wish every night were like this, because it feels like paradise. Deep down we're all tired. And deep down we all long for rest.

Tonight my topic is rest. In particular, I want to look at the question, "How can we find rest?" Especially because we're all so busy, tired, and exhausted. How can we find rest, a deep rest that will last forever?

Last week I visited a friend who had just given birth to a baby. The baby was only two weeks old. But he was asleep and looked so relaxed. Even though his eyes were shut, he was smiling! The baby was at rest. Why can't I be like that? How did my life get so busy and out of control?

Maybe we can find rest by pampering ourselves like we're doing tonight. This is what my family likes to do when we go on vacation to China. We book a massage for ourselves—as an entire family—and relax by having our tired muscles soothed, from head to toe. But what makes a massage so relaxing? Is it the massage alone? It's actually not the massage by itself that's so relaxing. It's who we're with at the time. You see, I want you to imagine that you're getting a massage right now. Relaxing, right? But what if you turn around and find that it's your ex-boyfriend giving you that massage? Ouch! Suddenly it's not so relaxing. It's not so much what we do or don't do that gives us rest; it's who we're with at the time.

Or maybe we can find rest by unwinding. Last year, after I handed in a major assignment, I was mentally exhausted. I needed to unwind. So when a friend invited me out to sing karaoke with her, I accepted. But when I got to the karaoke place, I found that my friend had invited many other people I didn't know. Suddenly I wasn't relaxed. I was no longer in the mood to sing karaoke. Again, it's not so much what we do or don't do that gives us rest; it's who we're with at the time.

Or maybe we can find rest by going on vacation. A few months ago, I planned a road trip with a friend. But only a few hours into the trip, my friend and I got into an argument. We didn't talk to each other after that. So for the rest of the trip, we sat in the car in awkward silence. Again, it's not so much what we do or don't do that gives us rest; it's who we're with at the time.

So how can we find rest? Especially a deep rest that will last forever?

In the Bible, Jesus says, "Come to me, all you who are weary and burdened, and I will give you rest."

Jesus says, "Come to me." Rest is about being with Jesus. Jesus is the *who* that gives you the real rest you need.

But what does that mean? How can Jesus give us rest? He can because he knows the real reason why we're restless. Jesus is God. He is the God who created us. He understands us better than we know ourselves. What makes us tick. What we're unconsciously longing for in life.

And he is the God who loved us enough to meet those needs. He died for us on the cross. He is the God who saved us! He is God who loves and knows us.

No matter what we're going through, no matter how tough the situation is, we can find rest when Jesus is with us.

I grew up in a family where I couldn't find rest. My dad favored my younger brother more than me. I knew it was because he was a guy and I was a girl. It was probably because of my father's traditional Asian mindset. But I hated it. It hurt me to know that my father didn't value me.

So my life's ambition was to prove my father wrong. In high school, I worked hard to get top grades in math, to show my father that girls also can do math. I also worked hard to get into law school to become a lawyer. I wanted to show my father that I was better than who he thought I was.

But this only made my life more restless. I've been trying my whole life to prove my father wrong. I've been trying to win his respect and earn his approval. But deep down in my heart, I know that I will never be at rest because I will always have this grudge with my father.

But after I came to know Jesus, I found the real rest that Jesus gives. I know that Jesus loves me just the way I am. I don't need to win his respect or earn his approval. He loves me so much that he died for me to give me a new life. And now he's always with me, no matter what.

I still face times of peace and hurt from my dad. But Jesus' words bring comfort and encouragement to me. My value is found securely in Jesus alone. So I don't have to look anywhere else for my value.

You see, I've learned that rest is not about what I do or don't do. That's not how we find rest. It's about who I'm with. And Jesus will always be with me. And Jesus will always love me. And Jesus will give me the rest that I'm looking for. But it's more than that. This rest will lead to an eternal rest in heaven, where there's no more suffering, hurt, or hate. But even more amazing is that by knowing Jesus, I get a taste of heaven now, in this life.

Again it's not what we do or don't do that gives us rest. Rest comes from who we're with. And if we know Jesus, we have a deep rest that will last forever.

## CONCLUSION: ALISON AND HEALTH NIGHT

We began this chapter looking at the challenge Alison was facing. She had been asked to give an evangelistic talk at health night. It was now the evening of the event, and she was sitting up at the front of the hall. Everything was going great. The women who showed up had enjoyed a free medical checkup from the team of doctors, and the talks from the personal trainer and nutritionist were so helpful that even Alison was listening and taking notes.

But now it was her turn to give a twenty-minute evangelistic talk. What was she going to say? She began by affirming the importance of health. After all, isn't that why we make New Year's promises to eat less and exercise more? Isn't that why we take out one-year gym memberships? We all want to be healthy, but what does that really look like?

The problem with our pursuit of health is that it can feel so temporary. Alison shared how she runs in the city races to stay healthy, but every year her times get a little slower. Now she's being passed by people wearing costumes. Batman, the fairy godmother, and a caveman all passed her by on the last run.

Another problem with our pursuit of health is that there are so many components to consider. We want to have endurance, flexibility, and strength. A bodybuilder typically focuses on strength. If we were to challenge a bodybuilder to arm wrestle, they would beat us. But they might gain that strength at the loss of endurance. So we might be able to run up a hill and they wouldn't be able to catch us!

Alison then pointed out that there are also many complementary components to good health. There's our physical health: taking your blood pressure, checking your sugar levels, and getting regular cholesterol readings. Then there's psychological health: avoiding stress and anxiety and treating depression. Then there's relational health: How are we doing in our relationships with our family, friends, and loved ones? And there is an additional component that we sometimes ignore: How is our spiritual health? How are we doing relationally with God?

These components are not separate; they are interrelated. For example, if our relational health is unwell, it will affect our physical health. Or if our physical health is unwell, it can affect our psychological health. And if our psychological health is unwell, it can affect our relational health.

Alison then told the story about Jesus meeting the woman at the well in John 4. The woman was seeking physical health by drawing water from the well. But her relational and spiritual health were unwell. And on top of that, if she was to be completely healthy, she would need living water from Jesus, the secret of spiritual health.

Alison told the audience that we also have a similar need to be healthy. In the same way that we work hard on our physical health, we need to be just as concerned about our psychological, relational, and spiritual health. We can get physically healthy by exercising, watching what we eat, or working out at the gym. But if we want to get spiritually healthy, we need a person—Jesus—who promises to be our living water.

Alison paused as she let the words sink in.

Then she delivered her final appeal. Physical health is important. For sure, we need to monitor our blood pressure. We need to work on our endurance, strength, and flexibility. But we also need to work on our psychological and relational health. We need to get right with our friends and family. But we cannot ignore our spiritual health. Just as important, and maybe more important, we need to get ourselves right with God.

CHAPTER 9

# HOW TO GIVE EVANGELISTIC EXPOSITORY TALKS

## Weddings, baptisms, and funerals

Tom is a medical doctor. When he was at college, he was very involved
with the Christian groups on campus. Now with his long hours of
medical work, he struggles even to get to church on Sundays. Tom's college friends Scott and Kate are getting married next spring, and Scott
and Kate have asked Tom to speak at their wedding. Kate has picked out
Philippians 2:1–11 for the Bible reading, and Scott wants Tom to preach
an expository Bible message. But not only that, Scott and Kate want Tom
to use this opportunity to share the gospel with their non-Christian friends
and relatives who will be at the wedding.

How can Tom do this? There will be times when Christians have an
opportunity to give an evangelistic expository talk. In the last chapter,
we looked at evangelistic topical preaching, but in this chapter we will
outline some basic principles for crafting an evangelistic expository Bible
talk. My hope is that by following these principles, you'll be able to speak
the gospel powerfully and effectively as you explain and apply a particular
passage in the Bible.

I have many times been asked by a friend or the organizer of an event to
give a monologue, an oral presentation that formally explains and applies a
Bible passage. The length of a talk like this can range from 10–45 minutes.

Examples might include an evangelistic Sunday church service, evangelistic youth group events, Bible talk conferences, school chapel services,
after-dinner talks at a restaurant or coffee shop, men's breakfasts or dinners,

weddings, trivia or game nights, Christmas church services, and Easter church services.

When the situation lends itself to an expository-style talk, I have a method which I use to prepare and deliver the talk, a method I'd like to outline for you to consider. However, and this is extremely important, I am only *recommending* a method for crafting Bible talks. I am not prescribing this method, saying, "You must do it my way, or you're doing it the wrong way." This is a good method which has reliably helped me to generate expository Bible talks. But don't let it become your only method.

## HOW BIBLE TALKS WORK

In every Bible talk, there is a dialectic between two conceptual realms: the world of the text and the world of the hearer.

If we privilege the world of the text, then we tend to prefer the tools of exegesis to generate our expository Bible talk. But if we privilege the world of the hearer, then we tend to use the tools of theology to generate a topical talk. As I noted in a previous chapter, even this conception is simplistic because we can never separate the two realms. Every expository Bible talk must begin and end in the world of the hearer—this is the function of the introduction and application—and thus has some of the elements of topical preaching. And every topical talk should eventually communicate a biblical truth (or it's just a nice speech, not a sermon), and thus has some elements of expository preaching. The main difference between so-called topical and so-called expository preaching is the proportion and sequencing of the elements.

All talks—topical and expository—have these basic elements:

| Introduction | Bible's Message | Application |
|---|---|---|
| Acknowledges context: "the world of the hearer" | Acknowledges the Bible: "the world of the Bible" | Acknowledges context: "the world of the hearer" |
| Demonstrates the significance of the message for this context | Demonstrates that the message comes from the Bible | Applies the significance of the message for this context |
| Mainly uses the tools of cultural exegesis and systematic theology | Mainly uses the tools of grammatico-historical exegesis | Mainly uses the tools of cultural exegesis and systematic theology |

For a hostile audience—people who haven't warmed to the gospel in their hearts and minds—we need to work hard at establishing common ground before we can give them the gospel message. This means that the introduction might even be longer than the message, possibly twenty minutes long while the message might be just ten minutes.

For a nonhostile audience—people who are already warm to the gospel in their hearts and minds—we don't need to spend as much time on the introduction. If we spend too long (longer than a few minutes), the audience may grow restless and wonder, "Why isn't the preacher getting us to open the Bible yet?" For this audience, the introduction can be shorter and the message might be longer, around 20–25 minutes.

We should keep in mind that people at different stages of life might seek out one approach or method more than the other. For example, a non-Christian might need more time in the introduction so that their existential cries, defeater beliefs, and plausibility structures are articulated. But Christian college students might need more time in the Bible's message. They are presented with huge amounts of data from their other college courses—statistics, anatomy, chemistry—and might have a similar hunger for data from the Bible. But Christians at a later stage of life might need more time in application. They're already familiar with much of the exegesis of Bible passages. They already know about the *hina* clause in Mark 4:12. Now when they come for a Bible talk, they want to know, "How can I be a good parent?" or "How can I care for my aging parents?" or "What should I do with my money?"

## PREACHING AS SCREENWRITING

A metaphor that has helped me to understand the heart of an expository approach to preaching is the task of screenwriting, and specifically the screenwriting of a book-to-film adaptation of a story. Now that I've thoroughly confused you by suggesting this metaphor, let me try to explain why I find it helpful. In screenwriting the adaptation of a book to the big screen, the screenwriter moves from the book to the film.

After watching the film, people might say, "That wasn't like the book at all!" My response when I hear people say that is usually, "Of course the film wasn't like the book. It was a film. If you want the book, read the book. But don't expect the film to be exactly like the book. It's a different genre. It's a different medium." The screenwriter is converting from one medium (a written book) to another medium (an enacted, visual film).

If the film was just like the book, it would be terrible, probably too long with far too much dialogue and way too many characters that you'd have trouble following. That's why screenwriters have to leave out dialogue and some of the characters. They have to remove some scenes and maybe even change the order in which events are presented.

I find this analogy useful because in expository preaching, we are moving from the book (Bible) to oral speech (usually a monologue).

Like a screenwriter, we may have to leave out some dialogue, possibly a few characters. We may edit out some scenes or even change the order in which events are presented. That's the art of writing a sermon. What do we leave in and what do we leave out? What do we emphasize? In what order do we present the points and events?

## HOW TO DEVELOP THE TALK

The macro structure or order of a 20–25 minute expository talk is often the same as a topical message. There is an introduction (3–5 minutes), a body (10–15 minutes), a bridge (1–3 minutes), and a conclusion (3–5 minutes). Beyond that, however, they are quite different. Let's take a closer look at how to write and deliver the content of the talk.

Books on preaching often like to talk about a big idea.[1] The big idea is the simple, clear, single idea that we are trying to communicate in a talk. It gives our talk unity, focus, and clarity. It is the organizing principle for the entire talk. It is the elevator summary of what we are trying to say. Unfortunately, some teachers have a limited view about what can qualify as the big idea, as if everyone should get the same big idea from the same Bible passage. For example, if we all prepared a sermon from John 4, they would argue that we should all have the same big idea in our Bible talk. I think much of the confusion preachers experience comes about because we quickly realize that there are different categories of big ideas.

> **The exegetical big idea:** The first big idea is the exegetical big idea, and it answers the question, "What is the biblical author saying?" It is a single idea used by the author of the Bible passage to organize all the other ideas in that passage. To get the exegetical big idea, we engage in the task of hermeneutics and utilize the tools of

---

1. I owe the concept of trying to get a big idea from the text—to aid communication—from Haddon Robinson, *Biblical Preaching: The Development and Delivery of Expository Messages* (Grand Rapids, Mich.: Baker, 2014), 15–26.

grammatico-historical exegesis. What makes this confusing is that there might not be one single big idea because the author might have had multiple ideas that he intended to communicate in that particular passage. For example, in Romans 3:21–31, Paul communicates multiple ideas. He communicates that "the righteousness of God has been made known," "to which the Law and the Prophets testify," pronouncing that "all have sinned," but that "all are justified freely by his grace through the redemption that came by Christ Jesus," "apart from works of the law," so that there is no "boasting," and that this is for both Jews and gentiles. But we can still summarize all of these ideas in one single, coherent exegetical big idea, staying as close to the original wording in the Bible as possible. For example, in Romans 3:21–31, this might be, "All have sinned but are justified freely by God's grace, through Christ's redemption, apart from the law."

**The theological big idea:** The exegetical big idea is not the only big idea we can talk about, however. There is also what we might call the theological big idea. This answers the question, "What timeless truth is the biblical author saying?" It tries to summarize the exegetical ideas in a passage or section of Scripture into a universal concept that is true for all peoples at all times and in all places. Getting the theological big idea is an exercise in conceptual thinking. We use the tools of systematic theology. Let's look at Romans 3:21–31 again. The theological big idea might be, "Sinners are justified by grace alone, through the means of faith, based on the atoning death of Christ, apart from good works."

**The homiletical big idea:** The homiletical big idea is another way of approaching a passage. It answers the question, "What is this talk saying?" It's an attempt to find a single, sharply focused idea that will serve as the organizing principle for the entire talk. Getting the homiletical big idea is an exercise in homiletics. We use the tools of pedagogy, communication, and contextualization. This means that if we look at Romans 3:21–31 and take into account different audiences, contexts, and situations, we might come up with different homiletical big ideas from the same Bible passage. For example, in the passage we've been considering, our homiletical big idea might be, "We can be right with God not because of what we have done but because of what Jesus has done."

**Bumper sticker big idea:** Finally—and this is my own original category—we also have the bumpersticker big idea or take-home big idea. It's an attempt to answer the question, "What do I want the audience to remember?" This looks at the text and tries to find a sticky, catchy, easy-to-remember meme for the audience to remember as the organizing principle for the entire talk.[2] For us to get the bumpersticker big idea is an exercise, again, in homiletics. We use the tools of pedagogy, contextualization, and communication. For example, in Romans 3:21–31, our bumpersticker big idea might be, "I don't have to be perfect because Jesus is perfect." It's similar to the homiletical big idea, but phrased in a catchy or memorable way.

## Choose a Bible Passage

We begin with a Bible passage. Sometimes you are given a text, and sometimes you get to choose. Your choice should be guided, in part, by your audience. What concepts of sin, salvation, Jesus, and conversion will best suit the audience, setting, and occasion? What learning style will the audience prefer—didactic or narrative?

Here's a handful of passages that I've used for various contexts:

| Bible Passage | Setting |
| --- | --- |
| Eccles. 3:1–14 | Wedding |
| Eccles. 4:9–12 | Wedding |
| Matt. 20:1–16 | Youth group |
| Mark 4:1–20 | High school chapel |
| Luke 8:22–56 | Church service |
| Luke 12:13–21 | City workers |
| Luke 14:15–24 | Youth rally |
| Luke 16:19–31 | Church service |
| Luke 18:9–14 | City workers |
| Luke 19:1–10 | Youth rally |

---

2. Chip Heath and Dan Heath, *Made to Stick: Why Some Ideas Survive and Others Die* (New York: Random House, 2007).

| John 3:16 | High school chapel |
|---|---|
| John 4:1–26 | Church service |
| John 20:1–10 | Youth group (in a dark cave!) |
| Acts 17:31 | Youth group |
| Rom. 5:6–8 | Wedding |
| Rom. 6:23 | Church service |
| Rom. 8:14–17 | Youth conference |
| 1 Cor. 15:50–58 | Airport chapel (Chicago O'Hare) |
| Eph. 5:21–33 | Wedding |
| Phil. 2:1–11 | Wedding |
| 1 Peter 3:18 | Church service |
| 1 John 4:10 | Wedding |
| Rev. 21:1–4 | Wedding |

## Find the Homiletical Big Idea from the Text

After choosing a text, the next step is finding the homiletical big idea. Again, this gives you the *what* of the talk, as in, "What is the talk about?" Let's look at examples from John 3:16, Romans 3:21–31, and Luke 12:13–21.

### John 3:16

*Exegetical big idea:* God loves the world by sending his Son, Jesus.

*Theological big idea:* The incarnation is the demonstration of God's love.

*Homiletical big idea:* God shows his love by sending his Son, Jesus.

### Romans 3:21–31

*Exegetical big idea:* Sinners are justified by God's grace through Christ's sacrifice.

*Theological big idea:* Justification by faith.

*Homiletical big idea:* Sinners can be right with God not by their works but by Jesus.

*Luke 12:13–21*

> *Exegetical big idea:* The man was a fool because he stored up for
> himself but wasn't rich toward God.
>
> *Theological big idea:* We are saved not by works (or wealth) but by
> faith in God.
>
> *Homiletical big idea:* A fool worships the gift, but a wise person
> worships God the Giver.

## Convert the Big Idea into a Question and Answer

The next step is to convert the big idea into a question with an answer.
The question gives the *why* of the talk, as in, "What question is the talk
answering?" Use trial and error to determine what question best fits the
big idea. Try starting your question with *what, where, who, why, when, how*
to see what works best. Here are some examples using the passages we've
been looking at.

> **John 3:16:** Homiletical big idea: "God shows his love by sending his
> Son, Jesus" might become:
> Q: "How does God demonstrate his love?"
> A: "By sending his Son, Jesus."
>
> **Romans 3:21–31:** Homiletical big idea: "We can be right with God,
> not by our works but by Jesus" might become:
> Q: "How can sinners get right with God?"
> A: "Not by their works but by Jesus."
>
> **Luke 12:13–21:** Homiletical big idea: "A fool worships the gift, but
> a wise person worships God the Giver" might become:
> Q: "Why does God call the rich man a fool?"
> A: "Because he worshiped the gift, not God the Giver."

## Convert the Question into an Existential Question

After you have your question, the next step is to convert it into an
existential question. The existential question is the need addressed by this
passage. You may need to reflect on the passage and the question you've
developed to work out what existential need is addressed by the big idea.
This gives the *want* of the talk, as in, "Why do I want to listen to this talk?"
To do this, we need to know our audience. What are the existential needs
of our audience? What existential questions are they asking? One simple
way to get at this is to personalize the question you are asking. Here are
several examples to consider:

**John 3:16:** Q: "How does God demonstrate his love?" might become:
> **Existential question:** "How do I know if God loves me?"

**Romans 3:21–31:** Q: "How can sinners get right with God?" might become:
> **Existential question:** "How can I get right with God?"

**Luke 12:13–21:** Q: "Why does God call the rich man a fool?" might become:
> **Existential question:** "How do I know whether I'm a fool?"

## The Sinful Problem

Another aspect to consider is the sinful problem that is being addressed by this Bible passage. Why did the author write this in the first place?[3] The answer to this question gives us the *need* of the talk, as in, "Why do I need to hear the gospel?" Why do I need to hear what God is saying in this passage?

> **John 3:16:** The sinful problem might be "not believing." Those who don't believe will perish and miss out on eternal life.
>
> **Romans 3:21–31:** The sinful problem might be trying to get justified through good works.
>
> **Luke 12:13–21:** The sinful problem is storing up for ourselves and not being rich toward God.

## The Gospel Solution

Finally, you'll want to have a clear grasp of the gospel solution. What is the gospel solution offered by the passage? How is God's grace the solution to our sinful problem, and what must we do in response to God's grace? This gives us the *must* of the talk, as in, "What must I do to be saved?"

> **John 3:16:** The gospel solution is that God has sent his Son, and now I must believe in Jesus.
>
> **Romans 3:21–31:** The gospel solution is that God will give me his righteous status based on the atoning sacrifice of Jesus, and now I must put my trust in Jesus and not my works.
>
> **Luke 12:13–21:** The gospel solution is that God offers me a relationship with him through Jesus, and now I must put my trust in Jesus and be rich toward him.

---

3. Bryan Chapell calls this the Fallen Condition Focus (FCF) in *Christ-Centered Preaching: Redeeming the Expository Sermon*, 2d. ed. (Grand Rapids, Mich.: Baker, 2005), 48–54.

## Using the Big Idea, Existential Question, and Sinful Problem

Let's pull all of these pieces together. From the Bible passage, we now have:

| Big Idea | What? | What are we talking about? |
|---|---|---|
| Question | Why? | What question is this talk answering? |
| Existential Question | Want? | Why do I want to listen to this talk? |
| Sinful Problem | Need? | Why do I need to listen to this talk? |
| Gospel Solution | Must? | What must I do to be saved? |

Now when we write our talk:

1. We write the introduction of the talk to set up the existential question as the need in the introduction.
2. We write the body of the talk to reveal, point by point, the big idea as an answer to the existential question.
3. We write the conclusion of the talk to raise the sinful problem and offer the gospel solution.

The existential question is what gets us into the talk. If we only tell people what we're going to talk about, we won't have their attention because they will have greater existential needs in their subconscious (or conscious!) minds: "I'm hungry." "I need to study for an exam." "I need to pay the bills on the way home." "I need to find a babysitter." But by stating an existential question that they want to know the answer to, we will gain their attention.

The existential question then functions as the question which the rest of the talk will answer. Without this question at the start, the rest of our talk will sound like a college paper being read, but one where the title page is lost, so we don't know what question is being answered.

The big idea is in the main body of the talk. The big idea is the organizing principle for the body of the talk. All the points in the talk are developments from the big idea. The sinful problem may (or may not) have already been addressed in the body of the talk. But we definitely raise it again in the conclusion so that the listener is aware that this is a problem that cannot go away. It is fundamental to their human condition. The gospel solution may (or may not) have also been explained in the body of the talk. But we offer it again in the conclusion so that listeners know they must choose this solution if they ever want their sinful problem to go away. Our talk should thus end with grace: God's offer of salvation.

## HOW TO WRITE THE INTRODUCTION

According to my friend Malcolm Gill and author and preacher Haddon Robinson, we do at least five things in an introduction to a talk or sermon:

- Tell a story that sets up an image.
- Introduce the subject that you're going to talk about.
- Raise a need for why we need to listen to this subject.
- Declare the biblical text that you'll be exploring.
- Give a preview of the outline of your talk.

Or in summary form:

- Image
- Subject
- Need
- Text
- Preview

For example, an introduction to John 3:16 could go like this:

They've done studies on guys. Single guys are more likely to rate themselves less good looking than they really are. For example, let's say a single guy is eight out of ten for looks. If you ask him, he might say he is only a four. But married guys are more likely to rate themselves more good looking than they really are. For example, let's say a married guy (like me) is only a three. If you ask him, he will say he's a ten! Why is this? Because, apparently, if you are loved by somebody, you will have a high rating of yourself.

It's very important that we are loved. It affects who we are. It affects how we live. It affects the choices we make. That's why we look for love from our partners, parents, family, and friends.

The question that drives us in life is, "How do I know whether I am loved?"

But if that's true, how much more important, then, is it that we know that we're loved by God? "How do I know whether God loves me?" It's the question that drives most world religions. It's the question that probably brought you to hear this talk today. "How do I know whether God loves me?"

Today we're going to answer this question from a passage in the Bible called John 3:16.

This will come in the form of a short ten-minute talk from me now. And in this talk, I'm going to make three points.

"How do I know whether I'm loved by God?" My first point is this . . .

Notice how this introduction covers all five of the aspects we mentioned earlier:

- The *image* is guys rating themselves.
- The *subject* is love.
- The *need* is, "How do I know whether God loves me?" (which is the existential question).
- The *text* is John 3:16.
- The *preview* is a ten-minute Bible talk with three points.

Now that we've finished the introduction, it's time to write the body of the talk.

## HOW TO WORK OUT WHAT OUR POINTS ARE GOING TO BE

To keep things simple, we'll adopt a three-point structure to organize the body of our talk. But what are the three points that best communicate our big idea?

### Preaching from Epistles

The epistles are the letters in the Bible, such as Romans, Ephesians, 1 Peter. As a genre, the epistles are didactic: they teach and explain ideas by presenting them in a logical argument. They lend themselves to expository talks, which similarly present ideas (or points) in a logical argument.

The body of our talk will usually have three points. But what should our three points be? I usually choose from one of three options:

### Option 1: Unpack the Big Idea Point by Point

In this first option, the big idea is three points which answer the existential question one point at a time. For example, if our passage is John

3:16, our existential question might be, "How do I know God loves me?" In this option, we answer the question with three points: (1) I know God loves me because he sent his Son, (2) I know God loves me because all I have to do is believe in his Son, and (3) I know God loves me because God will give me eternal life.

As another example, if our passage is Romans 3:21–31, our existential question might be, "How can I get right with God?" In this option, we answer the question with these three points: (1) We won't get right with God by our own works, (2) but we get right by what Jesus has done for us, and (3) we get right by our faith in Jesus.

### Option 2: Problem, Solution, Application

In the second option, the big idea also consists of three points, but these set up the sinful problem, offer the gospel solution, and specify the application for the audience. For example, if our passage is John 3:16, our existential question might change to, "How can I have eternal life?" In this option, we answer with these three points: (1) Right now we have the problem of death, (2) but God's solution is to send us his Son, (3) so if we believe in his Son, we will have everlasting life.

As another example, if our passage is Romans 3:21–31, our existential question might still be, "How can I get right with God?" In this option, we answer the question with these three points: (1) Our problem is we are guilty before God, (2) but God's solution is Christ's sacrifice for us, (3) so if we have faith in Jesus, God will justify us.

### Option 3: Resonance, Dissonance, Gospel Fulfillment

In the third option, the big idea again is three points. However, the aim of the first point is to resonate with the audience, to say something they will agree with. The aim of the second point is to dissonate the audience, to say something that demonstrates that they have a problem. The aim of the third point is to offer the gospel as the fulfillment for the problem created in the second point.

For example, if our passage is John 3:16, our existential question might be, "How do I know whether I am loved by God?" In this option, we answer with these three points: (1) God sends us his Son because he loves us, (2) but God sends us his Son because he also disagrees with how we live (that's why we're destined to die), (3) so we need to believe in his Son if we are to have eternal life.

As another example, if our passage is Romans 3:21–31, our existential question might be, "How can I get right with God?" In this option, we answer with these three points: (1) We need to be right with God, (2) but we can't get right with God by our own works, (3) so we need to have faith in Christ's death for us.

As you can see, the choice of points is as much an art as a science. This is something that is learned through trial and error, combining experience and cultural analysis. We need to develop discernment to sense our audience's existential cry, cultural storyline, and sinful problem. And while the tools of grammatico-historical exegesis might give us the meaning of the text, we need the skills of homiletics, communication, pedagogy, and contextualization to sense how best to present the meaning.

## Preaching from Narratives

The narratives are the stories in the Bible with characters, plots, dialogue, narrators, drama, and action. Their message is often implicit rather than explicit. Their aim is more to win over our imagination than to present an argument with a logical presentation of ideas. When preaching from narratives, we should be free to explore other models of preaching, ones that don't rely on a logical presentation of points.

When we preach narrative, we usually have three basic elements in our talk. At some stage in the talk we will:

1. *Retell* the story in the Bible.
2. *Explain* the story.
3. *Apply* the story.

The proportions of these elements will be determined by the story, audience, context, setting, and situation. For example, if we preach to high schoolers at a summer camp, we might have this proportion:

**Retell: 80 percent**
Explain: 10 percent
Apply: 10 percent

But if we preach to college students in a lecture room, which is a more didactic environment where the expectation might be for propositional learning, our proportions might be:

Retell: 10 percent
**Explain: 80 percent**
Apply: 10 percent

And if we preach to busy, tired, exhausted working parents on a Friday night, where the expectation might be for practical guidance and wisdom, our proportions might be:

Retell: 10 percent
Explain: 10 percent
**Apply: 80 percent**

Keep in mind that these proportions are descriptions and not prescriptions. The point is that narrative preaching will typically have three elements—retelling, explaining, applying—and we are free to vary the proportions based on our audience and context.

If—and only if—we decide to go with a three-point structure in our approach to narrative preaching, I typically choose from one of four options:

### Option 1: Retell the Story Point by Point

This is often the simplest option. After the introduction, where we set up the existential question, we promise an answer from the story itself. Then we simply retell the story in the body of the talk, point by point. We then explain the story in the bridge—the transition between the body and the conclusion. And then we apply the story in the conclusion of the talk.

For example, if our story comes from Luke 12:13–21—the parable of the rich fool—we can set up the existential question in the introduction of the talk: "How do I know whether I'm a fool?" We then promise an answer from the story in Luke 12:13–21. In the body of the talk, we retell the story one point at a time: (1) There is a man who became rich, (2) so he stores up his riches so that he can be happy and secure, (3) but God calls him a fool. We explain why God calls him a fool in the bridge of the talk. And then we apply the principles of the story to ourselves in the conclusion of the talk: Are we also fools, like the man, by storing up riches for ourselves when we should be rich toward God instead?

### Option 2: Explain the Story by Unpacking the Big Idea Point by Point

In the second option, we spend only a brief time retelling the story in the introduction of the talk. And then we use the body of the talk to explain the story one point at a time. We finish with a conclusion of the talk in which we apply the story.

For example, if our story comes from Luke 12:13–21—the parable of the rich fool—we can use the introduction to retell the story and then set up the existential question: "Why does God call this man a fool?" It's a good question, isn't it? Think about it! The man has done what our parents tell us to do. Work hard. Don't spend everything at once, but save what you have for the future. So why does God call this man a fool?

We answer this question by explaining the story in the body of the talk with three points: (1) God calls him a fool because he lives for himself, (2) God calls him a fool because he stores up what can't last, and (3) God calls him a fool because he lives as if he will never die. We can then apply these three points to ourselves in the conclusion.

### Option 3: Apply the Story Point by Point

In the third option, we spend only a brief time retelling and explaining the story in the introduction of the talk. And then we use the body of the talk to apply the story one point at a time.

For example, if our story comes from Luke 12:13–21—the parable of the rich fool—we can use the introduction to retell and explain the story and then set up the existential question: "How can I live wisely?" We answer this question by applying the story in the body of the talk with three points: (1) We live wisely by thanking God for our successes, (2) we live wisely by being generous with what we have, and (3) we live wisely if we are rich toward God.

### Option 4: The Points are Resonance, Dissonance, Gospel Fulfillment

In this final option, we similarly spend only a brief time retelling the story in the introduction to the talk. But then in the body of the talk, we explain the story with three points. Our first point aims to find resonance with the audience, something that they will readily agree with. But the second point will find dissonance with the audience, something that demonstrates that they have a problem. And the third point will offer the gospel as the fulfillment for whatever they are looking for.

For example, if our story comes from Luke 12:13–21— the parable of the rich fool—we use the introduction to retell the story and then set up the existential question: "Why does God call this man a fool?" We answer this question by explaining the story. But our three points might be: (1) The man wanted security, and isn't that what we all want? (2) But his riches can't guarantee him security—that's why God calls him a fool. (3) So if we want security, we don't store up riches but are rich toward God instead. We then apply these three points to ourselves in the conclusion of the talk.

## HOW TO FLESH OUT THE POINTS

To flesh out the points, we need to revisit what we learned in the previous chapter about the basic building blocks of communication. As an example, I used this tongue-in-cheek, nudge-nudge, wink-wink self-deprecating statement:

> *Statement of the idea:* Many Asians cannot swim.
> *Illustration:* Asians sink like rocks in the water.
> *Explanation:* Swimming is not big in the Asian culture.
> *Example:* I was the only kid who could not swim.
> *Payload or application:* At a pool party, don't push me into the pool.

Each building block has complementary but different functions, genres, and moods:

| Building Block | Function | Genre | Mood |
| --- | --- | --- | --- |
| Idea | Something to *believe* | Abstract | Neutral |
| Illustration | Something to *imagine* | Concrete | Winsome, humorous, self-deprecating |
| Explanation | Something to *understand* | Abstract | Serious |
| Example | Something to *see* | Concrete | Serious, intimate, vulnerable |
| Payload | Something to *do* | Concrete | Serious, intimate, vulnerable |

Now let's use these building blocks to build up each point. Our points will look like this:

*Point 1*
- State the idea.
- Show me where you got this idea from the Bible passage. (This is the explicit aim of expository preaching.)
- Illustrate.

- Explain.
- Provide an example and/or a payload.

### Point 2

- State the idea.
- Show me where you got this idea from the Bible passage. (This is the explicit aim of expository preaching.)
- Illustrate.
- Explain.
- Provide an example and/or a payload.

### Point 3

- State the idea.
- Show me where you got this idea from the Bible passage. (This is the explicit aim of expository preaching.)
- Illustrate.
- Explain.
- Provide an example and/or a payload.

For example, our second point in our talk on Luke 12:13–21 could go like this:

The second reason why the rich man is a fool is because he stored up things that do not last.

The Bible hints at this reason in Luke 12:21. Read along with me: "This is how it will be with whoever stores up things for themselves but is not rich toward God."

The man has stored up things that will not last!

My wife and I are from Australia. But we also lived for five years in Chicago. We loved the winters. We especially loved the snow. We would run outside and make snowmen. Have snowball fights. My wife loved to do the snow-angel thing. But as much as we loved snow, here's one thing you won't find us doing. You won't find us storing up snow. You won't find us filling our pockets with snow. You won't find us taking snowballs to the bank and asking the bank teller to put them away somewhere safe. You won't find us renovating our homes with snow: "Hey, do you want to see what I've done with my house? Look! Snow! Do you like it?" And why's that? Because snow melts. Only a fool would store up what doesn't last.

And that's exactly what this man has done. He's stored up things that do not last. That's why God calls him a fool.

But isn't that what we do? We store up things that don't last. And then we're shocked when they don't last. We buy the new car, and then we're shocked when someone runs their keys down the side and scratches it. We buy new clothes, and then we're shocked when they're out of fashion. We get a degree, and then we're shocked when they tell us that we need yet another degree. We too have stored up things that do not last.

This is the second answer to our question, "How do I know whether I'm a fool?": a fool will store up what doesn't last.

Notice the following elements and how they are represented in this example:

*State* the point: "The man is a fool because he has stored up what doesn't last."

*Show* me the Bible passage: Luke 12:21.

*Illustrate* with a story about how we don't store up snow.

*Explain* that only a fool stores up what doesn't last.

*Give examples* of how we also store up things that don't last.

## HOW TO WRITE THE BRIDGE

The bridge is a critical moment in any presentation. It is the montage in a romantic comedy movie. Or it is the training montage in a sports movie. Or it is the moment when the evil genius does his monologue in an action movie.

In an expository talk, the bridge is the transition between the body of the talk and the conclusion. The function of the bridge is to pause to summarize the talk up until now. We remind the audience of the existential question that we posed at the start of the talk. Then we sum up the points that we've visited in the body of the talk as the answer to our existential question. All of this anticipates a climactic finish to the talk.

Here's an example of a bridge that we can use for a talk from Luke 12:13–21:

Do you remember our original question? It is, "Why does God call the man a fool?" To answer this, we have looked at Luke 12:13–21. And we've seen three reasons why God calls him a fool: (1) He lives only for himself,

(2) he stores up what doesn't last, and (3) he lives as if he will never die. But hang on! Isn't that how we too live? If so, we've got a problem! So where do we go from here?

The bridge should get the audience on the edge of their seats, highly anticipating the climactic conclusion to the talk.

## HOW TO WRITE THE CONCLUSION

The conclusion is the climactic finish to the talk, so it will be the last thing that the audience hears and, we hope, remembers. It usually has a simple, single—what I call bumpersticker or take-home—big idea for our audience. We will then give illustrations, examples, or payloads of this idea.

- State the bumpersticker big idea.
- Illustrate it.
- Give examples of it (maybe a negative how not to do it and a positive how to do it).
- End with a final clear statement of the bumpersticker big idea.

For example, if I was preaching from John 4, let's say my take-home idea is, "We are thirsty for Jesus." My conclusion could go like this:

We are thirsty for Jesus.

    Whether we realize it or not, we're all thirsty for Jesus.

    Have you ever seen the image of a man in a desert? He is so thirsty for water that he drinks the sand around him. But the sand won't satisfy his thirst because it's not water. The sand only makes him more thirsty. He needs water. Without water he will die.

    We are the same. We are thirsty for Jesus. We can try to satisfy that thirst for Jesus with other things that are not Jesus. But that will only make us more thirsty. We need Jesus. Without Jesus, we will die.

    I was once at a wedding reception. The man sitting next to me said, "I'm a lawyer. For my whole life I've wanted to be a lawyer. I studied hard in high school and got the grades I needed to get into law school. I graduated and became a lawyer. Since then I've traveled all over the world. I've just bought a house. But do you know what? I still haven't found what I'm looking for."

    Do you know what I saw in front of me that night? I saw a man thirsty for Jesus. He had tried all the other things that are not Jesus. But he was still thirsty for Jesus.

But I've also met another man. His name is Spiro. He told me that in his twenties, he got into finance and investments. He made all the money he needed to make and then he traveled the world. But in his thirties, someone told Spiro about Jesus, and Spiro decided to trust, know, and follow Jesus.

But Spiro tells me that every now and then he meets people who say that they've been a Christian "for as long as they can remember." Ever since they were children, they have trusted, known, and followed Jesus.

Spiro says to me, "Do you know what I do when I hear people say that? I envy them. I wish I had known Jesus for as long as I can remember. I would give up all the money I made in my twenties if I could have known Jesus earlier."

We all have a thirst for Jesus. We can try to satisfy that thirst with other things. But that will only make us more thirsty. Come to Jesus. He offers us living water. He will satisfy our thirst. He will give us life.

We are thirsty for Jesus.

Notice how each element is represented in this example:

- State the bumpersticker idea: "We are thirsty for Jesus."
- Illustrate with the analogy of a man in the desert.
- Negative example of the lawyer
- Positive example of Spiro
- End with the bumpersticker big idea: "We are thirsty for Jesus."

## STORYTELLING THE NARRATIVE

If these options seem too propositional and didactic, you can also attempt storytelling the Bible story. You can use the methods of storytelling outlined in chapter 7 of this book to retell the whole story.

I usually do this by using the introduction to set up an existential question. I then promise an answer in the Bible story. And then I tell my listeners I'm going to tell them the story from the Bible. After I've told them the story, I say something like, "Wow, what a story. But if you're like me, you've probably got questions that you want answered. Let's answer them now."[4]

---

4. For more information, consult my section in Christine Dillon's *Storytelling the Gospel*.

The body of my talk has these elements:

1. Storytell the story.
2. Ask three questions from the story.
3. Answer these three questions.

For example, I once preached from Luke 16:19–31—the story of the rich man and Lazarus. My introduction set up the existential question, "What are we supposed to believe about hell?" I promised them an answer from Jesus' story in Luke 16:19–31.

In the body of the talk, I told the story from Luke 16:19–31.

I then set up the questions by saying, "Wow, if you're anything like me, you're probably now wanting to ask these three questions: (1) Is hell a real place? (2) What did the rich man do to deserve to be in hell? and (3) How do I make sure I don't end up in hell? Well, let's go back to the story to see if we can find the answers to these questions."

I then answered the three questions in the rest of the body of the talk.

The key here is to anticipate what three questions our audience wants to ask. Obviously, the questions will differ depending on our audience and their cultural, social, and existential contexts. Again, this shows us the added importance of cultural exegesis and contextualization.

## HOW TO LEAD THE SINNER'S PRAYER

We can end our talk with an offer for people in our audience to make an immediate decision to follow Jesus. They can do this by praying the so-called Sinner's Prayer.

You may have strong opinions as to whether it is appropriate to end a sermon or evangelistic talk with the Sinner's Prayer. I believe this is a pastoral decision that is determined by whether those in the audience are at a stage where they understand sufficiently what they are deciding.

In our post-Christian culture, it is difficult to see how a 20–30 minute talk can provide sufficient content for someone to make an informed decision to follow Jesus, especially if they have never previously heard the gospel. On the other hand, there will sometimes be people in the audience who have been on a long journey of hearing the gospel, and the talk you give may be the final piece of the puzzle for them. So while it's unlikely that a person hearing the gospel for the first time will respond, there may be some who are ready to make a decision, and an offer to pray with them may be the catalyst they need to move from nonbelief to belief. With this in mind, I'll offer you the following formula for praying the Sinner's Prayer. I call it a formula because it follows a pattern, but I encourage you to avoid formulaic language and seek to make sure that you are sensitive to the attitude and desire of the person you are praying with.

## A Simple Formula for the Sinner's Prayer

A simple formula for the Sinner's Prayer follows the pattern of "sorry, please, and thank you."

*Sorry:* Confess to the metaphor for *sin* in the talk.
*Please:* Ask for the metaphor of *salvation* in the talk.
*Thank You:* Thank God for the metaphor of *Christ* and his *work* in the talk.

Here are a few examples of what this looks like based on several passages from the New Testament.

**Romans 3:21–31:** "O God . . .
"Sorry for falling short of your glory.
"Please declare me innocent.
"Thank you that Jesus died for my sins."
**John 3:16:** "O God . . .
"Sorry that I have not believed in Jesus.
"Please give me eternal life.
"Thank you for sending Jesus to save me."
**Luke 12:13–21:** "O God . . .
"Sorry that I have been storing up for myself.
"Please let me be rich toward you instead.
"Thank you for sending Jesus so I can be rich toward you."

If you have never led someone in a Sinner's Prayer, you can start by saying something like this: "I am going to give us a chance to respond to God's call with a prayer." Then read the prayer to them so that they know what they are about to pray. After you've read it once, say something like, "If that sounds like what you want to say to God, then pray the prayer with me. I'm going to pray the prayer one sentence at a time. Then I'm going to pause, and you can say that same sentence in your heart to God."

Then simply pray the prayer one sentence at time with a long pause between each sentence. After you've prayed the prayer, say something like, "If you prayed that prayer, maybe you feel different, or maybe you don't. But God has heard you, and he is rejoicing."

Hopefully, the organizers of an event or a service have something arranged for follow-up. If that's the case, point the person toward that next step: "Today you have started the new day of a new life. It's like you're a child taking your very first steps. The organizers of this event will help you to find the support, help, and friends that you need."

You can then ask them to give their contact information to the organizers. Usually there will be a response form that they can fill out. The response form should be really simple. For example:

Name:
Contact Details:
Tick a box:
    ☐ I prayed the prayer.
    ☐ I want more information.
    ☐ I'm already a Christian.

I like to keep it at three boxes or less for simplicity. Negative options are left out to keep things in a positive mood. They can simply leave the boxes unchecked if they don't want more information or don't want to become a Christian.

Sometimes the organizers want those who prayed the prayer to walk out *en masse* to another room for follow-up. In these situations I say something like:

"I'm going to ask those who prayed the prayer to do something public. I'm going to ask you to walk out and meet me in the room next door. The reasons I'm going to ask you to do this are:

- "To give you a memory of your decision to follow Jesus.
- "So you can see you're not alone. Many others also decided to follow Jesus.
- "So we can connect you with a group of Christians who can support you.
- "So I can pray for you."

## PREACHING AT WEDDINGS

Occasionally you might get invited to speak at a wedding for a Christian couple. Sometimes this might happen because the couple wants you to preach evangelistically to their family and friends. My strategy in these situations is to use stories from the couple to function as my introduction, illustrations, examples, and conclusion in my Bible talk.

There's a good reason for this. Whatever stories we usually use will not work in a wedding talk. That's because the guests are not used to listening to a conventional Bible talk. So they will be wondering, "Why is this bozo telling us these stories that have got nothing to do with the couple?"

The guests have turned up for the couple. So they will be engaged if we use stories from the couple in our Bible talk. I usually meet the couple at least once before the wedding and ask them for stories to include. To get at these stories, I ask questions like:

- How did they meet?
- Who chased whom?
- What was their first date like?
- How did they declare their love for each other?
- What gifts have they given each other?
- What is each person's "language of love"?
- What adventures have they had together?
- What annoying habits does each person have?
- Who cooks, and what do they cook?
- What are their special likes and dislikes?
- What do they like to do together?
- What car do they drive?
- What's it like to be a passenger in their car?
- Where will they live?
- How have they furnished the house or unit?
- What are their plans for after the wedding?
- What's something romantic that they've done?
- What's the most unromantic thing that they've done?
- How did he or she propose?

From this pool of stories, I will choose one for the introduction, one for each point as an illustration, and one for the conclusion. For a ten-minute three-point talk, I need five stories from the couple! And a tip: usually the story about how they met is good for the introduction, and the story about how he or she proposed is good for the conclusion.

As we preach the gospel, guests who are not used to hearing a Bible talk might get offended that they are hearing something so explicitly Christian at a wedding. So we need to announce in advance that our message has been authorized by the couple. I usually do this in the introduction. In the place where we usually highlight the need, text, and preview, I make this brief pronouncement:

- Introduce myself as a friend of the couple (say how I know them).
- Say that the couple are Christians (or that they "trust and follow Jesus").
- Say that they have asked me to give today's message based on this Bible passage.
- Say that the Bible passage is a favorite passage of the couple.
- Say that this is what the couple have asked me to say to their friends and family on their special day because this will explain who they are and what makes them tick.

This gives warrant for you to say what you're about to say at a wedding talk.

## CONCLUSION: WEDDING BELLS

The wedding bells were ringing. It had been a great wedding service for Scott and Kate. The bridal party looked stunning in their wedding attire. The flowers were gorgeous. The vows were meaningful and memorable.

And besides the lovely couple, everyone was talking about the message given by the couple's old college friend Tom, the medical doctor. People who had never gone to church or read the Bible before were saying, "I've never heard a message like that before. It was so interesting!"

Tom's introduction was a story of how Scott and Kate met. Scott's romantic first question to Kate was, "What's your favorite vegetable?" It must have worked! Because here were Scott and Kate, getting married.

Tom used this story to ask the question, "But what sort of marriage will this be?" To answer this, Tom pointed the audience to Philippians 2:1–11, which was a favorite Bible passage for Scott and Kate. Tom let everyone know that he was going to preach a message on behalf of Scott and Kate to their friends and family, on their special day, based on this Bible passage.

From Philippians 2:1–11, Tom said that we have three choices for a marriage. Marriages can be, first, a love story. Tom illustrated this with the different languages of love that Scott and Kate have. Scott's language is to do acts of service, such as cooking. Kate's language of love is . . . well, ahem . . . to eat the cooking. This illustrates the acts of service in Philippians 2:1–8: love, humility, and looking out for the interests of others as modeled by Jesus' becoming a servant and dying for us on the cross.

But second, marriages can also become a horror story. Things can go from functional to dysfunctional in the blink of an eye. Tom illustrated this with a story of Scott and Kate on a date night. It was meant to be a romantic night. But as they were crossing the street, Kate was knocked over by a cyclist. And Scott had to decide whether to do mouth-to-mouth on Kate on their first date! Would this be taking advantage of the situation? Fortunately for Scott, Kate regained consciousness before he had to perform mouth-to-mouth.

Marriages can also go from functional to dysfunctional. And this is what we see in Philippians 2:1–5 if we read between the lines. We read words such as "selfish ambition" and "conceit." Why is that? Because by nature everyone is self-serving. Marriage vows alone cannot remove this from our nature.

Third, the only way to prevent marriages from going bad is if the marriage becomes an adventure story. The couple needs to serve someone else. To illustrate this, Tom illustrated with how Scott and Kate stay at home and play board games. Sounds boring. No! Because the board games become the adventure. In the same way, if the married couple serves the risen Jesus of Philippians 2:9–11, they won't have to become self-serving. They will be worshiping Jesus instead of themselves. Jesus will be the adventure, direction, and purpose that their lives crave.

Tom concluded the talk with the story of Scott's proposing to Kate on a sunset beach. But what was Scott asking Kate to commit her life to? Was it love? Or was it also an adventure? In the same way, Philippians 2:1–11 is asking everyone if they want to commit their lives not just to loving each other but also to serving and worshiping Jesus. And Jesus will give our lives the adventure, direction, and purpose that we both want and need.

# CHAPTER 10

# RELIGIOUS EPISTEMOLOGY, APOLOGETICS, AND DEFEATER BELIEFS

## Why won't people believe?

Michelle is spiritual. She believes in life after death. She also believes that there must be a loving personal God who made the universe. But Michelle would never call herself a Christian. Not if the Christian God sends people to hell! Not if the Christian God oppresses women. And certainly not if the Christian God won't allow gays to get married.

Michelle is not alone. Many people today cannot believe in the gospel because of "defeater beliefs." Until these are addressed by Christians, people like Michelle will refuse to believe the gospel of Jesus. But if Christians can hear, understand, empathize with, and address Michelle's presuppositions, then the unbelievable news of Jesus might become more believable for people like Michelle.

### RELIGIOUS EPISTEMOLOGY

Why do we believe some things but not others? For example, once upon a time, we believed that the earth was flat. But now we believe it's round. Yet most of us have not been in a spaceship orbiting the earth to see for ourselves that the earth is round. Yet we believe that it is. What is the mechanism for our belief?

Why do we believe some things and not others? This field of study is called epistemology. But when we apply it to religious beliefs—why do some people believe in the existence of God, but others don't?—it is called religious epistemology. In this section, we will outline some basic building blocks of religious epistemology.

## Which of These Truth Claims Is True?

Here are several truth claims. Which are you happy to believe as true?

Two plus two equals four.
Washington is the capital of the USA.
Salt is a compound of sodium and chlorine.
The MRI scans show the cartilage in my knee is worn away.
I live in Sydney, Australia.
I went to elementary school in Adelaide, Australia.
I have a cousin called John.
I know where you can find a good coffee shop in Vancouver, Canada.
I cook a good pancake.
I love my wife.

At the top of the list are facts that can be verified logically, empirically, and scientifically. But as we move down the list, it becomes harder to verify the claims with only logic, empiricism, and the scientific method. You have to rely more and more on trust, testimony, and personal experience. You have to know me to trust my words. You have to take me at my word.

So what do we do with religious truth claims? For example, "Jesus Christ is the Son of God" or "God loves you." Where in the spectrum of truth claims do they belong? Are these claims verified by logic, empiricism, and the scientific method? Or do they rely more on trust, testimony, and personal experience?

## How Do We Choose to Believe Someone?

In the previous list of truth claims, often we had to decide whether we could trust the person making the truth claim. How do we decide? According to the ancient Greeks, there are three components to my message:

- *Logos:* what I say
- *Pathos:* the way I make you feel (your emotions, passions)
- *Ethos:* the way I live (my character)

Look at the following list of truth claims. Let's say someone makes these truth claims to you. Which of the three—logos, pathos, ethos—is most influential in helping you to decide whether the claim is true?

Two plus two equals four.

Washington is the capital of the USA.

It will rain tomorrow.

USA needs to get a new national anthem.

Buy this car—it's only been driven by an elderly lady to church on Sundays.

I've done the bungee jump in New Zealand.

I cook a good pancake.

I am your father!

I love you.

For the claims that are easy to verify based on empirical facts— "Washington is the capital of the USA"—you rely chiefly on logos. But for the other claims, when you have to decide whether to trust the speaker, you rely more and more on pathos and ethos.

So what does this mean for religious truth claims? How do we decide whether to believe these claims: "Jesus Christ is the Son of God" and "God loves you"? What roles are played by logos, pathos, or ethos in helping you to believe them? Notice in 1 Thessalonians how Paul appeals to pathos and ethos, as well as logos, in making his appeal: "Because our gospel came to you not simply with words [logos] but also with power, with the Holy Spirit and deep conviction [pathos]. You know how we lived among you for your sake [ethos]" (1 Thess. 1:5).

When we are evaluating religious truth claims, all three aspects come into play, affecting how we determine whether they can be trusted. Why does this matter? Because if we think our friends are not becoming Christians because of lack of cognitive information about the gospel, then we will concentrate on giving them logos. But if we think our friends are not becoming Christians because their hearts are closed to the gospel, then we may want to concentrate on pathos and ethos.

**The Obama Heckler**

Have a look at this YouTube clip of the "Obama Heckler": https://youtu.be/9cP-FTX5tVg.

As a Christian, I believe—at a purely ontologically, cognitive informational level (the logos)—that what the heckler shouts is true: "Jesus Christ is the one and only true living God." I think most of us would agree with him and tick the box that "Jesus Christ is the one and only true living God." But if we didn't share the heckler's presuppositions, then the heckler is unpersuasive—it is difficult at an epistemological level to believe his ontological claim—because he has not won us over at the level of ethos or pathos. This clip also supports the claim that I was making in a previous chapter on contextualization. What we say is not always what others hear. It is not enough to transfer information when we evangelize. We need to speak in ways that our culture can hear and understand.

The way we choose to communicate reveals our anthropology (our understanding of what it means to be a human being). If we reduce human beings only to rational minds, then we will think that we only need to transfer ideas and cognitive information. But if we believe that human beings are holistically bodies, minds, and emotions, then we will try to communicate the gospel at the level of information (logos), body (ethos), and emotions (pathos). This is what James is getting at in his New Testament letter. He points out that it's no good only telling someone the idea—"God loves you"—without also feeding their bodies (James 2:14–17). Psychologists today would agree. They say that we need both IQ (cognitive intelligence) and EQ (emotional intelligence). Some people more naturally connect with people intelligently—logos—but we also need to connect with them emotionally—pathos and ethos. It's not an either-or; it's a both-and.

That said, I'm emphasizing the need to include the pathos and ethos because in the modern Western church, we've traditionally encouraged smart and gifted people—doctors and lawyers—into full-time paid Christian ministry. But cultural changes suggest that maybe we should also encourage emotionally smart people—those in the creative arts—into full-time paid Christian ministry. Conversely, rather than encouraging people into seminary, where we learn the cognitive aspects of Christianity, we may want to encourage some people to pursue the creative arts, where we learn to express ourselves through body and emotions.

## The Role of Community

Whether we like it or not, for right or for wrong, community plays a large role in determining what we believe is true. We tend to adopt the beliefs of our community, as we saw in chapter 2. So what do we do with religious truth claims? The postmodern critique of religious belief is uncomfortably close to the truth: "Had you been born in India, you would be a Hindu. Or had you been born in Indonesia, you would be a Muslim. But you were born in the USA, so that's why you're a Christian." In reply we can say that a statement like this doesn't preclude a belief from still being true. We have to decide whether a religious belief is true based on other grounds. And similarly, we can say to the person making this accusation, "And you're a secular humanist because our society is secular humanist." The critique cuts both ways.

But we should also acknowledge that the Bible, to some degree, agrees with this postmodern critique. The Bible recognizes the role of community in shaping our beliefs. Parents are told to pass on their beliefs to their children (Deut. 6:20–25). Paul passes on his beliefs to the Corinthians (1 Cor. 15:1–11). The Hebrew Christians must not stop the habit of meeting together (Heb. 10:24–25). Those who don't meet together soon find themselves cut off from the truth (3 John 9–10).

So there is truth in the postmodern critique that our beliefs are shaped by our community. And I hope that you're sensing that, more and more, we tend to believe what trusted people tell us. Consider the following truth claims:

Water boils at 100 degrees Celsius.
The MRI scans show that your knee needs an operation.
I am your father.
I didn't kill him.
I love you.

We all likely believe the claim that water boils at 100 degrees Celsius. Yet most of us have not done a legitimate scientific experiment to prove this is true. And if you have, you likely found that water doesn't always boil at exactly 100 degrees. So why do we still believe the statement that water boils at 100 degrees Celsius? Because we trust what teachers and books tell us. We don't have access to the empirical data. And we know that it's an approximation that is influenced by other factors like altitude and environment. But we also trust that our teachers and books do have access to this knowledge and it still functions as a trustworthy statement. So we end up believing what they tell us to believe.

Let's say a doctor says to us, "The MRI scans show that your knee needs an operation." We will tend to believe her at face value, especially if she has degrees and experience. Of course, you can also ask for a second opinion. But doing this only moves the goalpost back a few feet. Who do you believe now, the first doctor or the second one? Why would you trust one over the other? Of course, you can try to read the MRI scans for yourself, but most of us are not trained to do this. So at some stage, we all have to decide, "Do I trust what this doctor tells me?" We don't have access to perfect knowledge or expertise in every area, so we end up believing what a trusted person tells us to believe. And it's not even about trusting the doctors, really. It goes back even farther. The truth is that most doctors don't know how an MRI scanner works. They can read the MRI, but they are also trusting what the engineers and physicists have designed and built and what they've told them about the workings of an MRI scanner.

Most of us believe that our biological parents are indeed our biological parents. Yet very few people have done a DNA test to prove this scientifically. Why have we not done this? Because we trust what our parents and those present at our birth (through a signed certificate) tell us. We take it at face value, trusting that they are telling the truth. If we do take the DNA test, it is likely because we have reason to doubt, because trust has broken down. We tend to believe our parents—if we trust them—and accept that they are our biological parents.

When I was teaching a class at seminary, I did a thought experiment with the married men in my class. I said to them, "Imagine you came home early today. But you notice that something's wrong. The door is open. There's a dead body lying in the hall. Your wife is standing over the dead body with a bloody knife in her hand. She looks at you and says, 'You're home early! Okay, I know this looks bad, but you have to believe me; I didn't do it.'"

Then I ask them, "Would you believe her?" And every married man said, "Yes." They chose to believe their wife because they trusted her against the evidence.

But a lawyer in my class spoke up at that moment. He said, "My answer is no! I've seen this too many times in criminal cases where a spouse wrongly believes their partner instead of the evidence." So I pushed him a little deeper and asked him pointedly, "Let's say it was your wife. Would you believe her?" He was silent for a few moments, thinking. And then he finally answered. "Yes. You've got me. I would believe her."

Or what about when I come home and my wife says to me, "I love you." What do I do with that truth claim? Do I ask her to prove it with a scientific experiment? Do I ask her to show me an X-ray of her heart or give me a blood sample of this so-called love? No, I take her at her word because I trust her. I've lived with her. I know her.

We believe the testimony of people we trust—teachers, doctors, family, friends, and spouses. We take them at their word. We know that we often don't have perfect access to the facts, data, or evidence. But that's okay because we believe the testimony of those that we trust. This is what philospher Alvin Plantinga calls warranted belief.[1] We believe things not because we have perfect unassailable evidence that they are true but because we have valid reasons and they are enough to convince us that they are true.

That's why the Bible places so much emphasis on the Word. We are told that Jesus is the Word in the flesh. When Jesus says that he is the Son of God, we have to take him at his word. But it's more than that, isn't it? Our access to the person and words of Jesus can come only through the words of other eyewitnesses, through the testimony of the apostles who saw, heard, and wrote it down or shared what they had seen and heard with others who wrote it down (John 21:24; 1 John 1:1–3). So we have to decide, "Can I trust the testimony of the apostles?"

## The Role of Facts, Evidence, and Data

Facts, evidence, and data play a role in determining belief. But often it's a secondary role. In his book *The Righteous Mind*, Jonathan Haidt observes that people often shape the data they receive to fit a preconceived worldview. Behavioral psychologists have all sorts of terms for this—post-hoc reasoning, confirmation bias, and motivated reasoning, just to name a few. In his book, Haidt uses the analogy of a human rider sitting on the back of an elephant. The rider represents reason and the elephant emotions. We often assume that our rational mind is in control and can dictate what is true to our emotions. But Haidt says that it's actually the other way around. The elephant goes where it wants and determines where the rider ends up. That's why we fabricate post-hoc reasons for what we believe based on our emotions.[2]

---

1. Alvin Plantinga, *Warranted Christian Belief* (New York: Oxford Univ. Press, 2000), 167–98.
2. Jonathan Haidt, *The Righteous Mind: Why Good People Are Divided by Politics and Religion* (New York: Penguin, 2012), Kindle edition.

If Haidt's analysis is correct—and I believe it to be so—this means that we wrongly concentrate on logos at the expense of pathos and ethos. And when it comes to evangelism, it means that we won't win over the mind until we first win over the emotions. If anything, we need to win over the emotions before we win over the mind. Pathos and ethos are chronologically prior to logos.

The book *Five Views on Apologetics* presents us with a thought experiment. Let's say that tomorrow we wake up to the headline, "The Bones of Jesus Have Been Discovered!" Among Christian believers, who would believe a statement like this? Which of us would leave behind our faith and adopt a pre-Christian or pagan life and worldview under the belief that Jesus was never raised from the dead? I presented this thought experiment to my seminary class, many of whom had given up promising careers to enter the ministry. I asked them, "Who here would stop training to be a minister or a missionary and go back to law, dentistry, engineering, nursing, teaching, and medicine?" Not a single person raised their hand.

Why not? Because we have prior truth commitments that override what we are hearing and seeing. We find ways to explain away the evidence, knowing that it must be a hoax or thinking that there needs to be more evidence before a conclusion is firmly reached. It's probably a mistake, a nice story, but not a true story.

But what's the point of going through this thought experiment? It's to show a group of committed Christian believers exactly what it's like when we present facts, evidence, and data to our non-Christian friends about Jesus' resurrection. It's no different for them. When they hear us talk about Jesus and the resurrection and our belief in God and the Bible, we are announcing what is contrary to fact for them. The headline in the paper reads, "Christ Discovered to Have Risen from the Dead," and they find it difficult, if not impossible, to believe. Surely they are mistaken. Let's wait for more evidence before drawing any conclusions. We may try to demonstrate the historical reliability of this claim, but they still aren't convinced. So why aren't they converting from their unbelief to belief? Because, like us, they will find ways to explain away the evidence. It must be a hoax. There needs to be more evidence. Maybe it's a mistake. A nice story, but not a true story.

But it's even more than this. We don't just shape the evidence to fit our preconceived worldviews. Our worldviews shape how we interpret the evidence. For example, if we show the evidence for Christ's resurrection to a person of Hindu faith, they will think, "That's no big deal. In my worldview people are always reincarnating. What happened to Jesus is exactly what's supposed to happen to everyone on the planet." Harold Netland points out that a Hindu has a low view of historical evidence. It's mundane data to them, so they find it hard to see what the big deal is about a historical event. If the Christian faith was really worth believing, it would be founded upon something more supranatural than a very natural and historical event.[3]

By and large, whether we know it or not, what we end up believing is an explanation of best fit. This is the explanation that best explains the evidence, what trusted people tell me, and what I've experienced. It's why people believe in global warming, the causes of World War II, and love!

It's also how courts of law operate. What verdict best fits the evidence, the trusted testimonies, and our own experiences? It's also how books on history are written. What account best fits the evidence, trusted testimonies, and our experiences? It's also how relationships work. It's why I believe that my wife loves me. It's the explanation that best fits the evidence, trusted testimony, and my experiences.

## The Cumulative Case Method

If this is true, then how do people change their minds? If we have preconceived worldviews that shape the evidence, how do we ever change our worldviews? What will generate a paradigm shift?

One explanation is the cumulative case method.[4] After a while, bit by bit, if there's enough evidence that cannot be accommodated by the preconceived worldview, we might eventually jettison our worldview for another worldview that better accommodates the new evidence. We need an explanation of better fit![5] For example, if every day for the next ten years, they discovered more evidence supporting the claim that Jesus' bones have been discovered, then many of us might end up leaving the faith. Or if every day married men found yet another dead body lying under the bloody knife clutched by their wives, they might soon believe that their wives were not telling the truth when they said, "It wasn't me."

The gospels also operate on this cumulative case method. After yet another sign by Jesus, people need an explanation of better fit: that Jesus

---

3. See discussion by Harold Netland, *Encountering Religious Pluralism: The Challenge to Christian Faith and Mission* (Downers Grove, Ill.: InterVarsity, 2001), 209–10.

4. Paul Feinberg, "Cumulative Case Apologetics," in *Five Views on Apologetics*, ed. Stanley N. Gundry and Steven B. Cowan (Grand Rapids, Mich.: Zondervan, 2000), 147–72.

5. For example, see Paul Hiebert's examples of changing our "paradigmatic or configurational nature of knowledge" in Paul Hiebert, *Transforming Worldviews: An Anthropological Understanding of How People Change* (Grand Rapids, Mich.: Baker, 2008), 48–49.

really is the Messiah sent by God. How else can they explain what they see Jesus doing? When John the Baptist asks Jesus, "Are you the one who is to come, or should we expect someone else?" Jesus points to the evidence—the blind see, the deaf hear, and the dead are raised—and asks if John has a better explanation (Matt. 11:3–6). The old paradigms must go, to be replaced by new paradigms (Mark 2:22).

When I went through medical school, I was taught that stomach ulcers are caused by too much acid in the stomach. We were taught to treat stomach ulcers with strategies to reduce the acid in the stomach. But in the 1980s, Australian doctors—Robin Warren and Barry Marshall—made a different claim. They claimed that ulcers are caused by bacteria—*Helicobacter pylori*—and not by acid. Stomach ulcers are an infectious disease that can be cured by antibiotics.

Though Warren and Marshall produced evidence for their claim, the medical community did not believe them. This is because the claim that ulcers are caused by bacteria did not fit any of the paradigms in the medical community. It would have overturned everything that doctors had been taught, everything that they had told their patients, and everything that they had done to treat ulcers. We had too much invested in the status quo. So the evidence was ignored, explained away, ridiculed, or rejected.

But bit by bit, as more evidence accumulated, the medical community was forced to change its views. A paradigm shift occurred. Now the established view is that stomach ulcers are caused by bacteria and should be treated by an antibiotic. But this shift occurred only after decades of cumulative research and evidence from the initial discovery.

People largely have their minds already made up. They have preconceived worldviews with presuppositions, interpretive lenses, plausibility structures, and defeater beliefs. Evidence plays only a secondary role. Evidence ends up being interpreted and shaped to fit the preconceived worldview.

But there is still a dialectical relationship between evidence and presuppositions. By and large, our presuppositions shape the evidence, but there can also be a cumulative case effect where after a while the person encounters enough evidence that cannot be neatly explained away. When this happens, there can be instances of worldviews being transformed into new worldviews in the search for an explanation of better fit.

What does all of this mean for our efforts at evangelism? It means that there is a place for both gently dismantling the person's worldview (presuppositional apologetics) and presenting them with evidence for the

Christian truth claims (evidentialist apologetics). These two approaches can work together, from different directions, to bring about a shift in worldview. Let's take a closer look at how this happens.

## DISMANTLING DEFEATER BELIEFS

Let's begin by looking at an issue that sharply divides people in the United States: gun ownership and gun control. Let's say that I am pro gun control, and you are pro gun ownership. How can I persuade you to change your mind? I could try presenting facts, evidence, and data to you. I could point out the high number of shootings and gun-related deaths in the USA. I could use as evidence the 2012 mass shooting at the movie theater in Aurora, Colorado. The cold, hard facts are that twelve people were killed and seventy others were injured. The data is that the gunman fired seventy-six shots into the audience. From my worldview, this seems to be overwhelming evidence in favor of gun control. If we had less guns in the USA, we would have less gun shootings and gun deaths.

But what will you say in response to this? Will my evidence overwhelm you into a worldview change? No, you will respond, "Exactly. That's why we need more guns, not less." In your worldview, if everyone had guns that night in the movie theater in Aurora, Colorado, the gunman would not have fired off seventy-six shots. And twelve people would not have been killed. From your worldview, this seems to be overwhelming evidence against gun control. If we had more guns in the USA, we would have less shootings and gun-related deaths.

So we argue in circles. Same evidence. But two opposite conclusions. Again, people do not change their worldviews because of evidence alone. Their minds are made up. So they interpret and shape the evidence to fit their worldview. The evidence ends up reinforcing whatever worldview they already have.

This has immediate application for evangelism. Let's say our non-Christian friend has a hard time believing in hell. We can present to them facts, evidence, and data. We might say, "Do you know who speaks more about hell than any other person in the Bible? Jesus! So if Jesus talks about hell, then there must be a hell."

But they might respond, "Exactly. Jesus is so loving. So if he talks about hell, then there must be some other explanation. A loving Jesus would never send people to a place of eternal punishment. So hell can't be real."

Can you see what has happened? Same evidence. But two opposite conclusions. Our worldviews determine how we shape the evidence. Our starting point will determine our endpoint.

## The Chicken and Egg of Apologetics: Evidence or Presuppositions?

So how can we get people to change their views? Do people believe what they believe because of evidence? Or because of presuppositions? This is the chicken-and-egg argument that divides the Christian world in the field of apologetics. Just like people can be divided over Coke and Pepsi, Ford and Chevy, Christians can be divided over the two dominant approaches to apologetics: evidentialism and presuppositionalism.

### Evidentialism

Evidentialism is the apologetic approach that believes that if we give people evidence for what we believe—that Jesus is the Son of God, for example—then this evidence will compel them to belief (1 Peter 3:15; Matt. 11:4; Mark 2:10–12; John 20:8, 27, 30–31; Acts 14:17, 27). An evidentialist will tend to be optimistic about the enterprise of apologetics, believing that if we clearly and accurately present the evidence, it will move a person from nonbelief to belief in the gospel. Those who take a more evidentialist approach believe in the importance of using reason, arguments, logic, facts, evidence, and data in evangelism.

### Presuppositionalism

The counter to evidentialism is the observation that many people don't believe because of evidence, even when it is clearly presented to them. As I shared in the examples earlier, this is because people have preconceptions through which they interpret and shape the evidence to fit their views. And they explain away whatever evidence doesn't fit.

Worse, the Bible suggests that there are what theologians refer to as the noetic effects of sin. This refers to the effect that sin has on our ability to think, reason, and use our minds. The doctrine of total depravity teaches that every aspect of us is affected by sin (Rom. 3:9–20), and it implies that our ability to reason from evidence is somehow impaired. We have sufficient evidence about God and his existence and nature to condemn us, but that evidence is not enough to lead us to belief in a way that saves us from our sin (Rom. 1:18–20). The Bible also teaches that in our sinful state we are blinded by our sin (2 Cor. 4:4). This means that we suppress the truth (Rom. 1:18), unless the Spirit sovereignly intervenes and illuminates us. We will see (or understand the meaning at some level) but not perceive (understand

and believe or commit to that truth). We will hear but not understand (1 Cor. 2:14). Only those with the Spirit can discern the mystery and the foolishness of the gospel (1 Cor. 2:6–16).

Those who advocate a presuppositionalist approach argue that instead of presenting evidence, we should simply assume Christian presuppositions and start from there. Our method should be to present the gospel and pray for the Spirit to do his work. The rationale is that the gospel will change the worldview of the nonbeliever, and this will open their eyes to seeing the evidence from a Christian worldview. But until this happens we are, at best, wasting our time with apologetics or, at worst, not trusting enough in the gospel and relying on human arguments.

A presuppositionalist will tend to be pessimistic about the enterprise of apologetics, believing that there is little place for using reason, arguments, logic, facts, evidence, and data in evangelism.

## Cumulative Case Method

The counter to presuppositionalism is to say that the noetic effects of sin (impairing our mind and mental capacities) would similarly blind a nonbeliever from seeing both the evidence and the Christian worldview. And if the Spirit does his supernatural work, why can he not also work through the natural means of our presentation of the evidence and the Christian worldview? It is certainly important that we don't confuse the supernatural personal agency of the Spirit with the natural human means by which he does his work. But they can be mutually compatible and don't need to be pitted against each other. Both the evidentialist and the presuppositionalist can argue that they are relying on the Spirit's sovereignty and efficacy.

Instead of having to choose between presenting either evidence or presuppositions, some would say that we need both evidence and presuppositions in the work of evangelism. Instead of a purely inductive (evidentialist) approach or a deductive (presuppositionalist) approach, we can utilize an abductive to-and-fro (cumulative case) approach. With the cumulative case method, the strategy is to deliver an informal argument that presents the evidence, surveys how different worldviews might explain the evidence, and then present the Christian worldview as the hypothesis that best explains the evidence. The aim is to provide an explanation of best fit. Paul Feinberg and Harold Netland, professors at Trinity Evangelical Divinity School, have described this method as similar to a lawyer making their case before the court or a literary critic arguing for a particular interpretation of a book.

If the strategy of using the cumulative case method is correct—and I believe it is—then this implies that conversion in our post-Christian era is more of a journey to belief. It will likely be experienced by the convert as a series of moments—possibly lasting several years—rather than a single moment of conversion. It also means that our role as an evangelist may vary and shift depending on the context and the individual. We may be present in one of those single moments when the Spirit brings a shift and then trust God to send along other evangelists at later times, or we may be there for our non-Christian friend over the next few years' worth of moments. This also means that there isn't a silver-bullet answer that we can give that will convert our friend. Instead, evangelism is a cumulation of all the things that we do to promote the gospel, such as listening, inviting, offering hospitality, having coffee or dinner, going to the movies, being there for our friend, as well as presenting a reasoned case for our belief. And more than that, it may not be one single evangelist who brings our friend to the faith but a series of multiple evangelists. As an evangelist, we will in God's sovereignty be merely one piece of the puzzle. This is both empowering and humbling at the same time![6]

## Modified Presuppositional Apologetics

The method I use and teach is what I called a modified presuppositional apologetic approach. It borrows heavily from the writing and preaching of pastor and author Timothy Keller, especially as he has modeled in his books *The Reason for God* and *Making Sense of God*. I've also learned a great deal from several of his podcasts in which he lays out the specifics of his approach.[7]

What is a modified presuppositional apologetic? From presuppositionalism I begin with the assumption that presenting evidence alone will typically not be very effective. Why? Because the other person probably does not share my presuppositions. They have different plausibility structures, different defeater beliefs. But unlike the early advocates of presuppositionalism, I do believe that there is a valid place for using reason, arguments, logic, facts, evidence, and data in our evangelism. Our reasoning and arguments become one of many pieces that we utilize in evangelism. As a practical matter, I frequently use reasoning and arguments and evidence to dismantle

---

6. *The Secret Thoughts of an Unlikely Convert* by Rosaria Champagne Butterfield. This seems to be how she journeyed into belief. See Rosaria Champagne Butterfield, *The Secret Thoughts of an Unlikely Convert* (Pittsburgh: Crown and Covenant, 2014).

7. Most notably Keller's Preaching Christ in a Postmodern World series of talks, delivered at Reformed Theological Seminary, DMin program, 2002, which can be found on iTunes.

a nonbeliever's presuppositions. Once we've established some common ground, I can present the Christian worldview as an attractive alternative to their faulty worldview, one that better completes their cultural storyline. Here is a summary of the method:

1. *Resonate:* Describe, understand, and empathize with their presuppositions.
2. *Dismantle:* Show a deficiency or dissonance in their presuppositions.
3. *Gospel:* Complete their cultural storyline with the gospel.

Now let's say a friend says to me, "I can't become a Christian. Not if it means all that stuff in the Bible that says homosexuality is wrong. How can a loving God not accept people just for who they are?" What do we say in response? We could use evidence to mount an argument to support the traditional Christian position on homosexuality. For example, we could quote Bible verses that support our Christian position. We could appeal to reasoning: it seems unnatural. But none of this seems convincing to our friend. If they don't share our presuppositions, who cares what the Bible says? And who's to say what's natural and unnatural? Surely they are only social constructs. What we can do instead—in addition to things we'd do in any friendship or close relationship—is to resonate with their beliefs, dismantle their worldview, and then share the gospel.

### 1. Resonate

The first step is to resonate with their presuppositions. We must demonstrate that we have heard their objections, understood them, and empathized with them. Until we feel the same emotions they feel, we haven't really heard their objections.

Why do they think it ought to be okay for someone to be gay? What presuppositions—not so much the evidence—must they hold to come to this conclusion? How does it fit their cultural storyline? What is so emotionally compelling about their point of view? What is so morally repugnant and offensive about Christianity?

Here is one possible answer to that question. The gay debate represents the issue of freedom for many non-Christians. They read the Declaration of Independence and it boldly declares, "We hold these truths to be self-evident, that all men are created equal, that they have been endowed by their Creator with certain unalienable Rights, that among these are Life,

Liberty and the pursuit of Happiness." Article 1 from the United Nations' Universal Declaration of Human Rights (1948) states, "All human beings are born free and equal in dignity and rights." So the focus for the unbeliever is typically on questions of freedom and a specific understanding of freedom. This is why it's important that people have equal rights—free from traditional authority—to pursue happiness on their own terms. This is a foundational principle of the modern Western Enlightenment. Nonbelievers believe that this is what brought us out of the Dark Ages, when we used to burn witches and believe in magic potions. Our soldiers fought, bled, and died to preserve our freedoms. So being gay means that one is now able to enjoy these freedoms.

The gay debate also represents a specific understanding of love. Love and community are core to who we are. Being able to love and be loved is one of the needs in Maslow's hierarchy of needs. The non-Christian thinks, "If you're loving someone in the privacy of your own home and no one is getting hurt, who am I to tell you what to do?"

The gay debate also represents the values of tolerance and acceptance. I remember the incipient racism and microaggressions I experienced as an Asian growing up in a chiefly white Australia in the 1980s. I know what people mean when they talk about the need for tolerance and acceptance. Many people believe that if we shouldn't discriminate against people of different skin colors and genders, why should we discriminate against people of different sexual identities?

Stop for a moment and try to listen to what is being said, to the concerns being raised. Don't immediately look for a way to poke holes in this worldview or argue against a specific understanding of love or freedom or tolerance. Seek to understand where someone is coming from. A Christian's preaching against gay love represents hate, intolerance, and bigotry. Worse, it threatens to take away freedoms that people died for and return us to the Dark Ages. You may disagree, but can you hear the concern and take it seriously?

I say this because I don't think we have successfully resonated with a person until we feel the emotional burden of their objection. We have to feel the sheer horror of how a Christian worldview feels to our non-Christian friend. My aim is not merely to echo their objection but also to restate that objection in a stronger version—both emotionally and intellectually—so that our friend is now thinking, "Yes! That is exactly what I'm saying. He's saying it better than what I'm trying to say!" If you can resonate in this way, you show that you are someone worth listening to. Now they will want to know how you're going to answer their objection. Try to dig a deeper hole than the hole your friend dug for you so that your friend will be thinking, "I wonder how they're going to find their way out of this!"

## 2. Dismantle

Now that we have articulated our friend's presuppositions back to them, the next step is to dismantle them. We do this by gently showing them that there is a deficiency in their presuppositions. Often, our friend has unknowingly taken the presupposition to be simply true—as an *a priori* fact—with no supporting evidence. In this sense, their beliefs are faith-based beliefs that may not accord with the evidence.

You can also do this by gently showing that there is a dissonance with their presupposition. There is something else that they hold to be true which clashes with this presupposition. So they can't both be true. Our friend has to give one of them up. I call this the "you can't have it both ways" method of dismantling a presupposition.

So what does this look like? Let's consider where we get our views on freedom, love, and rights from. The US Declaration of Independence says that such freedoms and rights are self-evident. But what if that makes us guilty of question begging? Can these beliefs really be self-evident if not all cultures share our Western views on freedoms and rights? Interestingly, the US Declaration of Independence has another basis for these rights. It says that such freedoms and rights are endowed by God—"their Creator." This is a *deus ex machina*—introducing God into the context seemingly out of nowhere. But that raises the question, Which god are we talking about? Not all gods believe in freedom and rights. In Greek mythology, the gods were more likely to take away your freedom and rights as a human being. In Asian mythology, the gods are capricious and malicious.

So where do we get our views on freedom, love, and rights? They are not so self-evident to many people today. What proof do we have of their existence? Where would we even find this proof? And how would we even prove the existence of metaphysical concepts such as freedom, love, and rights if all we are is physical atoms and molecules?

What am I doing by dismantling all of this? I'm trying to show how Western the common view sounds. Because most people we interact with in the West have been brought up with Western principles, they can't see how Western they are. It's just part of our cultural milieu, like the fish not noticing the water it swims in or an American asking me, "Do I have an accent?" when of course they have an accent.

Some Westerners are surprised to learn that the Dalai Lama has often opposed our Western views on gay issues. While he has recently changed his views, it may be to bow to Western pressure, since for many years he held the opposite view. The Dalai Lama is famous for his views on tolerance, love, and happiness, so for him to hold those views and still be against homosexuality suggests that this must be about more than tolerance, love, and happiness. What if our views on homosexuality and sexual freedom are nothing more than a Western social construct that we're imposing on the rest of the world, telling the rest of the world what to believe? Our view that this is progress might be yet another form of patronizing Western colonialism. To say that our view of morality is the right view or that it's the progressive belief that all should eventually hold could be a thinly veiled form of intolerance. We should always be nervous when someone tells us that their views are "on the right side of history." Others have used that phrase to justify cultural imperialism, which represents the height of cultural superiority and arrogance.

The goal of this dismantling is to show that we can't have it both ways. We can't argue that we should tolerate all beliefs and then not tolerate the beliefs of those who also believe in love and happiness, especially those with traditional worldviews that oppose homosexual practice, people who live in the majority world. We can't tell others they don't have the right to tell us what to do, and then use our rights to tell others what to do. We can't call their views primitive and ours progressive. This is a tool that governments and cultures of power have used to oppress those without power for centuries.

## 3. Gospel

We've raised objections to show that there are problems with their worldview, that the presuppositions may not lead to the conclusions or beliefs that they truly want. And here is where we complete our friend's cultural storyline with the gospel. We can do this in two ways. If we previously demonstrated a deficiency in their storyline, we should now replace that deficiency with the gospel. Or if we previously dissonated their storyline, we now replace the dissonated presupposition with the gospel.

So let's return to our example of homosexuality by first looking at the deficiencies in the storyline. We might say to them, "Where you and I differ, actually, isn't in our view on gays. Where you and I differ is where we think we derive freedom, human rights, and love from." We would then explain to them that freedom, human rights, and love—as the concepts we've come to love and celebrate in Western culture—actually come to us from the Bible. Before we dismiss the Bible, we have to realize how much of what we hold to be true—which isn't as self-evident as we think it to be—actually comes to us from its pages.

For example, the Western belief that humans have inherent rights originates from a biblical understanding of human beings and what they are. The Bible teaches that God has made us in his image and that our worth and value—and our rights—are something given to us by God. They are not something given by the government or by other people. They are inherent, meaning that we possess them by virtue of being human. If we want to say that marriage is being able to marry the person we love, the Bible supports this. It commands husbands to love their wives, which was quite a revolutionary concept for marriage in a culture where women were married as property. And if we want to support the rights of the individual over their collective, tribal responsibilities, the Bible supports this idea as well, emphasizing the importance of personal, individual decisions. I'm briefly touching on each of these concepts here, but all of them could be further unpacked and discussed, pointing toward the unique and revolutionary worldview the Bible presents us with.

Right now, the Christian faith is exploding in majority world places such as South America, China, and Africa. People are converting because they've discovered the freedom, rights, and love that come from knowing and following Jesus. They are not finding Christianity to be a tool of oppression and hate. The opposite is true. They experience it as a tool of liberation, justice, and love.

The point is that if we're thinking that Christianity is a tool of oppression, then maybe we've been reading the Bible with a specific lens, a postmodern Western lens, for too long. Or maybe we've been hanging around the wrong Christians. All that we're trying to do is open up their mind to consider leaving aside some of the prejudices we might have against Christianity and consider reading the Bible on its own terms. Perhaps we'll be surprised to discover for ourselves an objective basis for freedom, rights, and love. What many have found over the years in reading the Bible is that the greatest demonstration of freedom, rights, and love is found in Jesus' coming to die and then live for us. Our goal is to invite them to investigate this claim and to see if this can be the objective basis for what we know, love, and need to be true.

Another way to approach this is to show where the dissonance is in the storyline and how the gospel resolves it. I might begin by saying, "Where you and I differ actually isn't on our views on gays but on who has the right to tell anyone what to do." I go on to explain that typically, we say that an individual has a right to decide for themselves what to do. But this is just arrogance and selfishness. Often as individuals we make mistakes. Being openminded means being open to correction. So it can't be just me as an individual who should decide what's right or wrong for my life. Doesn't that seem arrogant and selfish?

Sometimes people will say that our society has the right to tell us what to do. Right now in our culture we have a majority opinion on the gay issue. Surely our morals should be dictated by the majority in society. But what if society or the majority gets it wrong? Australia once had a white Australia policy, supported by the majority opinion, but now we realize that it's wrong. In the history of nations, moral reform has often begun with a lone moral hero, a minority opinion. So can we really trust society to tell us what to do? With the majority, what is right today might be wrong tomorrow.

Sometimes we argue that we should let Mother Nature tell us what to do. We should do what's most natural for us. But what is this, exactly? Penguins are supposedly monogamous. Is that what we're to be like? What about the serially unfaithful dog, the misogynist elephant, or the male-eating black widow spider? Just because something is found in nature doesn't mean we ought to emulate it.

Where does this leave us? We need to ask the bigger question: Is there an objective basis—something that transcends the choices of the individual, society, and Mother Nature—for determining what we can and can't do in love, sex, and marriage?

What if there is a God who made us and loves us, and he has the right to tell us what to do? I might not agree with him on everything, but if he loves me, then I have to trust that what he tells me is the most loving thing for me. And if he made me, then I have to trust that what he tells me is the wisest thing for me.

Jonathan Haidt, in his book *The Righteous Mind*, says that there are three main ethical systems employed in the world: the ethics of the individual, the ethics of society, and the ethics of the sacred.[8] Haidt says that our present Western views on sex and morality are based only on the ethics of the individual. But he says that this makes us WEIRD, an acronym for Western, Egalitarian, Individualistic, Rich, and Democratic. We are statistical outliers compared with the rest of the world. No one else in the

---

8. Haidt, *The Righteous Mind*.

world shares our ethical system. The rest of the world has a much richer ethical vocabulary, employing the ethics of the society and the sacred as well as the individual. This is why they hold different views on sex and morality. Haidt cautions us in the West from presuming that we are any more advanced or happy than those in other parts of the world.

We in the West need to be aware of our potential to be arrogant and imperialistic in our views on sex and morality. We should seek to be more humble and open to inquiry about what the rest of the world—and what the great thinkers of the past who drew inspiration from the Bible—say about sex and morality.

## ANSWERING TODAY'S DEFEATER BELIEFS

These are only brief, sample answers, not exhaustive enough to answer objections or convince anyone of the gospel. They might not even be great answers, and they are certainly not silver-bullet answers. I've borrowed from others some of the specific answer in the language or the concept and how it was used. But what I want to focus on is not the specific way to answer objections about homosexuality. I want you to note how the principles are applied in my answer: resonate, dismantle, gospel.

Knowing this process is helpful as you think through how to come up with your own answers to objections and beliefs. To help you get into the habit of this three-part process, let's look at a few more common objections, the defeater beliefs that many in the West hold today.

### Example 1: What about Other Religions?

We could attack this question head-on, evidentially, by showing that not all religions are the same—some believe in one God, while others believe in many gods. But this misses the point! We also have to address the underlying presuppositions that (1) ontologically, God might be ephemeral and unknowable, and (2) epistemologically, how would we ever know anyway, since we're so blinded by our culture?

**Resonate:** One strategy is to resonate with the presupposition that we are blinded by our culture: "Yes, I know. All religions do look the same. They all seem to say the same thing. Any differences could be explained by cultural starting points. And besides, who are we to impose our cultural preferences and say which one is right and which one is wrong? We should accept them as all true, just different paths to the same God."

**Dismantle:** Another strategy is to demonstrate the dissonance in their presuppositions: they can't have it both ways. They can't believe both that others are blinded by their culture and that they themselves haven't been: "But to say that all religions are the same is to do exactly that: impose our cultural preferences (cultural relativism) upon them and make them say something that they themselves are not saying. A devout Muslim would be horrified if we said they believed in the same God as the Hindus. A devout Jew would be horrified if we said they believed in the same God as the Buddhists. What gives us the right to say we can see something that they can't see for themselves? As if they're blinded by their religion, but we're the all-wise, all-knowing ones? We need to let each religion speak for itself. And many religions do say that they are right and other religions are wrong."

**Gospel:** A final strategy is to offer the gospel as the best completion to their storyline. If we're looking for God but are all blinded by our culture, then the only way to find God is for him to find us: "The real question is, 'How can we know?' What if it doesn't depend on our trying to find God, but it depends on God's finding us? This is the Bible's claim. It's not a journey with many paths to the same God but God's journey to us. What if God actually talks and reveals himself in person to us? What if God sent us his Son, Jesus, so we can know?"

Again, the point I want to emphasize is that there is more than one way to respond to the same issue or concern. To illustrate this, I'll share another way of responding to the same question.

**Resonate:** We can resonate with the presupposition that a loving God should let us approach him in whatever way we want: "Yes, I know. If God is a loving and personal God, why should he care how we approach him? He would accept us just the way we are, no matter what our beliefs are."

**Dismantle:** We can also demonstrate the dissonance in their presuppositions: they can't have it both ways. They can't believe both that God is loving and that he doesn't care how we approach him: "But that's just it. If we can believe whatever we want about God, then either he doesn't exist or he's so uncaring that it doesn't matter. But if God is loving and personal, then the facts matter. For example, my wife is a real, live, loving person. That's why there are facts about her. Her name is Stephanie. She was born in Australia. She studied at the University of Sydney. But if I said to you that her name is Rachel, she was born in Finland and studied at Northwestern University, you would say to me, 'Either your wife doesn't exist and you're just making her up as a fantasy, or I don't think you know your wife.' When it comes to living, loving persons, the facts matter. We can't just make up facts to suit ourselves."

**Gospel:** Finally, we can offer the gospel as the best completion to their storyline. If they want to believe in a God who loves them, but for whom the facts matter, then they also have to accept Jesus as the only way to this loving God: "And the facts matter so much to God that he sent us his Son, Jesus, so that we could know the facts about God. And the facts matter so much to God that Jesus died for us on the cross, because there really is no other way to this God."

## Example 2: How Can a Loving God Send People to Hell?

Here is another example to consider. Again, we can try to show that many verses in the Bible, especially spoken by Jesus, talk about hell. But this misses the point! We need also to address the underlying presuppositions that hell is unfair, hell is unloving, hell is excessive, and hell is the opposite of tolerance, love, forgiveness, and inclusiveness.

**Resonate:** The strategy here is to resonate with the presupposition that hell is unloving: "Yes, hell sounds so wrong, doesn't it? How can a good, loving, forgiving God send people to hell, just for what they believe? It sounds so unfair and unloving. It sounds so excessive. Who is God to judge us for who we are?"

**Dismantle:** The strategy here is to demonstrate the deficiency in this presupposition. Where is the evidence for a loving God? Is it an *a priori* assumption? If so, why should we accept it as true? "But that's just it. We all want to believe that God ought to be good, loving, and forgiving. But where do we get this idea from? In Greek mythology, the gods are immoral. In Asian mythology, the gods are mischievous. Out of all the major and minor world religions, it's only the God of the Bible who is good, loving, and forgiving."

**Gospel:** The strategy here is to offer the gospel as the best completion to their storyline. If we want to believe that God is loving, then the gospel is the best guarantee that such a God exists: "So if we want to believe the bits in the Bible where God is good, loving, and forgiving, we have to believe all the other bits in the Bible about God. We can't just choose the bits we like. It's either all of the Bible or none of the Bible. That means we also have to believe in the bits in the Bible about hell."

And again, there is more than one way to respond on this issue.

**Resonate:** The strategy here is to resonate with the presupposition that God should be inclusive, tolerant, and not exclusive: "Yes, hell sounds so wrong doesn't it? How can a good, loving, forgiving God send people to hell, just for what they believe? It sounds so unfair and unloving. It sounds so excessive. Who is God to judge us for who we are?"

**Dismantle:** The strategy here is to demonstrate the dissonance in this presupposition. We can't both believe that there is a difference between right and wrong (based on whatever definition you choose) and expect God to be inclusive of everyone: "But what if God is more inclusive than what we are? If I were God, and if I ran the universe, who would I let into heaven? I might want to let everyone into heaven.

"But you would then say, 'Are you going to let people like Pol Pot and the Bali bombers into heaven?' I will then say 'Okay, maybe not them.'

"But you would say, 'Based on what? What are your criteria? Who would you let into heaven if you can't let everyone into heaven?'

"Suppose I say, 'Whoever is good enough.'

"You would then say, 'Whoah! You're a very exclusive God, excluding people based on their moral behavior! How good do I have to be before I get into your heaven?'

"Suppose I then say, 'Okay, okay! Let's not make it morality. How about everybody gets in if they're a sincere believer in whatever gods they believe in?'

"You would then say, 'Whoah! You're a very exclusive God, excluding people based on the strength of their sincerity! How sincere do I have to be before I get into your heaven?'

"Suppose I then say, 'Okay, okay! Let's not make it about religion. How about everybody gets in if they are true to themselves? They kept it real. They were authentic.'

"You would then say, 'Whoah! You're a very exclusive God, excluding people based on their authenticity! How authentic do I have to be before I get into your heaven?'"

**Gospel:** The strategy here is to offer the gospel as the best completion of their storyline. If their storyline champions inclusiveness but still has to distinguish between right and wrong, then the gospel offers the best way of God's including the most people into heaven: "But God is more inclusive than what you and I could ever possibly be. His criteria is on whether we know Jesus. And based on this criteria, more people are going to get into heaven than what you and I could have let in based on our criteria. The scandal of the Bible isn't that people go to hell. The scandal is that God lets people into heaven that you and I would not let into heaven. The scandal of the parable of the wedding banquet isn't just who misses out. It's also who gets let in [Luke 14:15–24]!"

Or I can utilize a third approach.

**Resonate:** The strategy here is to resonate with the presupposition that love and righteous anger are incompatible: "Yes, hell sounds so wrong, doesn't it? How can a good, loving, forgiving God send people to hell, just for what they believe? It sounds so unloving. It sounds so excessive. Who is God to judge us for who we are?"

**Dismantle:** The strategy here is to demonstrate a dissonance in this presupposition. They can't believe that God is loving and that he should never get angry: "But what if this is what love is all about? True love means that if we love someone, we don't turn a blind eye to their wrong actions. True love means that when we are wronged by our loved ones, we are rightfully angry.

"I once watched the TV series *House of Cards* where a husband-and-wife couple no longer loved each other. The wife had an affair with another man. When the affair was exposed, the husband didn't really care. So what if his wife had an affair? The wife confronted her husband and said, 'I thought that you would be more angry.' The husband's lack of anger showed that he didn't love his wife. Sometimes, the loving thing is to be rightfully angry.

"So what if it's the other way around? If God were unloving, there wouldn't be a hell. But hell exists because God is loving. It's because he loves us that he is rightfully angry at how we've shamed, dishonored, and wronged him."

**Gospel:** The strategy here is to offer the gospel as the best completion of their storyline. If they want a God who is loving but who also necessarily gets righteously angry, then they also need to believe that the gospel is the only way to be saved from hell: "The Bible says that God's most powerful demonstration of love is sending his Son to die on the cross for us [John 3:16; 15:13; Rom. 5:8; 1 John 4:10]. But how is this a loving act? It's loving only because Jesus is dying in our place to save us from hell. If there were no hell or if there were any other way to be saved, then Jesus' death on the cross would be foolish, wasteful, and disturbing. But it's because there is a hell and there is no other way to be saved that Jesus' death is a demonstration of God's love."

## Example 3: Science Disproves Christianity

Another common objection you might hear is that science disproves Christianity. You can try to show how much the Bible aligns with archaeological, historical, and cosmological claims. But you cannot ignore the underlying presuppositions that (1) we can rationally believe only what science can prove—we have a commitment to naturalism and a rejection of any metaphysical claims—(2) everything we believe comes from science, and (3) faith is antiscience.

**Resonate:** Again, we can resonate with the presupposition that we should believe only what is scientifically proven: "Yes, we need to be rational and scientific. Otherwise we'll just believe anything. We'd end up believing in unicorns and fairy godmothers. This was the whole point of the Western scientific revolution—to rescue us from the Dark Ages and superstitious belief."

**Dismantle:** We can also demonstrate a dissonance with this presupposition. We can't believe both that we should believe only what is scientifically proven and still believe a range of truth claims that can never be scientifically proven: "But at the same time, there's more to life than what we can prove scientifically. For example, we believe it to be true that it's good to be generous to the poor, wrong for a white person to discriminate against a black person, and wrong for a man to be violent to a woman. But we can't prove this with a scientific experiment. Yet all of these beliefs that we hold to be reasonably true are not self-evident by science, because they are the opposite of what we see in the natural world of animals and insects, where the stronger animal picks on the weaker animal.

"But it's more than this. When my wife tells me, 'I love you,' this is something that I can't prove scientifically. But I believe it to be true. And you would say my belief is reasonable.

"Science is good. It has given us cures for cancer, the microwave oven, and the smart phone. But if all we have is science, then this would be a very cold, hard universe with no such thing as generosity, charity, justice, mercy, and love."

**Gospel:** Finally, we can offer the gospel as the best completion to their storyline. If we want to believe in a world of love, then we also need to believe in the God of the gospel: "So where do we get generosity, charity, justice, mercy, and love from? These are metaphysical and personal concepts that are derived from elsewhere, apart from science. But if they are to be more than a social construct or wish fulfillment, then they need to come from an objective person who transcends society and wishes.

"What if they come from a personal and loving God? What if we even have an objective historical basis for this claim, which can be proved by the conventions of historical and legal evidence, such as the Bible? If so, such a belief would be reasonable.

"There's one other thing that science can't prove for us. It's what happens to us after we die. If we say, 'Nothing,' how do we know? This answer is something that science can't give us.

"We all go to our graves with a so-called faith-based belief in either an afterlife or no afterlife. If we say there is nothing, where is the objective basis for this claim? But if we say there is eternal life, at least we have the objective word of Jesus, who came back from the dead. If so, a belief in eternal life would be more reasonable than a belief in no afterlife.

"So it all comes down to this. Do I trust Jesus' word? In the same way I have to trust my wife when she says, 'I love you,' I have to choose whether I'm going to trust Jesus' word."

## Example 4: Christians Are Judgmental Hypocrites

Let's consider the objection that Christians are judgmental hypocrites. Maybe you've heard that one before. I could show examples of loving Christians, unloving atheists, or how this isn't what the Bible teaches. But we will also need to address the underlying presuppositions that (1) Christianity is about being a good person, and (2) belief in objective truth is what brings out the worst in people, because absolutism makes people narrowminded, intolerant, and judgmental.

**Resonate:** The strategy here is to resonate with the presupposition that Christians should be good people: "Yes, some of my worst enemies are Christians. They can be selfish, brooding, grumpy, and nasty. Often when I give a public talk, the general public gives me encouraging feedback, but the Christians give me the most unkind comments."

**Dismantle:** The strategy here is to demonstrate a deficiency in their presupposition. Where do they get the idea that Christians ought to be good? If Christianity were a religion of works-based salvation, then this presupposition might be true. But where is the evidence for this? The evidence actually points the opposite way: Jesus offered grace to those who are humble and broken, not to the self-righteous: "But that would be like complaining that a hospital is full of sick people. Jesus came saying he was like a doctor coming to heal the sick, not the healthy. If so, then

Christians are those who recognize their brokenness. They are a work in progress.

"But here's the thing. What if we're all broken and sick? Jesus didn't divide the world into those who needed him as a doctor and those who didn't. He divided the world into those who were humble enough to come to him and those who were too self-righteous to come to him."

**Gospel:** The strategy here is to offer the gospel as the best completion to their storyline. If they have a problem with self-righteous Christians, then they too might need to be humble and accept the gospel, lest they also be accused of self-righteousness: "God's message to us in the Bible isn't to make ourselves good enough for him. That's God's job. The message from God in the Bible is that we don't have to be perfect, because Jesus is perfect. God loves us just the way we are because of Jesus. But God loves us too much to leave us the way we are. So if we can be humble enough to see that we, just like the hypocritical Christians, also need Jesus, then we too can be a work in progress where God makes us more and more like Jesus everyday."

Again, there is more than one way to respond to this objection.

**Resonate:** The strategy here is to resonate with the presupposition that absolutism is the cause of evil: "Yes, those Christians with their belief in objective truth come across as so smug and arrogant. They are so intolerant, bigoted, and narrowminded because they think they have the truth and everyone else is wrong. This is what causes religious hatred and violence."

**Dismantle:** The strategy here is to demonstrate the dissonance in their presuppositions. They can't believe both that it's wrong to hold to absolutes and have their own absolute truths: "But we all have absolutes, so it can't just be absolutism alone that causes violence; it all depends on what our absolutes are.

"According to a TED talk by Karen Armstrong, the author of *Fields of Blood*, it's not religion that causes violence but politics. This is also the observation of George Orwell in *Animal Farm*, that it's power that ends up causing violence and persecution. Whoever wins the revolution ends up in power, and the oppressed become the oppressors. This is also the observation of history, where both the religious and the nonreligious become awful oppressors once in power."

**Gospel:** The strategy here is to offer the gospel as the best completion of their storyline. If they want a loving world but at the same time can't escape absolutes, then only the gospel can offer the absolutes that best guarantee a world of love and forgiveness: "So what absolutes can possibly stop such violence? What about the absolutes taught by Jesus and the Bible to love your enemy, forgive those who persecute you, don't repay evil with evil, and turn the other cheek? What about the story of when Jesus is arrested and Peter pulls out a sword and cuts off the ear of the priest's servant? Jesus tells Peter to put away his sword and then heals the servant's ear. I once heard John Lennox use this story to show that Jesus was telling all his followers that they were to conquer the world with words and acts of mercy rather than violence.

"I once stood in a church hall in St. James Church, Kenilworth, Cape Town, South Africa. In 1993, four gunmen entered the church during the Sunday evening service and fired assault rifles and threw grenades into the audience. They killed eleven people and wounded fifty-eight. The gunmen were arrested. But members of the church, many of whom lost family members in the attack, publicly forgave and reconciled with the attackers. What sort of absolutes would do this? What about the absolutes of Jesus from the Bible?

"Tim Keller points out that Desmond Tutu, when opposing apartheid, and Martin Luther King Jr., when supporting the civil rights movement, preached more Bible at their opponents rather than less Bible.

"If we hold more rather than less to Jesus' teachings in the Bible, we would have less violence rather than more. So the answer to judgmentalism, intolerance, bigotry, racism, hatred, and violence isn't less Jesus but more Jesus."

## Example 5: The Bible Is Wrong

A fifth example is the objection that the Bible is wrong or unreliable. Many will address this objection by focusing on the historical reliability of the Bible. But you can show that the Bible is reliable and still fail to address the underlying presuppositions that (1) the Bible says stuff that we would no longer hold to be true—we are more culturally advanced than the original writers of the Bible, who were limited in what they knew because of their culture—or (2) that what the Bible says is objectionable.

**Resonate:** The strategy here is to resonate with the presupposition that the Bible's culture is limited by its time and place: "Yes, I know! There are many things in the Bible that we might find hard to believe or agree with."

**Dismantle:** The strategy here is to demonstrate the dissonance in their presuppositions. They can't believe both that the Bible's culture is limited and that our own culture is not similarly limited: "But it's not just us. Every culture in every time found things in the Bible that were hard to believe or agree with. For example, in the early centuries, some groups found it hard to believe that Jesus could be a human. They liked to believe he was God, but struggled with the idea that he was also a real human who needed to eat just like us. But in the twentieth century, some groups found it hard to believe that Jesus could be God! They liked to believe that he was human, but struggled with the idea that he was also really God, who could do miracles. But now in the twenty-first century, we find other things hard to believe about Jesus: for example, that he might be the only way to God.

"A lot of our objections to the Bible might be a product of our present Western cultural viewpoint. So maybe we need to be less culturally imperialistic and not impose our cultural wishes upon the Bible, and just let the Bible speak to us on its own terms."

**Gospel:** The strategy here is to offer the gospel as the best completion of their storyline. If they want God to be a loving God, and if they don't want to impose their own culture on other people, then they will need to let the Bible speak to us on its own terms: "Did you know that right now, Christianity is growing at a rapid rate in non-Western countries in Asia, South America, and Africa? Why is that? Maybe they can see that Jesus in the Bible offers them freedom, hope, and joy.

"So maybe we need to read the Bible on its own terms and not impose our Western culture on it. Most of our objections to the Bible are products of our culture and time. Each culture will have its peculiar things that it finds hard to believe in the Bible, but this changes as cultures come and go. What if we missed out on knowing God or having eternal life because of a cultural hangup that our grandchildren won't have?"

Or here's another way to respond.

**Resonate:** Here the strategy is to resonate with the presupposition that what the Bible says is objectionable: "Yes, I know, there are some things the Bible says that I find hard to agree with."

**Dissonate:** Here the strategy is to demonstrate the dissonance in the presupposition. They can't believe in both a loving God and a God who never disagrees with them: "But we can't have it both ways. If we believe God is a loving personal God, then he also will disagree with us from time to time. That's what it means to be in a loving and personal relationship. Otherwise God would be our puppy dog, taking orders from us."

**Gospel:** The strategy here is to offer the gospel as the best completion to their storyline. If I want God to be loving, but he will often disagree with me, then the gospel is the only way I have of trusting this God: "So how do I know if I can trust this God when he says things that I think are wrong, outdated, or objectionable? God demonstrates his love for us by sending his Son, Jesus, to die for us and live for us. Jesus was prepared to die for God's version of the truth. That's how I know I should trust God's version of the truth rather than my version."

## Example 6: How Can a Loving God Allow Suffering?

As a final example, we might get the objection that a loving God would never allow the horrible suffering that we see all around us. Attacking this evidentially, we might try to give people reasons for why God might allow suffering—he has given humans free will, he might be working good out of bad, he is patient. But not only is this pastorally disastrous and insensitive; it also misses the point. We also need to address the presupposition that the existence of evil disproves the existence of God.

**Resonate:** The strategy is to resonate with the presupposition that a loving God shouldn't allow suffering: "Yes, how can a loving, powerful God allow suffering? And it's not just that suffering exists. It's the type of suffering. Suffering is unfair: Why should a loved one get cancer or why should a drunk driver kill a friend or why should innocents die in a tsunami? Suffering is also disproportionately evil and painful: Why cancer and not a head cold? Why death and not a broken arm? Why a tsunami and not a rainstorm? Why should children die at all?"

**Dismantle:** The strategy here is to demonstrate the dissonance of this presupposition. We can't have it both ways. We can't believe both that there is no God and that there is a problem of the existence of suffering: "But that's just it. The problem of suffering exists only if we hold all of these truths to be true at the same time: (1) suffering is real, (2) suffering is unfair, (3) God is loving, and (4) God is powerful.

"We can remove the problem by removing any one or all of the above four truths.

"For example, we can deny truth 1 and say suffering is only an illusion. We need to transcend our pain and get over it. But this is no comfort to anyone who has lost a loved one to cancer, a car accident, or a tsunami.

# HARD AND SOFT THEODICY

The traditional Christian defense against the question, "How can God allow suffering?" is called a theodicy. We can distinguish between a hard theodicy and a soft theodicy.* A hard theodicy will try to specify the reasons God has for allowing suffering, whereas a soft theodicy will say that God has reasons for allowing suffering, but we don't know what they are.

In the answers I gave earlier, I followed the approach of the soft theodicy. First of all, a hard theodicy is hard to defend theologically.** For example, what could God's reasons be? If we say it's because God has given humans free will, then this means that our human choices are more powerful than God's will. It is also open to the *reductio ad absurdum* question: "Will there be free will in heaven? If so, what's to stop another fall?" So free will alone can't be the reason for the existence of suffering.

If we say it's because God works good out of suffering, then this means God is a consequentialist. The ends justifies the means. Does this mean we can use good results to justify our choices to do evil? Or if we say that it's because Satan causes suffering, does this mean God can't completely control Satan? But then if we say that God is ultimately glorified in our suffering, then this makes God out to be cruel. In the end, a hard theodicy fails to give a theologically satisfactory single reason for the existence of suffering.

Although the Bible gives us multiple hints as to why God might allow suffering, it doesn't give us a single reason, and we can't possibly know what that single reason for suffering might be at this particular moment for this particular person.

Second, a hard theodicy is pastorally cruel and insensitive. Imagine that someone asks us why their sister died of cancer. If we try the free-will defense, she will say, "Are you saying my sister chose to get cancer?" If we try to say that it's because of sin in the world, she will say, "Are you saying my sister died of cancer because she was more sinful than others?" If we try to say that God is working good out of our suffering, she will say, "What good can come out of this for my sister? My sister is dead."

Therefore, pastorally it's best to show compassion and empathy instead. Echo their pain and tears. Affirm the suffering person's right to ask questions. That's what the writers in the Bible did in the midst of their suffering. And avoid trying to give neat answers when we can't possibly know the loving and powerful reason that God has for allowing suffering in this moment.

---

* I learned this distinction from my PhD supervisor, Graham Cole, who is now the academic dean at Trinity Evangelical Divinity School.

** I owe this insight to John Feinberg in his book *No One Like Him*.

"We can deny truth 2 and say that suffering is fair. But this is cruel. How can a loved one deserve to die of cancer or a car accident or a tsunami?

"We can deny truth 3 and say that God is unloving. God wills our suffering but doesn't care enough to remove it. So we have to learn to get over the impersonal will of God. But this is close to fatalism. It robs us of personal agency, love, and mercy. Why care at all for the sick and dying if it is the will of God that they suffer?

"Or we can deny truth 4 and say that God is powerless. He watches us helplessly but can't help us. We have to help ourselves. That's why there's suffering. But the fact that we are outraged at God shows that we sense he can remove suffering.

"So we can remove the problem of suffering if we remove any one or all of the four truths. But this seems to make the problem worse. The problem exists because suffering is real and unfair, and we sense that there is a loving and powerful God who can and ought to do something about it.

"If we were in a random, impersonal, godless universe, we should just get over the pain, disease, and loss of loved ones. But our pain is real, not imagined. Our suffering is not a social construct. The problem of suffering exists only because a loving and powerful God also exists."

**Gospel:** Here we offer the gospel as the best completion of their storyline. If we want to believe that suffering exists and yet there is still a loving God behind it, then we also need to accept that the gospel is the best way of resolving this tension: "But that's just it. We can't have it both ways. If there's a loving and powerful God, then we also have to trust that he has a loving and powerful reason for our suffering. We don't know what that reason is. And it would be cruel and insensitive of me to try to give you an ignorant guess. But it must be a loving and powerful reason because even his own Son, Jesus, entered our world and suffered for us.

"If God is loving and powerful, it also means there's more to this story than we can see. There's another chapter still to come. And if we trust in this loving and powerful God, then we can be part of that chapter that is still to come."

## A FINAL WORD ON APOLOGETICS

The sample answers that I have presented in this chapter are, admittedly, heavy on reason, logic, and argumentation—logos. But as I've mentioned, our non-Christian friends will be persuaded just as much, if not more, by stories, emotions, experiences, and actions—pathos and ethos.

As I mentioned in the chapter on postmodernity, I once heard Ravi Zacharias say that the best answers to give are stories. This is because people can't argue against a story. And stories win over the imagination and the emotions. Stories make our argument not just more conceivable (logos) but also imaginable and attractive (pathos and ethos).

In addition to the evidentialist and presuppositionalist approaches to apologetics I outlined earlier in this chapter, the field of apologetics can also be divided into negative apologetics and positive apologetics. The aim of negative apologetics is to make a defense against our friend's objections against Christianity: "How can you trust the Bible?" or, "How can a loving God send people to hell?" Whereas the aim of positive apologetics is to promote the gospel by giving our friend reasons for believing.

In the answers I gave earlier, I used a combination of negative and positive apologetics. In the dismantle part of the answer, I practiced negative apologetics. But unlike traditional evidentialism, I did this by dismantling the presuppositions rather than providing evidence to address the objection head-on. And in the gospel part of the answer, I practiced positive apologetics. But instead of the evidentialist approach of providing logical reasons for belief—the historical reliability of the Bible or reasons for God's existence—I provided existential reasons for belief; I showed how the gospel completes their cultural storyline. So if our friend wants their cultural storyline to be completed, they will need (and want) the gospel also to be true.

For help learning how to engage in positive existential apologetics, I've found James K. A. Smith's book *How (Not) to Be Secular: Reading Charles Taylor* quite helpful.[9] In this book, Smith helpfully summarizes the massive work by Charles Taylor, *A Secular Age*.[10] The main claim of the book is that we live in a secular age with only an immanent frame: there is no transcendence. But our secular friends live as if this house is still haunted with the spiritual realm. Our friends still live—borrowing from transcendence—as if there is hope, purpose, and meaning.

Although our secular friends believe in only an immanent world, they live as if there is a transcendent world. Although they believe in only a physical world of atoms and molecules, they live as if there is a metaphysical reality. If we can articulate this to our friends and then show that they need a transcendent world, we can begin to show them how God and a belief in Jesus might complete their secular cultural storyline.

---

9. James K. A. Smith, *How (Not) to Be Secular: Reading Charles Taylor* (Grand Rapids, Mich.: Eerdmans, 2014).

10. Charles Taylor, *A Secular Age* (Cambridge, Mass.: Belknap Press, 2007).

## USING CULTURAL TEXTS

In Athens, Paul quoted to the Athenians their own cultural texts (Acts 17:23) and poets (Acts 17:28). In a same way, we can find common ground with our audience if we can quote their respected authors. For this reason, I regularly read the *New York Times* and the *New Yorker*. I listen regularly to podcasts from NPR. I also regularly scan the *New York Times* bestsellers.

I have found three immediate payoffs in doing this. First, I find immediate common ground with and respect from my audience. I demonstrate that I've read their canon of literature as well as my own. They are also surprised that I am using their texts to agree with them rather than to attack and disagree with them. This is different from the culture-wars model that they might have expected.

Second, many of the authors are already respectful and sympathetic to Christianity. For example, David Brooks and Nicholas Kristof in their columns in the *New York Times* are graciously supportive of the Christian claims. As another example, Malcolm Gladwell in his book *David and Goliath* ends up returning to his Mennonite faith halfway through writing the book. As another example, Jonathan Haidt's *The Righteous Mind* demonstrates the plausibility of Christian ethics—or as he calls it, "the ethics of the sacred." And David Brooks in his *Road to Character*, in the chapter on Augustine, clearly and sympathetically articulates the gospel.

Third, many of these books support James K. A. Smith's (and Charles Taylor's) claim that our secular age still borrows from our transcendent Christian worldview. For example, Jennifer Senior's *All Joy and No Fun* ends with a woman of deep Catholic faith as the example of how to survive as a parent in today's busy age. Malcolm Gladwell's *David and Goliath* uses examples of the French Huguenots and a Christian family as models of love, survival, and forgiveness. Charles Duhigg's *The Power of Habit* claims that we can break a destructive habit only if we believe in a God or some sort of transcendent purpose. Paul Dolan's *Happiness by Design* says that true happiness can come only if there's both purpose and pleasure. Stephen Biddulph's *Manhood* claims that we need purpose if a job is to be satisfying, and he ends his book with a whole chapter on the topic of spirituality. Angela Duckworth's *Grit* argues that grit is possible only if there's also purpose and hope.

We can use these books to articulate and affirm our audience's cultural storyline. And then we can show how their storyline still requires transcendence: hope, purpose, love, forgiveness, community. And then we can show how the gospel completes this storyline for them.

If they want a world where love, mercy, hope, justice, community, and purpose are realities, then they also need (and want) the gospel to be true.

## BE READY TO GIVE AN ANSWER

Michelle cursed her luck. Her college roommate this year was going to be a Christian named Helen. Of all the rotten luck. A full-blown, born-again, fundamentalist, Bible-believing, narrowminded Christian.

But as Michelle got to know Helen, she found Helen didn't fit her preconceived ideas of Christianity. And as Michelle got to hang out more and more with Helen's Christian friends, the Christian faith became less and less foreign. And Helen seemed to have read all the same books Michelle read. She was far from the isolated, misinformed Christian that Michelle had in mind.

Thanksgiving came around, and Helen invited Michelle to her family's for dinner. There Michelle saw a family that loved, respected, and functioned well. And she was curious as to how Michelle's mother was able to pray out loud personally to God before the meal, giving thanks on behalf of everyone. Michelle had never thought you could pray to God like that! And during the meal, the family took turns to say what they were thankful to God for in the previous year.

This got Michelle thinking. Thanksgiving is all about giving thanks. This is a good thing. Psychologists, more and more, are stressing the importance of giving thanks. David Brooks, in his *New York Times* column, said that thankfulness stops us from becoming self-entitled, self-interested, utility-maximizing creatures. Thankfulness is the social glue that acts as an antidote to our capitalist meritocracy.[11]

But who are we giving thanks to? If all we are is matter—atoms and molecules—what or whom are we thanking? Mother Nature? Luck? Random chance? Is thankfulness a social construct? Or a useful social contract to keep us all well behaved? If so, thankfulness is a tool of oppression wielded by those in power to keep the masses in check. Another opiate for the masses! These hardly seemed likely or persuasive reasons to be thankful.

But what if there really is a loving and personal God? A God who is interested in us enough to hear and answer our prayers? This would change

---

11. David Brooks, "The Structure of Gratitude," *New York Times*, July 28, 2015, http://www .nytimes.com/2015/07/28/opinion/david-brooks-the-structure-of-gratitude.html. Accessed January 2, 2017.

everything! But how did Michelle know if even this wasn't a mere social construct or a tool of oppression wielded by those in power?

But Michelle thought this unlikely. Not from what she saw in Helen and her family's life. God was real. God made a difference. But if Michelle wanted to know this God, what would it mean for her strongly held beliefs? Would she also have to believe in hell? But what if all of this would feel different once she knew God anyway?

The next day, Michelle swallowed her pride and said to Helen, "Tell me the reasons why you believe God is real." Helen said a quick prayer before she answered. She prayed, "Please God, help me to listen first to what Michelle has to say. Help me to hear, understand, and empathize with her. And then give me the words to say. And let this be the first in many moments in Michelle's journey to a saving faith in you."

# CONCLUSION

## Moving People from Hostile to Loyal

I have a friend called Tim. Tim wasn't always a Christian. But a few years ago he began a journey to belief, and he is now a loyal Christian. Looking back, Tim can see the sovereign and supernatural work of God in his life. If you ask Tim how he became a Christian, he will answer, "It was through God's grace, mercy, and power." But at the same time, Tim can see how God worked through natural human means: relationships, experiences, communication, emotions, existential cries, culture, and social and psychological forces.

Tim also works in marketing. It is his job to sell Bumper Gluten Free Bread. (I've changed the name for this book.) Tim uses natural human means to move people from being hostile to eating gluten free bread to becoming loyal to Bumper Gluten Free Bread.

So I asked Tim—assuming the primacy and overarching supernatural and sovereign work of God in his life—what factors led him to becoming a Christian. How did he move from being hostile to God to becoming a loyal Christian? I also asked him what we could learn from his conversion for my book on evangelism. And I asked him what we could learn from his experience in selling Bumper Gluten Free Bread.

Tim showed me that when it comes to buying Bumper Gluten Free Bread, people belong in the groups in table 11.1.

Tim identifies several categories for the way people relate or respond to Bumper Gluten Free Bread: hostile, open, considering, trying it out, entry level, switching, and loyal. Tim's job is to move people from one group to the next. For Tim, the two key "block points" are the transition from considering to trying it out, and from switching to loyal. If he can get you to try it out and just get you to place a slice of Bumper bread into your mouth, then that is a major breakthrough. And then if he can get you from switching to loyal, so that you are exclusive and evangelistic about Bumper, then that is the final breakthrough. His job is done. He has moved you from hostile all the way to loyal.

But how does Tim get you to go from one group to the next? He uses levers. Social forces might get you to move into the group that considers Bumper Gluten Free. There's a critical mass of people you trust who are eating gluten free products.

Next, trials (free samples are handed out in the supermarket), promotions (Bumper is half price this week), easy access (Bumper is conveniently placed at eye level near the checkout), wisdom (your friends seem to benefit from Bumper), felt need (you need a healthy diet), and perhaps a crisis (you've just had a health scare) might get you to move into the group that tries and begins using Bumper Gluten Free.

Next, benefits (you notice that you feel better) and behavior (you wear the logo on your T-shirt) might move you into the group that switches over to Bumper and finds belonging with other Bumper eaters. If this happens, you might become a daily eater of Bumper, and soon you will identify as a Bumper eater and become loyal to Bumper.

Tim applies this as an analogy for his journey to the Christian faith, where he moved along a similar path (table 11.2).

As he thinks about the process of becoming a Christian, Tim also sees people in several groups: hostile, open, considering, trying it out, entry level, switching, and loyal. I would argue that our role as evangelists is to move people from one group to the next.

But how do we move people from one group to the next? We can use evangelistic levers. Social forces might get people to move from hostile, to open, and finally to considering Christianity. There's a critical mass of trusted people who believe in Jesus.

Next, trials and promotions (introduction to Bible courses, a church sports team, a wine-tasting night), easy access to the "sacred" (carols night, family church service), wisdom (their Christian friends are wise and loving), felt need (they need a daytime play group), and perhaps a crisis (they've just had a health scare or lost a loved one) might get them to move into the group that checks out Christianity.

|  | Hostile | Open | Considering | Trying It Out | Entry-Level Acceptance | Switching Over | Loyal |
|---|---|---|---|---|---|---|---|
| Character-istics | "There's nothing to this gluten free diet. It's a fad and a waste of time." | "Maybe there's something to this gluten-free diet, but I'm not buying Bumper." | "Maybe Bumper Gluten Free is an okay brand." | "Bumper Gluten Free tastes okay. Maybe I should buy it." | "Okay, I've bought Bumper Gluten Free, and now it's in my repertoire of brands, but I'm not exclusive to it. I still buy other brands." | "Bumper Gluten Free is what I eat." | "I buy only Bumper Gluten Free, and I tell others they should eat it too." |
| Levers | Social Forces<br>• friends are eating gluten free | | Trials and Promotions<br>• free samples<br>• sale prices<br><br>Easy Access<br>• prominent on shelves<br>• near the checkout<br><br>Wisdom<br>• seems to work for friends<br><br>Felt Need<br>• need a healthy diet<br><br>Crisis<br>• health scare | Benefits<br>• notices benefits to eating<br><br>Behavior<br>• behaves as a Bumper eater (wears the T-shirt with the company's logo)<br><br>Belonging<br>• finds belonging with a community of Bumper eaters | | Daily Eating | |

Table 11.1

| | Hostile | Open | Considering | Trying It Out | Entry-Level Acceptance | Switching Over | Loyal |
|---|---|---|---|---|---|---|---|
| **Character-istics** | "There's nothing to religion. It's a fad and a waste of time." | "Maybe there's something to religion, but it doesn't have to be Christianity." | "Maybe Christianity is okay." | "I should check out Christianity." | "Being a Christian is okay, but I'm not exclusive about it." | "I've decided to become a Christian." | "I'm loyal to Christianity and want to tell others about Jesus." |
| **Levers** | Social Forces<br>• friends are religious or Christians | | Trials and Promotions<br>• "preevangelism" events<br>• church sports team<br>• introductory courses to Bible and Christianity<br>Easy Access to the "Sacred"<br>• carols church service<br>• family service<br>Wisdom<br>• seems to work for friends<br>• sees wisdom and love in Christians<br>Felt Need<br>• children's play group<br>• parenting seminars<br>• kids vacation club<br>Crisis<br>• health scare<br>• loss of job, relationship, health, house | Benefits<br>• good for children<br>• good for marriage<br>• cared for<br>• talks have meaning, wisdom, application<br>Behavior<br>• goes to church<br>• reads Bible<br>• prays<br>• signs up for rosters<br>Belonging<br>• finds belonging with a community of Christian believers | | Behaves as a Christian<br>• serves<br>• rosters<br>Church<br>• Christian friends<br>• Bible studies<br>• training<br>• conferences | |

**Table 11.2**

# THE GRAY MATRIX

Tim has brilliantly captured with his Bumper Gluten Free Bread analogy, in vivid concrete images, what the Gray Matrix (see figure) also tries to capture.*

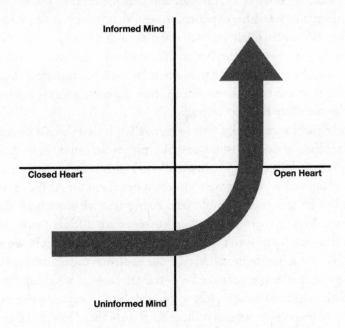

According to the Gray Matrix, the journey to belief begins in the bottom left quadrant (closed heart to the gospel and a mind uninformed by the gospel) to the top right quadrant (open heart to the gospel and a mind informed by the gospel). Our job as evangelists is both to open hearts and inform minds with the gospel.

In my observations and in my experiences doing evangelism, many post-Christian Westerners belong in the top left quadrant: they are informed already by the gospel but have closed their hearts to it. But many of our efforts as evangelists are spent still trying to inform them with the gospel when we also need to be opening their hearts to the gospel. Conversely, many Asian-Americans, when they grow up in the USA, already have their hearts open. So when we evangelize them with information about the gospel, they prove to be good soil, and our efforts at evangelism often lead to much fruit. This probably helps to explain at least one reason for the growing numbers of Asian Christians in Western churches today.

* http://thegraymatrix.org/. Accessed April 7, 2017.

Next, benefits (they notice that the Christian faith is good for their children) and behavior (they attend church and sign up for the cleaning roster) and belonging might help them to switch over to the Christian faith; they become followers of Jesus. If this happens, they might become daily followers and identify as a Christian and become loyal to Jesus.

Tim's analogy and his experience mean that most people journey into the Christian faith. Their journey consists of a series of moments rather than one key moment. Whether we like it or not, this means that people behave as a Christian first and then identify as a Christian later. They find belonging first and then believe later. Often the entry point is wisdom, and along the way they find salvation.

The significance of this for us as evangelists is that there is no one-size-fits-all method of evangelism. But it also means we can be more deliberate in our strategy: Who is our implied audience, what is their group, what lever are we using, and where are we trying to move them to? At the same time, we need to be generous to those who evangelize with methods different from ours. Maybe their audience and context are different from ours, so what works well for us won't work so well for them. Conversely, we need to be humble about our methods. Maybe our audience and context are unique to us, so our methods might not be as transferrable as we think they are.

This brings us to a good place to end this book, because we've explored a variety of levers that we can utilize. As we use these levers, we pray that the supernatural God, in his power, sovereignty, and mercy, might use these levers as his natural means for moving someone from unbelief to belief.

My hope is that after reading and studying this material, you will take away from it a profound understanding that God uses our humanity—our relationships, community, hospitality, communication, experiences, emotions, existential cries, and cultural texts—to communicate his gospel. As I mentioned in the first chapter, God uses all our natural, mundane, and ordinary presentations as the natural means for his supernatural regenerating work. This should keep us humble about our abilities, generous to those who use different methods, and encouraged that, if God wills it, he will use our words to move someone from death to life.

# APPENDIX

## Have You Heard of the Four Spiritual Laws?

Just as there are physical laws that govern the physical universe, so are there spiritual laws that govern your relationship with God.

## LAW 1

### God loves you and offers a wonderful plan for your life.

#### God's Love

"God so loved the world that He gave His one and only Son, that whoever believes in Him shall not perish but have eternal life" (John 3:16, NIV).

#### God's Plan

[Christ speaking] "I came that they might have life, and might have it abundantly" [that it might be full and meaningful] (John 10:10).

Why is it that most people are not experiencing that abundant life? Because . . .

## LAW 2

### Man is sinful and separated from God. Therefore, he cannot know and experience God's love and plan for his life.

#### Man Is Sinful

"All have sinned and fall short of the glory of God" (Romans 3:23).

Man was created to have fellowship with God; but, because of his own stubborn self-will, he chose to go his own independent way and fellowship with God was broken. This self-will, characterized by an attitude of active rebellion or passive indifference, is an evidence of what the Bible calls sin.

## Man Is Separated

"The wages of sin is death" [spiritual separation from God] (Romans 6:23).

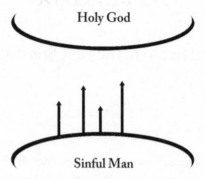

This diagram illustrates that God is holy and man is sinful. A great gulf separates the two. The arrows illustrate that man is continually trying to reach God and the abundant life through his own efforts, such as a good life, philosophy, or religion—but he inevitably fails.

The third law explains the only way to bridge this gulf . . .

# LAW 3

**Jesus Christ is God's only provision for man's sin. Through Him you can know and experience God's love and plan for your life.**

## He Died in Our Place

"God demonstrates His own love toward us, in that while we were yet sinners, Christ died for us" (Romans 5:8).

## He Rose from the Dead

"Christ died for our sins . . . He was buried . . . He was raised on the third day, according to the Scriptures . . . He appeared to Peter, then to the twelve. After that He appeared to more than five hundred . . ." (1 Corinthians 15:3–6).

## He Is the Only Way to God

"Jesus said to him, 'I am the way, and the truth, and the life, no one comes to the Father but through Me'" (John 14:6).

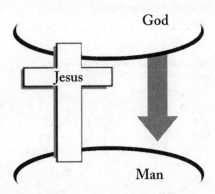

This diagram illustrates that God has bridged the gulf that separates us from Him by sending His Son, Jesus Christ, to die on the cross in our place to pay the penalty for our sins.

It is not enough just to know these three laws . . .

## LAW 4

**We must individually receive Jesus Christ as Savior and Lord; then we can know and experience God's love and plan for our lives.**

### We Must Receive Christ

"As many as received Him, to them He gave the right to become children of God, even to those who believe in His name" (John 1:12).

### We Receive Christ through Faith

"By grace you have been saved through faith; and that not of yourselves, it is the gift of God; not as result of works that no one should boast" (Ephesians 2:8–9).

### When We Receive Christ, We Experience a New Birth

(Read John 3:1–8.)

### We Receive Christ through Personal Invitation

[Christ speaking] "Behold, I stand at the door and knock; if any one hears My voice and opens the door, I will come in to him" (Revelation 3:20).

Receiving Christ involves turning to God from self (repentance) and trusting Christ to come into our lives to forgive our sins and to make us what He wants us to be. Just to agree **intellectually** that Jesus Christ is the Son of God and that He died on the cross for our sins is not enough. Nor is it enough to have an **emotional** experience. We receive Jesus Christ by **faith**, as an act of the **will**.

These two circles represent two kinds of lives:

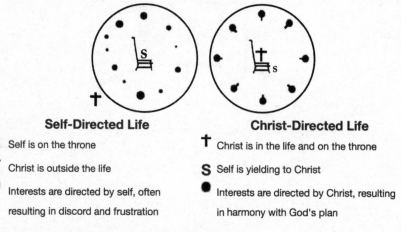

**Self-Directed Life**

**S**   Self is on the throne

**✝**   Christ is outside the life

●   Interests are directed by self, often resulting in discord and frustration

**Christ-Directed Life**

**✝**   Christ is in the life and on the throne

**S**   Self is yielding to Christ

●   Interests are directed by Christ, resulting in harmony with God's plan

Which circle best represents your life?
Which circle would you like to have represent your life?
The following explains how you can receive Christ:

## You Can Receive Christ Right Now by Faith through Prayer (Prayer is talking with God)

God knows your heart and is not so concerned with your words as He is with the attitude of your heart. The following is a suggested prayer:

> *Lord Jesus, I need You. Thank You for dying on the cross for my sins. I open the door of my life and receive You as my Savior and Lord. Thank You for forgiving my sins and giving me eternal life. Take control of the throne of my life. Make me the kind of person You want me to be.*

Does this prayer express the desire of your heart? If it does, I invite you to pray this prayer right now, and Christ will come into your life, as He promised.